DRINKING IN AMERICA

E. E. Cummings: A Life

Louisa May Alcott: A Personal Biography

Desire: Where Sex Meets Addiction

American Bloomsbury: Louisa May Alcott, Ralph Waldo Emerson, Margaret Fuller, Nathaniel Hawthorne, and Henry David Thoreau

My Name Is Bill: Bill Wilson—His Life and the Creation of Alcoholics Anonymous

As Good As I Could Be

Home Before Dark

Note Found in a Bottle

Treetops

Elizabeth Cole

Doctors and Women

The Cage

A Handsome Man

Looking for Work

DRINKING IN AMERICA

Our Secret History

SUSAN CHEEVER

TWELVE

New York   Boston

Twelve
Hachette Book Group
1290 Avenue of the Americas
New York, NY 10104

www.HachetteBookGroup.com

Printed in the United States of America

RRD-H

First edition: October 2015
10 9 8 7 6 5 4 3 2 1

Twelve is an imprint of Grand Central Publishing.
The Twelve name and logo are trademarks of Hachette Book Group, Inc.

The Hachette Speakers Bureau provides a wide range of authors for speaking events. To find out more, go to www.hachettespeakersbureau.com or call (866) 376-6591.

The publisher is not responsible for websites (or their content) that are not owned by the publisher.

Library of Congress Cataloging-in-Publication Data
Cheever, Susan.
  Drinking in America : our secret history / Susan Cheever.
    pages cm
  Includes bibliographical references and index.
  ISBN 978-1-4555-1387-1 (hardcover) — ISBN 978-1-61113-529-9 (audio download) — ISBN 978-1-4555-1386-4 (ebook) 1. Drinking customs—United States--History. I. Title.
  GT2883.U6C54 2015
  394.1'20973--dc23
                          2015025648

To my parents, John and Mary Cheever, who taught me how to think.

AUTHOR'S NOTE

Some of the spellings and punctuation in the quoted material in this book have been modernized to improve legibility.

CONTENTS

America had been awash in drink almost from the start—wading hip-deep in it, swimming in it, at various times in its history nearly drowning in it.

Daniel Okrent, *Last Call:*
The Rise and Fall of Prohibition

PROLOGUE

The Pilgrims landed the *Mayflower* at Cape Cod, Massachusetts, on a cold November day in 1620 because they were running out of beer. Their legal charter from King James was for a grant of land in Northern Virginia, but instead they anchored illegally and carved their first community from the sand, laying the foundation of the American character: flinty, rebellious, and inspired by adversity.

Since the beginning, drinking and taverns have been as much a part of American life as churches and preachers, or elections and politics. The interesting truth, untaught in most schools and unacknowledged in most written history, is that a glass of beer, a bottle of rum, a keg of hard cider, a flask of whiskey, or even a dry martini was often the silent, powerful third party to many decisions that shaped the American story from the seventeenth century to the present.

Like the Massachusetts climate with its steamy summers and icy winters, the American character is subject to wild extremes. This is true with our relation to the natural world and true with our connection to drinking. At times, we don't seem to be able to moderate our drinking. At other times we blame it for everything. We love it or we hate it. It is our big solution and it is our big problem. In some decades we banned alcohol, and in others we drank so much that foreign visitors were astonished. "I am sure the Americans can fix nothing without a drink. If you meet, you drink; if you part, you drink; if you make acquaintance, you drink; if you close a bargain, you drink; they quarrel in their drink, and they make it up with a drink," wrote Frederick Marryat in the nineteenth century.

Every century, our drinking pendulum—the radical change in our relationship to alcohol—swings. In the 1830s we were the drunkest country in the world. By 1930 we had outlawed drinking entirely, with disastrous results. The swings accelerated after prohibition—in the 1950s and '60s we were again awash in alcohol. Although in the twenty-first century there are more laws and more stringent social controls on drinking than there have ever been in our history, we are drinking enough to make alcoholism a significant public health problem.

In 2014, the Centers for Disease Control issued a scathing summation of the damage drinking does in the United States.[1] The CDC reported that 88,000 adults a year die of alcohol consumption. There are also, the CDC report says, more than a million alcohol-related emergency room visits as well as 10,000 traffic fatalities a year caused by drinking.[2]

Drinking is a cherished American custom—a way to celebrate and a way to grieve and a way to take the edge off. It brings people together. It makes social connection easy. It loosens inhibitions. "Alcohol has immediate and profound effects on behavior," writes Dr. James Milam in his classic study *Under the Influence*. "At low doses, alcohol stimulates the brain cells, and the drinker feels happy, talkative, energetic, and euphoric. After one or two drinks, the normal drinker may experience some improvement in thought and performance."[3] This is the alcoholic sweet spot, and its looseness and clarity have been woven into the fabric of American history. The American Revolution, the winning of the Civil War, and the great burst of creativity in American literature in the twentieth century were all enhanced by drinking.

Americans are also well acquainted with the dark side of drinking.

"After several drinks, the normal drinker may begin to show signs of intoxication," Dr. Milam writes of the sedative and toxic effects that occur when the drinker keeps on drinking. "He may become emotionally demonstrative, expressing great joy, sadness, or anger. He may also begin to show signs of motor incoordination, staggering slightly when he walks, knocking his drink over as he leaves the table, or slurring his words. If he continues to drink, his vision may blur, and his emotions, thoughts and judgment may become noticeably disordered."[4] When someone is drunk, the familiar suddenly seems unfamiliar, and the simple complicated. "I take out my phone," writes Adam Rogers in describing an experiment with drunkenness and its aftermath. "At this point [it] seems like utterly unfamiliar technology, like something aliens have left in my pocket."[5]

When does drinking become more than just a little harmless enjoyment? In history and in personal life, drinking has to be judged by its effects—not by the quantity imbibed or the attitudes of the surrounding culture. Alcoholism is a harsh diagnosis to make, and for most of our history this damning word was not used. The terms *alcoholism* and *alcoholic* were not even coined until the 1840s, and didn't become common until the temperance movements of the 1890s. Before then drunks were just drunks and drinking too much was called by many names, most of them picturesque. According to one source, Benjamin Franklin's *Drinker's Dictionary*, some synonyms for *drunk* can be: *afflicted, piss'd in the brook, had a thump over the head with Sampson's jawbone, cherry merry, hammerish, haunted with evil spirits, moon-ey'd, nimptopsical,* and *double-tongu'd.*

We know much more about alcoholism than we did just fifty years ago. Science and our modern temperance movements have pushed forward in defining both the brain chemistry and the social behavior of alcoholics. Alcohol creates what the scientists call a "hedonistic highway" in the brain of an alcoholic, so that the body is electrified with pleasure when alcohol is first imbibed. Soon it takes more and more alcohol to produce the same pleasure. After a while it takes a damaging amount of alcohol to produce what was once a normal state of being.

We now know that alcoholism has a genetic component and that it is passed from generation to generation within families. Sometimes it skips a generation or surfaces as an eating disorder, a gambling problem, or another addiction. What baffled eighteenth-century first lady Abigail Adams, who watched her brother waste his life through drinking, and was then heartbroken to see two of her sons and two of her grandsons die of drinking, makes sense to us now.

Alcohol also has an environmental component. People raised in societies where liquor is banned are less likely to drink as much as people raised in societies where liquor is freely imbibed and used as medication, mood elevator, social lubricant, and inspiration. Richard Nixon, raised in a nondrinking Quaker household, did not drink until he was an adult. He learned to drink in the Navy, and although he never drank very much, the effects of those drinks were catastrophic.

Alcoholism is not a measure of how much someone drinks but rather a measure of the effect the drinking has. Some drinkers—President Nixon is a good example—have a low tolerance for alcohol. Others have a high tolerance. Although the law judges drinking entirely on quantity—a breathalyzer measures only how much alcohol has been imbibed—whether or not a drinker is impaired is not predictable by quantity. The old-fashioned police field test for driving while intoxicated—can you walk in a straight line and turn on command, can you stand on one leg, can you sustain a horizontal gaze—is actually a more accurate measure than blood alcohol content (BAC). Many drinkers can appear to be unaffected by a great deal of alcohol, while others are unable to walk straight after a few glasses of wine.

We do know how alcohol affects the brain, first in pleasurable changes and then in less pleasurable changes, changes which sometimes end in alcoholic blackouts—periods during which an alcoholic appears to be functioning normally but has no memory of what he or she is doing. We also know that a hangover can cause even more drastic impairment than a drinking binge.

Despite all we know, there is still a mystery at the heart of alcohol's effects. We do not understand why some people with genetic or environmental markers for alcoholism can drink normally while others cannot. We are only beginning to understand the effects of an alcoholic family member on the nonalcoholic members of a family.

I have studied alcoholism for decades, beginning when I wrote about alcoholism as an editor for *Newsweek* magazine in the 1970s. My father was alcoholic, and he suffered from heart attacks and delirium tremens as well as the subtler forms of distorted behavior caused by alcohol. In 1975, my father got sober through Alcoholics Anonymous, and I saw firsthand the miraculous effects of sobriety. My father's drinking had destroyed his body, but it had also distorted his character—his soul. The restoration of one man through the simple measure of not drinking was revelatory.

My own alcoholism took a very different course. Like many women I controlled one addiction with another. When my drinking became a problem I cut back on booze and ate more. When I gained weight I went back to drinking more, or spending more money. I persuaded my Weight Watchers leader that a drink was a legitimate substitute for a fruit. What recovery guru Patrick Carnes calls "bargaining with chaos" kept me from seeing that I was drinking too much.

My father was addicted to alcohol and it showed. I was addicted to everything, and that was much easier to hide. I haven't had a drink in more than twenty years—twenty years during which I have obsessively studied both alcoholism and temperance and their effects on individuals and cultures. Temperance, the belief that all drinking should be prohibited, is the other side of alcoholism. Our country has a rich history of temperance movements and temperance crusaders— from Walt Whitman to Carrie Nation and Phineas Barnum—and this, too, is part of our drinking story.

Individual drinkers also experience a personal dark side: hang-overs. In many ways a man whose system is in withdrawal from alcohol can be less responsive than a man who is simply drunk. "The next morning is very, very terrible," Rogers writes. "My worst hang-overs sit heavily in my guts, with horrible nausea the main symp-tom…I get foggy, too—like, can't remember how to type…Even the attenuated sunlight of an overcast day is painful, and my forehead feels like it has a railroad spike embedded in it."[6]

Some addicts can switch substances in order to get high. As food philosopher Michael Pollan points out, one of the agricultural causes of American drunkenness has a modern parallel in our obe-sity epidemic. At the beginning of the nineteenth century, Amer-ican farmers were producing a huge amount of corn, which does well in our fertile soil. But corn is bulky and hard to transport. The farmers found a way to make corn easy to market and transport. Soon the country was flooded with corn whiskey, which got people drunk and was enticingly cheap to buy. "Before long the price of whiskey plummeted to the point that people could afford to drink it by the pint. Which is precisely what they did," Pollan writes in *The Omnivore's Dilemma*.

These days, our surplus of corn, subsidized by government help, is made into another liquid that is cheap and easy to transport—high fructose corn syrup. Pollan concludes that "corn sweetener is to the republic of fat what corn whiskey was to the alcoholic republic." We used to be the drunkest nation in the world; now we are the fattest na-tion in the world.

"Those who cannot remember the past are condemned to repeat it," wrote George Santayana. In the twenty-first century, as we swing back toward regulation and laws against drinking, we are repeating our own history. At the same time, because we often ignore the effects of alcohol in current events and in our own experiences, we are in the midst of a public education crisis. According to the *New York Times*, fewer than 10 percent of people needing treatment for alcohol and drug abuse get that treatment. The treatment itself is often untested and expensive.

Drinking is still on the American syllabus. Colleges have become the place where Americans serve a drinking apprenticeship. Even in the elite clubs of the Ivy League, binge drinking is approved of and sanctioned. This is nothing new. Founded in 1636, Harvard College, like many universities, had its own brewery, and as a result, one professor wrote, "lectures sometimes became unintelligible and commencement exercises so boisterous that rules had to be put into effect to limit 'the Excesses, Immoralities and Disorders.'" By the university's second century, Harvard professor George Ticknor told Thomas Jefferson that if the rate of drinking kept up, "we should be hardly better than a nation of sots."

Elementary school children no longer start the day with "flip"— grain alcohol and fruit juice—as they did in the nineteenth century, but according to the National Institute on Alcohol Abuse and Alcoholism, 25 percent of college students report that they have had academic trouble because of drinking. Today, although mothers would be horrified at the idea of putting vodka miniatures in their children's lunch boxes, a variant of flip remains a staple for teenagers in the form of alcopops and fruit-flavored beers and wines sold in convenience stores.

As drinking waned in the nineteenth century, the temperance movement grew. Proponents of temperance deplored American drinking habits and tried to change them, often by advocating that people drink only wine and beer. "We found intoxicating liquor used by everybody, repudiated by nobody," Abraham Lincoln told a temperance meeting in 1842. "It commonly entered into the first draft of an infant and the last thought of the dying man." Lincoln didn't drink, but he was personally and professionally destroyed by others' alcoholism.

During the Civil War drinking was also expected of many of the war's military leaders. Famous for his drinking and his attacks of remorse afterward, the great General Ulysses S. Grant was one of the most brilliant battlefield strategists of his age. After the war, Grant embraced sobriety with a great deal of difficulty and many slips. His was one of the most scandal-ridden and corrupt presidencies of the century.

The twentieth century in this country after Prohibition saw a blossoming of creativity and alcoholism linked together. This was a new and uniquely American phenomenon. During and after Prohibition, drinking almost became a prerequisite for great writing. All five of our twentieth-century literature Nobel laureates were alcoholics—Sinclair Lewis, Eugene O'Neill, William Faulkner, Ernest Hemingway, and John Steinbeck. "The presence of the disease in so many of our notable writers surely makes it appear that alcoholism is the American writer's disease," writes Tom Dardis.

The Cold War was the opportunity for another alcoholic episode of our history. Wisconsin-born senator Joseph McCarthy was famous for his drinking prowess and his struggles with booze—he repeatedly went on and off the wagon during his entire career, and died an alcoholic of cirrhosis of the liver.

In the post–World War II twentieth century, drinking continued to be what lubricated the dark side of American business practices. "Alcoholism is well represented in the executive suites of corporate America," writes James Graham.[7] "I have personally observed, from within more than one multinational corporation, powerful executive-alcoholics ruin...careers...[and] drive large organizations...to extinction." Lee Iacocca reported in his autobiography that Henry Ford II was prone to alcoholic rages. When Iacocca joined the company, he was warned, "You'll get fired some night when Henry's drunk. He'll call you a wop...it will be over nothing." After the fall of Lehman Brothers in the autumn of 2008, a camera panning through the empty offices showed an empty vodka bottle on one abandoned executive desk.

Now in the twenty-first century there are many signs that the pendulum is swinging back toward Prohibition—the control of drinking through the law. Alcoholics Anonymous, which was founded by two American businessmen in an Akron, Ohio, living room, is growing and becoming an increasing public force. Laws against drunk driving and drinking in public are being enforced more rigorously than any time since they were written. Rehabs and addiction specialists are everywhere. Many television shows—reality and otherwise—are devoted to watching people trying to stop drinking.

Each of us is a living dialogue about the benefits of drink and the dangers of drink, just as our nation has always had a similar dialogue. Masked by denial—the purposeful blindness that we sometimes bring to this subject as people and as a nation—this tension has changed our history. Even today, almost every day brings a news story in which drinking is important and in which drinking is ignored.

Whether we are the drunkest nation in the world as we were in the 1830s or a nation that outlaws liquor as we were in the 1920s, our national character is inextricable from our drinking history—and it started with the *Mayflower* back in the fall of 1620.

CHAPTER 1

THE *MAYFLOWER*:
A GOOD CREATURE OF GOD

E ven before the supporting beam at the foot of the main mast was shattered by a powerful wave in the middle of the stormy North Atlantic, the voyage of the creaky old *Mayflower* seemed cursed. She was a sweet ship, so called because she smelled of her previous cargo of wine, which she had carried from Spain to England up the Atlantic Coast of Europe for decades. When a group of exiled English separatists living in Holland stepped in to buy her, the sweetness evaporated. The voyage to the New World was a bitter vision of Calvinist Hell. When the Pilgrims finally arrived at their destination, their leader, historian William Bradford, who loved biblical parallels, wrote that what they found was far from a new Eden but "a hideous and desolate wilderness full of wild beasts and wild men."[1]

The ship was bulky and boxy with high, built-up fore and aft decks, four masts—foremast, mainmast, sprit, and mizzen—and six heavy, tattered square sails. The poop deck at the stern where the captain stood on a narrow ridge of planking was more than twenty feet above the water. From there he barked commands at the ship's helmsman below him in a tiny steerage compartment with a whip staff attached to the tiller through a hole in the deck. In 1957 at the helm of the *Mayflower II*, a replica of the *Mayflower*, experienced blue-water sailor Capt. Alan Villiers complained that even in less than gale winds the motion of the high poop aft cabin was so violent that he felt as if he might be thrown from his bunk.[2]

About a hundred feet from bow to stern, the *Mayflower*'s three acres of sails enabled her to manipulate the power of the wind when the ship wasn't caught in a series of westerly gales or completely becalmed. In high winds her captain, Christopher Jones, who was also one of the ship's four owners, just reefed the sails and lay "ahull," letting her drift on the ocean's turbulent surface. Jones navigated using an hourglass, a primitive compass, two sounding lines, and a backstaff, which crudely calculated latitude but not longitude. He knew roughly where he was, but not how far he had to go.

The ship had been built to transport almost two hundred wine barrels, not people. A quarterdeck at the back and an upper deck amidships were the roofs of the large room where the passengers lived in cramped quarters with no privacy, no bunks, no way to wash, and no facilities. Their bathroom was a bucket. Ladders connected the two decks. The living space, which was crawling with bugs, was so low ceilinged that most men could not stand up straight.

For food, the 102 passengers and about forty crew members had salt horse—salted beef or pork that was leathery and got tougher as the voyage progressed—and hardtack made from flour and water. There was some Dutch cheese as well as peas and beans.[3] They washed all this down with beer—a lot of beer. Although the ship was carrying water, it grew fetid and became covered with algae in the barrels. They weren't used to drinking water. In the seventeenth century in Europe, because of pollution in populated areas with no drains or sewers, water was not potable.

In the prow, barely above the water line, were the damp crews' quarters, while the captain's cabin was high up at the stern of the ship. Ever since they had voted to set out for the New World, the separatists, who had originally left England for Holland in 1608 in order to practice their religion as they pleased, had been in trouble. They were Protestants who did not want to be associated with the

Church of England—the official church. They became restless in Holland, although they had the religious freedom they craved. They were homesick, but they knew that in England they would be arrested or hanged. They imagined a wilderness where they could settle and establish a community on their own terms far from compulsory attendance at Anglican churches.

Some wanted to try to get to Guyana in South America, but most of them voted for Virginia in the New World, where communities of Englishmen had already settled. The Virginia Company of London had extended its northern boundary to the Hudson River and had just begun granting large tracts of land to groups who would go on the journey to populate and cultivate them. Against a lot of evidence, the British explorers defined the eastern coast of the New World as unpopulated—it lacked the farms and houses that signified population in the British Isles.

Under a British law called vacuum domicilium, unpopulated land was free for the taking; it could be claimed by anyone who was willing to live there and develop it. This extraordinary law allowed King James to grant licenses to lands that he did not own, land that had been populated for centuries by Native Americans. The two separatists who had been sent to London from Leiden easily obtained a charter from the Virginia Company, and with somewhat more difficulty wrenched a promise from King James I that, although he did not recognize their religion, if they settled in Virginia he would "not molest them, provided they carried themselves peaceably."[4]

The ease of getting a land grant in Virginia, a grant that turned out to be useless, was one of the few easy things the men encountered. First in the winter of 1618, they were swindled by an English businessman who promised to find them a ship and supplies, but tricked them into signing a contract which would turn over seven years of their labor and profits to another company. Then they set off for England in a small ship they had purchased in Holland—the *Speedwell*—thinking that she and the *Mayflower* would sail to America together. The separatists were ignorant of the demands of a trans-Atlantic voyage. Nor did they realize that the *Speedwell*'s captain, Master Reynolds, had no intention of sailing to the New World and had resolved to hinder their voyage rather than help it.

They planned to leave England in the early summer of 1620, but difficulties with supplies held them back. The *Speedwell* and the *Mayflower* met and loaded in Southampton, England, and set off for the New World for the first time in early August 1620. Their troubles continued. Master Reynolds had knowingly replaced the *Speedwell*'s masts with taller masts and increased the amount of sail the ship carried so that when it went at high speeds in the open ocean it would leak. "By overmasting the *Speedwell*," Nathaniel Philbrick writes, "Reynolds had provided himself with an easy way to deceive this fanatical group of landlubbers."[5] The *Mayflower* and the *Speedwell* were forced to turn back and find a harbor near Dartmouth on the west coast of England so that the *Speedwell* could be repaired.

Reynolds may have been working for Dutch businessmen who wanted to keep the best land in the New World for themselves, or he may have been afraid to sail to America. Whatever the reason for it, his deception fooled the Pilgrims and cost them valuable weeks.

The best time to sail across the North Atlantic was the summer, which had been the Pilgrims' plan for the *Mayflower* and, they hoped, the *Speedwell*. Slowly that plan began to evaporate. The group of landlubbers had grown beyond the original tight band of English separatists. Even before they left England, the Pilgrims had become a minority on the *Mayflower*. In order to finance the voyage, they had been forced to take on two other groups of passengers.

One of these groups, the Adventurers, was a group of Englishmen paying passage and in search of fortune in the New World. The other group, called the Strangers, was a polyglot mass of people who had crowded on board back in Southampton when the ship needed passengers. A fourth group on the *Mayflower*—after the Pilgrims, the Adventurers, and the Strangers—were the sailors. A tight social unit that served as the crew of the *Mayflower* under Capt. Christopher Jones, they were also a forceful presence. They planned to return to England as soon as possible with the ship. They cordially despised the Pilgrims and all their fellow travelers, calling them glib-gabbity puke-stockings. The Pilgrims were offended by the sailors' cursing.

Although the distinction of being a *Mayflower* descendent has become a badge of American aristocracy, the truth is that the aristocrats came over a decade later on the *Arbella*. The trash came on the *Mayflower*. Far from being members of the ruling class or the landed gentry, the Pilgrims and their hangers-on were outcasts in England, mostly impoverished and joined by dozens of mercenaries and men and women who were so desperate that they were ready to take almost any chance with their lives.

Once the *Mayflower* passengers had managed to build a town, live in peace with the local Native Americans, and start shipping profitable cargoes of lumber back to England, the possibility of immigrating to America became inviting to a very different group of religious separatists—the Puritans. Like the Pilgrims, the Puritans believed that the Church of England needed reforming, but the Puritans were followers of the strict teachings of John Calvin. They saw their journey to the New World as similar to the biblical story of the Israelites crossing the Red Sea. If the Pilgrims and the *Mayflower* passengers were riff-raff, the Puritans were aristocrats who had learned from the Pilgrims' mistakes. The Pilgrims had settled in Plymouth Harbor—a small inlet between two of the greatest harbors in the world, Boston and New York. The Puritans would settle their Plymouth Bay Colony south of Boston.

The Pilgrims had scraped together the money for one badly provisioned ship. Ten years later the Puritans sailed in fleet with a flagship, the *Arbella*, and ten smaller ships with more than 700 men and women as well as livestock. They brought 10,000 gallons of beer, 120 large casks of malt to jump-start the brewing industry, and, oddly enough, just 12 gallons of Dutch gin. Every member also brought one hogshead (large cask) each of wheat, rye, and barley seed. In an observation suggestive of the level of significant beer consumption, Dean Albertson in "Puritan Liquor in the Planting of New England" notes that "there was not sufficient barley mash produced, however, to slake the thirst of the entire colony, so they learned to derive a passable beer malt from oats, rye, old wheat, and even corn." Modern craft brewers will cringe at the last, because corn is scorned as a cheap adulterant resorted to only by industrial-scale producers of the proverbial beerlike "wet air."

The Puritans were well prepared and well born. Among their number were landed gentry, educated aristocrats and dukes and earls. The *Arbella*'s captain, John Winthrop, would become the governor of the Massachusetts Bay Colony on the gentle hills above what is now Boston Harbor, and the Puritans would imagine a growing new world in their "city on a hill."

Unlike the Pilgrims, the Puritans had a rigid code of daily living, and although they also depended on beer as a dietary staple and a thirst quencher, their idea of the good life did not include being drunk all the time. Soon after the establishment of the Plymouth Bay Colony, the new government became concerned about excessive drinking. Rules governing the hours when taverns could be open were put into place. This difference in attitude toward drinking between the Pilgrims and the Puritans would split the seventeenth-century Great Migration to America into two factions. These two factions—the prodrinkers and the antidrinkers—would each create ideas and identities that flow forward through American history and are still with us today.

There are two strains of American belief about drinking: the one that holds our freedom to eat and drink as an essential liberty, and the one that hopes to limit our drinking through law for the good of the community. The one created a level of drunkenness in the 1830s that shocked European visitors. The other instituted Prohibition in the 1920s. The one holds our right to drink the way we choose as sacred.

The other tries to legislate drinking habits by age, hours of availability, open-container laws, and general disapproval. All this began with the Pilgrims and the Puritans.

At last, in the late summer of 1620, the Pilgrims were ready to sail…again. Hopes were high. In a fine following wind the two ships headed west out of Dartmouth Harbor, sailing for the New World for the second time. "So with good hopes from hence, they put to sea again," wrote William Bradford.[6] Their good hopes were once again dashed. They had cleared Land's End off the coast of Cornwall and were out in the open Atlantic when the *Speedwell* hoisted all her sails and the leaks worsened. The doomed ship began to founder. Both ships were forced to turn back. This time they sailed farther north, seeing once again the headlands of Land's End, which they had passed so triumphantly on the wrong side of the ship. Both ships landed in the first harbor they could find near Plymouth to make repairs once again.

It was now September, and many of the passengers had been on board for almost two months without getting anywhere. Some of the ship's stores were already low. Morale was even lower. It was clear that they would have to abandon the *Speedwell* or abandon their entire trip. At this point the passengers—almost 150 people and two dogs, an obliging spaniel and an English mastiff—were forced to crowd into the *Mayflower* for the third try at sailing across the wild, unknown Atlantic.

Three months later than planned, with one ship missing and many fewer supplies than they needed, the *Mayflower* set sail for the last time with a prosperous wind on September 16. The third try seemed to succeed. By this time the travelers were exhausted and frightened. Everything that might have gone wrong, had gone wrong.[7] It can have been no surprise that most of the passengers were stricken with severe seasickness, which in the cramped confines of the *Mayflower* felt like a possession by the devil. It was also no surprise when the wind began to blow at gale strength. "In sundry of these storms the winds were so fierce and the seas so high as they could not bear a knot of sail," Bradford wrote. The *Mayflower* was blown off course and, unknown to the ship's captain, was now heading for New England instead of Virginia.

When the central timbers splintered, the damage was so severe that Captain Jones wanted to turn back. The passengers refused. Crammed into narrow quarters below the deck and above the hold with its dwindling supplies, they did not want to turn back under any circumstances. They had come close to rebellion, although many of them were still crippled by seasickness.

Almost a year of delays and misfortunes had dogged the voyage from Holland and England to the New World. They had been conned by men who stole their capital and a captain who tricked them. They had gone through almost half of their stores before even sailing, and their sister ship, the *Speedwell*, had to turn back before they were out of sight of land. Now when they were finally a few weeks into the miserable voyage they were not about to give up.

By this time the tsunami of adversity facing the Pilgrims seemed to have engendered a practical and enduring spirit. They examined the split timber and tried to figure out a way to repair it. Someone mentioned that in the hold were some tools which had been brought to build houses in the New World, including a huge jack, which used a screw attached to a wheel to push its top upward. This lever was unpacked and set under the cracked beam. Men turned the wheel, the top of the jack engaged with the bottom of the beam, and as the wheel turned the beam groaned back into shape. Using extra lumber to buttress the repair, the carpenter was able to reassure Captain Jones that the beam, with the screw jack in place, would stay put.

Two *Mayflower* passengers who became the historians of the *Mayflower*'s Atlantic Voyage—William Bradford, who wrote about it in *Of Plymouth Plantation*; and Edward Winslow, who with Bradford wrote about it in *Mourt's Relation*—each give the entire Atlantic crossing, which took more than nine terrible weeks, less than a paragraph. No wonder. There wasn't much good to say about the voyage.

Five weeks in, with no land in sight, the scanty provisions began to run out. This was a concern for passengers, and also for sailors who were traditionally promised a gallon of beer a day as part of their sailing wages. They could do without food; they could not do without drink.

On the evening of November 8, the endless sea began to change; the waters calmed, and their color went from oily, treacherous black to a paler green. Seagulls began to appear, cawing and circling in the sky. Although God did not send a dove with an olive leaf in its peaceful beak to land on the *Mayflower*'s rigging, the Pilgrims were as delighted as if he had.

The morning of November 9 was a clear late-fall New England morning, with a thin slice of moon overhead and a gentle wind out of the northwest that picked up at dawn. Captain Jones sent his lookout up the main ratlines. His leadman took his place outside the mizzen shrouds with his two deep-sea lead lines. The singsong of the leadman's voice called out fathoms—twenty—thirty—forty. Then suddenly: "The bottom at eight fathoms, sir!" Captain Jones was suddenly alert. Then he heard the shout from the maintop lookout. Land Ho! Land Ho! "Where away?" yelled Jones, and passengers began to crowd up from below and sleeping sailors woke up all over the ship. "Two points on the weather bow, sir," called the lookout. The ship's bell chimed out the hour of seven a.m.—*ding dong, ding dong, ding dong*—six bells.[8]

The Pilgrims crowded the upper deck and pushed against the portside rail as land came into view at the edge of the horizon. The briny smell of the ocean, the creaking of the ship's timbers, the clanging of the topsail halyard against the stays, and the fluttering of sails in the friendly wind were a dream of pleasant sailing. The water, once a murderous and crushing adversary, now whispered and gurgled as it slid past the battered hull. At first the land seemed a hallucination caused by desire, making the endless horizon just a slightly thicker line. Then as the sun rose, the horizon became more than a line and took on the features of a beach. After unimaginable hardships they had made it from the Old World to the New World.

"By [daybreak] we espied land which we deemed to be Cape Cod," Bradford and Winslow wrote, "and so afterward it proved. And the appearance of it much comforted us, especially seeing so goodly a land and wooded to the brink of the sea, it caused us to rejoice together and praise God that had given us once again to see land."[9] They had been on board for sixty-six miserable days during which one man had died and one child had been born. The journey had seemed endless. Now it was done. Lined at the edge of the hull they rejoiced and thanked God. The rising sun showed them a long barrier beach with dramatic hundred-foot-high sand dunes that Captain Jones recognized as the outer, windward edge of Cape Cod. Behind the dunes, wooded hills sloped down to the sea at the outer edge of the curved cape near what was then the Wampanoag village of Pamet and is now near Truro.

The edge of the dunes "was like the escarped rampart of a stupendous fortress, whose glacis was the beach, and whose champaign the ocean," Henry David Thoreau would write a century later in his book *Cape Cod*. He stood at the top of the dunes, he wrote, adding:

> Far below us was the beach, from half a dozen to a dozen rods in width, with a long line of breakers rushing to the strand. The sea was exceedingly dark and stormy, the sky completely overcast, the clouds still dropping rain, and the wind seemed to blow not so much as the exciting cause, as from sympathy with the already agitated ocean. The waves broke on the bars at some distance from the shore, and curving green or yellow as if over so many unseen dams, ten or twelve feet high, like a thousand waterfalls, rolled in foam to the sand. There was nothing but that savage ocean between us and Europe.

Although the Pilgrims' landfall was the cause of much gratitude—the boat was low on all provisions and lower on endurance—the separatists had no legal right to land on Cape Cod. They had won permission from King James to settle in Virginia, a territory that at the time spread from the current Virginia up to the mouth of the Hudson River.

So Captain Jones turned south, and sailed down the spine of Cape Cod toward the land in which the Pilgrims might peaceably and legally settle and begin their new lives. That calm afternoon there were many factors at play for the Pilgrims, their captain, and the other passengers on board ship.

They had been through a kind of Hell: a voyage beset with difficulties both human and natural that none of them could have imagined back in Leiden. One of the few things that brought relief to those miserable, crowded, sick people was a generous ration of beer for men, women, and children—often as much as a gallon a day dipped out of the huge barrels carried in the back of the boat in a dank storage space below the water line. Taken on board at Southampton, the beer was sometimes called "ship's beer" and probably had about 5 or 6 percent alcohol. Even when the wind blew so hard that the sails had to be taken down and the ship lay ahull, a swallow or two of beer calmed the body and eased the soul.

With enough beer, a man or woman was not only healthy but also often happy. Beer was also a problem on Captain Jones's mind. Not only did he need enough beer for the rest of the voyage, but also he planned to sail back to England as soon as possible, as soon as the Pilgrims had established a settlement, and he needed to husband his beer for passengers and crew during the return voyage.

Beer and wine are made through fermentation and are relatively easy to create compared to hard liquor, which requires distillation. Beer is made through the boiling and steeping of a substance—traditionally barley—and the addition of yeast, which causes the brew to ferment over time. "Beer in the 1699's was dark and cloudy, was flavored with hops, and in the popular version, it carried an alcohol level approaching 6 per cent," writes Gregg Smith in his book *Beer in*

America. In spite of its foul appearance, Smith writes, "The newcomers considered beer essential to the infant colony's social, cultural, and physical health. Beer was more than a necessity, it was as indispensable as breathing."[10]

Later, the Pilgrims would find a way to make beer out of many things that they found in New England, including corn and carrots. Their inventiveness when it came to creating this most necessary of drinks—beer—has been immortalized by an anonymous seventeenth-century American poet who wrote: "If Barley be wanting to make into malt / We must be content and think it no fault; / For we can make liquor to sweeten our lips / Of pumpkins and parsnips and walnut tree chips."

As Captain Jones knew from experience on many voyages, beer was essential to the well-being of his ship. As soon as he had started rationing the beer on the *Mayflower*, scurvy began to appear among the passengers. "They were down to their last casks of beer," Nathaniel Philbrick writes in *Mayflower*. "Due to the notoriously bad quality of the drinking water in seventeenth-century England, beer was considered essential to a healthy diet." The dwindling of the *Mayflower*'s beer supplies was one of the reasons the Pilgrims needed to land as soon as possible. Until they could start brewing their own New England beer, they would have to rely on the stores on the *Mayflower*.[11]

So as Captain Jones sailed south with the wind and made way for their original destination, getting the passengers ashore—to any shore—was becoming increasingly imperative for him both as the ship's captain and as one of its owners. There was no reliable chart of the water between Cape Cod, where the Pilgrims found themselves, and their official destination in Northern Virginia, but it was hoped that sailing south would get them there in a few days. The ocean had other ideas. With the wind pleasantly behind them from the Northeast they were headed, as Philbrick notes, "for certain death."

The nine-mile stretch of water between the end of Cape Cod at Monomoy and the end of Nantucket at the wide hook of Great

Point is a treacherous series of shoals and currents called Pollock Rip. Shifting sand changes the configuration of the shoals, and the tides can come roaring through the gap between the Cape and Nantucket in a way that makes the Rip difficult to navigate. Many ships have foundered and sunk in Pollock Rip. It is estimated that half of the shipwrecks on the eastern coast lie there. On the other hand dozens of ships a week sail through it without harm. But the Pilgrims did not have navigation or tidal charts. Their only navigational tool was Captain Jones's backstaff, a quadrant that he would line up with the sun to try and chart their course. Soon the ship was in trouble, battered by the rip tide and pushed toward the edge of what is now Handkerchief Shoal by the winds. "They fell amongst dangerous shoals and roaring breakers, and they were so far entangled therewith as they conceived themselves in great danger," Bradford wrote.[12]

Almost miraculously, as the afternoon shaded into evening, the wind shifted to the south. Captain Jones set his sails and turned the prow of the ship back up the coast of Cape Cod. "With the wind building from the south, Jones made a historic decision," Philbrick writes. "They weren't going to the Hudson River. They were going back around Cape Cod to New England."[13] Cape Cod had been their first landfall, and they had fallen in love with the idea of wooded hills and magnificent dunes. The decision to land illegally on Cape Cod had a huge effect on the later fate of the Pilgrims and the way in which the American character was formed. An illegal landing in a hostile place, partially caused because of a shortage of beer, was not an auspicious beginning.

Once they felt safe and out of the treacherous water of Pollock Rip, the *Mayflower* passengers were in an uproar over the decision to land well north of their original destination. The polyglot group—Separatists and Strangers—had lost one of their common interests. If they were to proceed, they needed to find a way to work together to build their settlement. They drew up the agreement that would let them go forward, an endorsement of civil law rather than law by divine right. A simple half-page document, the Mayflower Compact guaranteed a general democracy and pledged a civil "body politic."

On the morning of November 11, the *Mayflower* finally anchored in the harbor sheltered by the rounded arm of Cape Cod. Their small shallop, a boat brought along for exploration, was still stowed in the *Mayflower's* hold in pieces, so they waded in to the sandy beach. "We could not come near the shore by three quarters of an English mile, because of shallow water; which was a great prejudice to us, for our people going on shore were forced to wade a bow shot or two in going a-land, which caused many to get colds and coughs, for it was many times freezing cold weather," Bradford and Winslow wrote years later in their account of the *Mayflower, Mourt's Relation*. The outlook was not promising. "They came into the harbor at Cape Cod, and they saw nothing but a naked and barren place," Bradford wrote in his own journal. "They began to think what should become of them."[14]

For the first winter the Pilgrims spent on Cape Cod, the *Mayflower* would be the center of their lives. Captain Jones was not able to set back toward England until April 1621, by which time the settlers had written and signed the Mayflower Compact, found a place for their new settlement across Cape Cod in Plymouth Harbor, and begun building what would become their central town. Bradford called these awful months "the starving time." Famine was just one of their problems. Although only two passengers died during the *Mayflower's* voyage from England, a combination of hunger, illness, and exposure killed almost half of the *Mayflower's* passengers before spring; including Bradford's wife, Dorothy, who drowned in a way that suggested she might have killed herself.

Dorothy Bradford's death is a mystery that future generations have tried to solve. Perhaps Bradford, who would become the governor of the Plymouth Bay Colony, had fallen in love with someone else. Perhaps William Brewster, a fellow *Mayflower* passenger, made unwelcome advances to her. Certainly the fate of a woman whose husband had gone off in the shallop to try to find a new harbor, who had left her beloved son behind in Holland, and who must have thought she would never see home again, looked understandably grim. "But that which was most sad and lamentable was, that in two or three months' time half of their company died, especially in January and February, being the depth of winter, and wanting houses and other comforts," Bradford wrote, "being infected with the scurvy and…other diseases which this long voyage and their inaccomodate condition had brought upon them."[15]

Although Bradford believed that everything happened according to the Lord's plan, the first winter on Cape Cod may have tested his faith. The death rate, the misery and drowning of his own wife, the repeated skirmishes with unfriendly local Indians, the fire that consumed the first house the Pilgrims built at Plymouth, and the accidents and near disasters might well have discouraged a lesser leader. Yet during this time, Bradford and Captain Jones still had the energy to quarrel over beer. Beer in the *Mayflower*'s hold was clearly marked by owner, and the Pilgrims' share of the beer was gone by December, one month after their landing. The remaining beer belonged to Captain Jones, who encouraged his passengers to stay on shore instead of staying with the ship. They were, as Bradford wrote, "hasted ashore and made to drink water that the seamen might have more beer."

When Bradford came down with an illness that almost killed him, he begged Jones for a beer. Bradford was the community's de facto leader along with the soldier Miles Standish—who was also called "shrimp" for his diminutive stature. Although John Carver was officially the governor, the handsome and eloquent Bradford was already the man the Pilgrims looked to for guidance. He would soon become the actual governor of the Plymouth Bay Colony and rule it well until his death in 1657. Bradford had been on most of the dangerous trips to explore both the interior of Cape Cod and the possibilities of a place for the new settlement. He had been shot at by Indians and hoisted off the ground and turned upside down by an animal trap. His courage was unquestioned.

Captain Jones said no. Even if Bradford had been Jones's own father, none of the ship's beer could be spared. But even the steely Captain Jones had a change of heart when he saw how sick his former passengers became as they tried to live on land and drink the putrid water from the *Mayflower*'s storage barrels. Later he told Bradford that he would send beer to those who "had need of it" even if it meant the captain had to drink water on the way home to England.[16]

It took the better part of two months for the men of the *Mayflower* to assemble the shallop, the small sailing ship they carried in pieces in the hold of the *Mayflower*, and explore Cape Cod Bay, finally discovering the calms of Plymouth Harbor where they decided to settle. On their way to Plymouth they encountered their first Native Americans, and were again frequently shipwrecked and lost. They were in a hurry to begin building because of the *Mayflower*'s schedule, although their original plan—to send the ship home filled with furs and timber from the New World—seemed like a delusional dream. For one thing, the sooner they could build a brewery, the sooner they could produce their own beer. "In each of the new settlements the need for breweries was immediate. No matter how small the colony, the population expanded faster than imports of ale from Europe could provision. Of all the hardships endured (by the Pilgrims) the lack of beer was the one that caused the most displeasure," writes Smith.[17]

A brew house was one of the first structures built in Plymouth, and it was soon joined by a local tavern. The Pilgrims believed beer was an unalloyed good, a "good creature of God." People who did not drink were suspect and "crank-brained." After their first dreadful winter, the Pilgrims began to establish themselves and their drinking patterns with more success. The famous first Thanksgiving included enough to eat for all—and also enough to drink, since the Pilgrims' first barley crop had borne fermentable fruit. Their Indian friend Samoset joined them in a few beers and found that they made friendship very inviting. Soon enough the Pilgrims had more taverns—public houses that for years served as courthouses and centers of government throughout New England.

The Plymouth Colony Court records begin in 1623. As Plymouth grew, the courts began granting licenses to make and sell liquor. By 1635 drunkenness became against the law. The instigator was one John Holmes, who got so drunk that his punishment was time in the stocks and a twenty-shilling fine. Soon the Plymouth Court ruled "that the person in whose house any were found or suffered to drink drunk be left to the arbitrary fine and punishment of the Governor and Council, according to the nature and circumstance of the same." Later the laws were increased and refined.

One Thomas Lucas, a drunken repeat offender, was indicted for drinking with Thomas Savory's wife, Ann, at her home on a Sunday, after which she was found drunk "under a hedge, in uncivil and beastly manner." Ann was sentenced to the stocks. Soon enough Lucas's drunkenness provoked the Court into punishing anyone who sold him liquor: "It was ordered concerning him, that all that sell drink be strictly ordered and prohibited to let him have none." He was fined. He was sentenced to be publicly whipped. He was accused of abusing his wife. He sat in the stocks. Tavern owners were ordered not to serve him. Somehow he still got drunk, even on Sunday. On January 6, 1678, Lucas was found dead in a local ditch. The cause of death, the court records show, was "he being very ancient and decrepit in his limbs, and it being very cold, and having drunk some drink, got a violent fall into a ditch, in a very dangerous place, could not recover himself, but bruised his body, and lying all night in the cold, so he came by his end." He was the first Plymouth settler whose death was officially linked to alcohol consumption—more than fifty years after the gallon-a-day rations had been imposed on the *Mayflower*.[18]

Was the *Mayflower* truly cursed? Botched or cursed, afflicted with disease, indecision, suicide, and seemingly wrong-headed navigation, this small high-hulled boat certainly seemed to be a ship of fools, men and women befuddled by the beer that they drank almost constantly.

Often where there is a curse, there is a drink, and this was very much the case with the Pilgrims.

Their beverage of choice was beer, although they also drank plenty of whiskey and aqua vitae—a kind of gin—and later cider and rum. On the voyage from England, beer was their everything. Beer was their fruit and their vegetables in a diet that otherwise consisted of bread, cheese, and meat. Beer was their yogurt with its healing enzymes, and beer was their medicinal spirit. Beer was their water, and beer was their, well, beer.

The many misfortunes that crowded around the voyage—swindlers, robbers, accidents, dissension, and ultimately disease and death—seem to be more than the share of one small boatload of intrepid souls eager to find a new way to live. What of their many errors? Their excessive trust? Their inability to sail through Pollock Rip? Their eagerness to land where they were not legally able to land? Was this a curse, or did it have something to do with the fact that they were almost constantly drinking beer? By modern standards, the Pilgrims were sailing while intoxicated—a gallon of beer a day almost certainly yields a blood alcohol level of more than .08, which would make it illegal to drive in today's United States. The Pilgrims—men, women, and children—were all impaired a great deal of the time. Perhaps this was one of the factors that drove their bad decisions and incompetent preparations.

The fact that the *Mayflower* landed on Cape Cod had innumerable effects on American history and on the American character. With her bad luck, scruffy passengers and drunken sailing, the *Mayflower* is still our glorious origin myth. As William Bradford wrote in *Mourt's Relation*,[19] his and Edward Winslow's account of the voyage published in 1622, "We could not now take time for further search or consideration, our victuals being much spent, especially our beer." The winds and the Pilgrims' thirst for beer had sealed their fate and influenced ours.

CHAPTER 2

THE AMERICAN REVOLUTION, THE
TAVERNS OF THE NEW WORLD

The winter of 1621 cut the population of the New England colonists in half. Of the 102 men, women, and children who had arrived in Plymouth Harbor on the Mayflower, about fifty were left to build the town of Plymouth, figure out the vicissitudes of the New World, deal with the local tribes, and fend off the waves of disease that had decimated the Native American population and now threatened to end their glorious experiment.

For all their courage, the Pilgrims had little flexibility when it came to adapting. Their old habits seemed to survive in their hearts even when their bodies were barely surviving during the "starving time." Perhaps their fear made them inflexible.

Desperate for beer, they ignored the abundant freshwater. Even the Bible advised against drinking water in Saint Paul's epistle to Timothy: "Drink no longer water, but use a little wine for thy stomach's sake and for thine own infirmities."[1] In a jeremiad against drinking water, Plymouth's own William Bradford made a list of health hazards in the New World: "change of air, famine, or unwholesome food, much drinking of water, sorrows and troubles, etc."[2]

Desperate for food, they couldn't manage to net or eat the fish that swarmed abundantly around them in Cape Cod Bay. The whales playing in the distance represented money to be made from oil, not meat to eat. It took months for them to break down and eat the mussels, oysters, clams, and lobsters that almost begged to be captured. They hadn't eaten fish at home. They hadn't brought the right weapons to bring down the birds that sometimes filled the skies or to kill the animals—deer, rabbits, foxes—which teemed in the local forest. Their dreadful voyage had eliminated their sense of adventure. They were not looking for a new world but rather for a new version of the old world.

Even as a curse is often accompanied by a bottle, a resistance to change is also characteristic of alcoholic behavior. Drinking can cause one kind of courage to blossom—physical courage—but it can stunt another kind of courage: the courage to experiment, to try the unknown, and to use the imagination in new ways.

The Plymouth colony's governor, John Carver, a wealthy businessman who had originally chartered the *Mayflower* and who had managed to sign an early peace treaty with the Wampanoag tribe, was one of the winter's casualties. William Bradford, the newly elected governor, feared that the underpopulated, underprovisioned Plymouth would not survive. Other ships that were supposed to bring reinforcements either didn't make it to Cape Cod or arrived with passengers as hungry and needy as the existing colonists. The crew of one 1630 ship that was supposed to bring mead for making liquor landed with only six gallons left, "being drunk up under the name of leakage and so lost," reported an angry Bradford.[3]

The first barley crop, which was quickly made into the first beer, had also come in—but facing the winter of 1622, the Pilgrims were still far from prosperous. In the early years, when the *Fortune* and the *Anne* arrived at Plymouth Harbor, many of their passengers chose to return home to their impoverished and well-regulated English lives instead of staying to eke out a meager and difficult life in the Plymouth colony. The price they would pay for liberty had its limits.

Others, seeing the windswept sands and emaciated colonists, wept with disappointment as they disembarked. Hungry, cold, and grieving, the colonists seemed headed for the fate of another failed colony they had all heard about: Roanoke. Sponsored by Queen Elizabeth and Sir Walter Raleigh, the colony in Virginia had prospered, in spite of some friction with the local tribes. Then in 1590, Governor John White arrived to find it completely abandoned and dismantled. The lost colony of Roanoke still remains a mystery four hundred years later; it was certainly fresh in the minds of the colonists who disembarked on the hostile sands of Cape Cod in the 1620s.

But fate had other plans for Plymouth. Events in England were to change the history of the Massachusetts colonists in ways they could not have imagined. Angered by religious rebellions, King Charles I of England disbanded his own Parliament in 1629, creating a threatening and hostile climate for religious dissension. There were no longer any mitigating politicians to dilute his power. In an age when men were routinely tortured, killed, burned at the stake, or literally drawn and quartered for their religious beliefs, the specter of a king without a Parliament to rein him in was terrifying to anyone who hoped to reform the Anglican Church or to found a separate church.

This change in the way England was governed provoked a mass exodus of Separatists, Calvinists, and anyone with any doubts about the administration of the Church of England. This huge population shift is sometimes called the Great Migration—or the Great Puritan Migration. Less than a decade after Plymouth's first winter, when the English population of Massachusetts was down to about fifty terrified souls, twenty thousand English immigrants carried by dozens of ships joined the decimated band of Pilgrims on the shores of the east coast.

Because of the Great Migration, the Pilgrims went from being an isolated band of starving, thirsty, frightened men and women to being part of a tidal wave of immigrants. Mostly families with women and children, the new colonists, the Puritans, settled the astonishing natural harbor, which would become Boston, and founded the Massachusetts Bay Colony, which soon dwarfed Bradford's Plymouth, forty miles up the rocky New England coast.

One of the new immigrants was of particular interest to Bradford. After his wife's death he had written to an old friend, Constance Southworth, a recent widow who had been a childhood friend of Bradford's in England. She had married Robert Southworth, and a few months later Bradford had married Dorothy. His letter reached back across time and asked if she would come to the New World to be his wife. He knew she had two children, and he wasn't sure if she would bring them or leave them behind—just as he and Dorothy had left their three-year-old son, John, with Dorothy's parents in Amsterdam.[4]

He had no idea if she had received his letter, or if she would come to Plymouth even if she had. She might also have tried to come and been lost in an accident or shipwreck. When the *Anne* arrived in Plymouth Harbor, Constance Southworth was on board. It was a sunny morning, and Bradford, wearing his best cape with silver buttons, escorted Southworth formally uphill to the dirt track that ran between the houses the settlers had built and to his own board and thatch home. Two months later, they married.

In both the Massachusetts Bay Colony, which took root in and around Boston, and also in the Plymouth Colony just to the south, the tavern became the center of town. Usually the first public structure, the tavern was officially established for travelers but quickly became the center of all kinds of local activities. Taverns provided meals, good company, shelter, warmth, and local news that was sometimes read aloud in the tavern from a jointly owned newspaper. Taverns sometimes sponsored lectures and were the preferred spot for political discussions and campaign speeches. Some taverns were fancy two-story buildings with private rooms and comfortable bedrooms upstairs, while others were more like sheds built as protection from the brutal New England winters. Every tavern was an island of freedom, a comfortable place for conversation and of course the place to have a drink or two.

Drinking, as Eric Burns writes, was our first national pastime—long before baseball was invented. A great deal of the drinking took place in colonial taverns from Boston to Richmond. Homes, churches, town halls, and schoolhouses were often empty as the local taverns bustled with crowds of excited men. Virginia's Committee of Correspondence met and plotted against the king in the only safe place they could find in Williamsburg—Raleigh Tavern. Samuel Adams and John Hancock fomented their secret organization of the Sons of Liberty at the Black Horse Inn in Winchester, Massachusetts, and later at the Green Dragon Tavern in Boston's North End. Ethan Allen's headquarters was the Catamount Tavern at Bennington, Vermont. John Adams and George Washington met for the first time at the City Tavern in Philadelphia, and Thomas Jefferson began writing the Declaration of Independence at the Indian Queen Tavern, with an often-refilled glass of Madeira next to his inkwell.

Massachusetts Bay was founded by Puritans who frowned on drunkenness, but thought of drink and places to drink—taverns—as gifts from God. Puritan elder Increase Mather explained this incongruity in his popular tract *Wo to Drunkards*: "Drink is in itself a good Creature of God, and to be received with thankfulness, but the abuse of drink is from Satan; the wine is from God, but the Drunkard is from the Devil." This tension between the colonists' unabashed enjoyment of drink and their contempt for drunkenness was soon expressed in a series of laws, which are still part of the split American character.

The Pilgrims struggled with a two-sided definition of alcoholism—drinking is from God but the effects of drinking are from the devil—and we still struggle with this problem. Alcoholics Anonymous cofounder Bill Wilson faced this quandary when he and Dr. Robert Smith established AA in the 1930s. They neatly sidestepped it by decreeing that each person could decide whether or not their drinking was from God or from the devil. Alcoholism, they wrote, is a "self-diagnosed disease."

The difficulty of drawing a line between good drinking and bad drinking hasn't changed very much. The Pilgrims and the Puritans, unlike most professionals today, saw the bad kind of drinking as a moral failure. As a result, the only recourse they had when faced with the destructive nature of drunken citizens was physical punishment. It didn't work. They had no real treatment for alcoholism and no real understanding of what it was—they only knew that it was from the devil.

Mather, a respected elder, was horrified at the huge amount of drinking and drunkenness he saw around him in the towns that sprung up around Boston. "Time was when there was not need for Ministers to preach much against [drunkenness] in New England," he wrote. "Oh that it were so now!"

In many ways the American character was forged in those early taverns that also served as inns, courthouses, and town halls before those structures were built. "Taverns became a public stage upon which colonists resisted, initiated, and addressed changes in their society. Indeed, in these houses men gradually redefined their relationships with figures of authority."[5] The local taverns were the cradle of the American Revolution, the place where people allowed their anger at the king and his loyalists to surface and be supported by other drinkers. "The tavern could not but help but be the most venerated of early American institutions," writes Eric Burns in *The Spirits of America*. "The best people went to them. The best people owned them."[6]

The first government building didn't go up in Boston until 1658. Before that court was held in rooms at John Turner's Tavern and George Monck's Blue Anchor. "Upon all the new settlements the Spaniards make, the first thing they do is build a church," wrote the British captain Thomas Walduck in 1708. "The first thing the Dutch do upon a new colony is to build them a fort, but the first thing the English do, be it in the most remote part of the world, or amongst the most barbarous Indians, is to set up a tavern or drinking house."[7] Taverns were also places where rumors began and ended, where neighbors got to know each other, and where communities found an identity. If the taverns and the drinking fed the colonists' desire for independence from powers on the other side of the world, it was no wonder the desire grew rapidly.

By the early eighteenth century the Colonies had become world famous for their drinking. With their drinking customs firmly entrenched, the colonies were becoming a "nation of drunkards."[8] They drank in Boston and they drank in New York. Peter Stuyvesant wrote, "One quarter of New Amsterdam is devoted to houses for the sale of brandy, tobacco, and beer."[9] Judges were so frequently drunk at the bench that special fines were instituted for those who were "incapable" during legal proceedings.[10] Liquor was inexpensive, but the average colonist spent a quarter of his household income on alcohol.

Although the amount they drank was staggering, and there were many, many occasions for drinking as each day progressed, it is the use of alcohol throughout the population that is even more unusual. They drank the way they breathed. "Excessive drinking occurred among a broad spectrum of society, not just particular groups," writes David Conroy in *In Public Houses*, his discussion of the dozens of laws that began to be written in the mid-seventeenth century to control both tavern behavior and general drinking. "Excess drinking continued despite all of the laws devised to contain it."[11]

Everyone drank, beginning at birth—infants were plied with rum to help with sleep—and ending at death. At funerals, even if there were huge debts, money was set aside for the hard-drinking mourners. Most colonists began the day with a drink, either a tankard of cider— as John Adams liked to drink upon waking—or some "stonewall," a mixture of rum and hard cider, which was Ethan Allen's favorite. Breakfast was also washed down with beer. Schoolchildren started the day with a potent mug of flip. Smaller children were not excluded and "toddies for toddlers," as Burns remarks, were endorsed by many great men, including the British philosopher John Locke. At eleven a.m., four p.m., at dinner, and after dinner, the colonists drank. At home and in taverns, at work in their fields or taking care of their children, the colonists drank. They drank Rattle-skull and Bombo, Cherry Bounce and Whistlebelly Vengeance, Sillabub and Madeira. Soldiers drank, and the weekly drills held by the fledgling military of Plymouth Colony to help protect them against Indians often ended in drunkenness. "As these afternoons progressed...the volunteer soldiers tended to fight one another after getting 'drunk as David's sow.'"[12] When they established a college—Harvard, in 1636—they equipped it with its own brewery.

They drank when the minister dropped by—after a long day on the circuit, local ministers were often three sheets to the wind. Kegs of whiskey with attached cups were at the disposal of many ships' passengers on the flatboats that plied the new nation's rivers. Barrels of rum stood by the door for the enjoyment of many shops' favorite customers. Inexpensive and effective, liquor made the hard winters and other difficulties of the new colonies seem bearable. No celebration was complete without enough drinking to leave a few men and women legless at the end of the party. They drank at weddings and they drank at funerals and they drank when they went to the polls. There was a feeling that voters should be repaid in booze for the effort of voting. As historian Arthur Schlesinger points out, this had the "beneficial effect" of drawing large crowds to democracy.[13]

By the middle of the eighteenth century, the Colonies were famous for their abundance of furs, wood, and wool, but they were equally famous for their drinking. They were, as Benjamin Franklin, born in 1706, was to write in his famous list of synonyms for drunkenness: "addled, afflicted, boozy, drunk as a wheel-barrow, drunk as a beggar, had a thump over the head with Sampson's jawbone, cherry merry, chipper, dipp'd his bill, dagg'd, fishey, glad, groatable, hammerish, jolly, juicy, lordly, rocky, raddled, stitch'd, in the sudds, stewed, soaked, right before the wind with his studding sails out, wet and weary." The *Old American Encyclopedia* described the wildness of the drinking citizenry. "A fashion at the south was to take a glass of whiskey, flavored with mint, soon after waking…At eleven o'clock, while mixtures, under various peculiar names—sling, toddy, flip— solicited the appetite at the bar of the common tippling shop, the offices of professional men and counting rooms dismissed their occupants for half an hour to regale themselves…with punch…At the dinner hour…whiskey and water…or brandy and water introduced the feast; whiskey or brandy and water helped it through; and whiskey or brandy without water secured its safe digestion."[14]

Or, as historian W. J. Rorabaugh puts it, "They drank from the crack of dawn to the crack of dawn."

As energy and anger bubbled up against England in a way that would lead to the American Revolution, American drinking habits hit their first peak. Starting at that time, we began to swing forward in the first arc of the pendulum that has taken us from being one of the drunkest countries in the world to being a country where liquor has been outlawed.

By the time of the Revolution, the colonists' drinking habits had escalated until each colonist was drinking almost twice as much as the average person drinks today. Drinking diminished after the Revolution. Between the decrease of the West Indies trade and taxes on whiskey and other liquors instituted by the new federal government, drinking became more expensive and less tolerated. At the beginning of the nineteenth century, Americans slowly began to drink more again, so much that the backlash to drinking—jeremiads by men no one took too seriously—began to reach into the American mind. Temperance societies grew larger, and drinking diminished.

Already in the 1640s there were those who thought the taverns and the drinking needed to be better controlled. The earliest punishments were primitive: flogging, time in the stocks, or the wearing of a huge D for "drunkard." There were also fines for those who, like William Reynolds, vomited "in a beastly manner," under a neighbor's table. Drunkenness, the legislators agreed, caused "lisps or falters" in a person's speech, or "staggers in his going, or [vomiting] by reason of excessive drinking."[15] The earliest drinking laws required taverns to shut at nine p.m., except for out-of-towners. Tavern owners were fined for serving liquor to a list of "habitual tipplers."

Both the Pilgrims and the Puritans imposed dozens of laws to try to control both taverns and individual drunks. This led to a lot of confusion. First, they had to define drunkenness. What was the difference between the respected ministers who had trouble walking because they were drunk after riding the circuit to adjudicate arguments according to the law, and a scoundrel who drank too much in a tavern when he should have been at home…and had trouble walking?

Brought before the magistrates, colonists protested that they had not been drunk. They had "the falling sickness." They had intestinal problems. But colonists had lower standards, and a catchier definition was immortalized in anonymous ditty. "Not drunk is he who from the floor, / Can rise again and still drink more, / But drunk is he who prostrate lies, / Without the power to drink or rise."[16] Maryland poet Ebenezer Cook was more specific. "A Herd of Planters on the ground, / O'erwhelmed with Punch, dead drunk we found."[17]

Drinking is a progressive disease, and the Pilgrims and Puritans understood that the worst offenders were bound to be repeat offenders. Names of drunks were posted over the doors of taverns. In a legal twist reminiscent of our modern twenty-first-century liability laws, tavern keepers were fined for their customer's drunken behavior after they left the tavern.

The colonists struggled to draw a line between good drinking and bad drinking, and they failed to come up with a universal definition. This is hardly surprising, since even today the definition of an alcoholic is as fuzzy as a drunk's vision after a few too many. Our drunk driving laws pin down drunkenness as having a blood alcohol level of .08—about what a person has if they have been steadily drinking a drink every hour.

This is problematic since each driver is different and each situation is different. The police field test for alcoholism is hauntingly like the definition the Pilgrims came up with—can the person walk a straight line, do they stutter, can they see straight? It's clear that the early colonists struggled to define drunkenness just as we do, but it's also clear that their definition was far more lax than ours. Many of the great men of the seventeenth and eighteenth centuries in Colonial America were, by our modern definition, impaired quite a lot of the time. Without cars, their definition necessarily was predicated on the drunk's ability to walk and talk, and they seemed ready to tolerate a blood alcohol level two or three times higher than the one we have set as law.

The Pilgrims had no medical or psychological treatment for alcoholism, and it was clear even then that their punishments were remarkably useless. It wasn't just the New England colonists who drank a lot, but colonists everywhere in the United States. In New Amsterdam and in Jamestown, Virginia, and as the colonies spread west into Kentucky and Illinois and south into Georgia and Florida, colonial life was characterized by a defiant attitude fueled by plenty of cider, whiskey, and rum distilled from the river of molasses pouring in from the Caribbean and the southern states.

Certainly the mixture of drinking and politics that grew up around the colonial taverns was unique to the new world. The Pilgrims and the Puritans were not ordinary colonists. Driven away from home by religious fear, they were unusually well educated, and most of them were part of a family. This high seriousness combined with alcohol created a dangerous idea: independence. Why should they be governed by men who were not only far away, but not necessarily more intelligent or better informed? Defiance is a characteristic of drinkers, and the response of King George II (during his reign in 1727–1760) and his loyalists in Massachusetts—to punish those who disobeyed his laws—was not very useful.

In 1686, in the wake of a damaging war with the Indians—King Philip's War—and a series of state boundary disputes, the king of England thought it would be a good idea to bring the unruly colonies back under control. King James II appointed Edmund Andros, formerly the bailiff of Guernsey, to sail to the New World and tame the increasingly obstreperous colonists. Andros would become governor of what would now be called the Dominion of New England, automatically revoking previous charters and unseating the existing governors, respected men like William Bradford in Plymouth and Edward Winthrop in Boston.

Probably no one could have reconciled the colonists with the idea of a government imposed by the king, but Andros made a lot of mistakes. First he asked if the Puritan churches could be used for Anglican services. Then he instituted a tax on liquor imports. Although the colonists were making their own beer, they still imported whiskey, rum, and molasses for the creation of rum. Finally, he outlawed the town meetings which were at the heart of the colonial democracy—restricting them to one a year. Drunk or temperate, the colonists hated all this. Perhaps James II should have known better than to try to govern a city like Boston, which had almost a hundred public houses—or one for every twenty adult males. When news of James II being overthrown reached New England in April 1689, the colonists rose up against Andros, who tried to escape dressed as a woman, was captured, escaped again, and was finally sent to England for trial.

The two strains of the new American character—temperance and sober well-educated family life versus drinking freely—were reflected in the colony's newspapers. The Plymouth colonists and the Massachusetts Bay colonists were family people whose literacy rate—almost 98 percent among men—was unusually high. By the middle of the eighteenth century, Boston's four newspapers, as well as many booksellers and pamphleteers, were as unregulated as its worst drunk. The first settlers tended to be well-mannered, devout, and clean—the *Mayflower*'s first foray onto the shore of Cape Cod was made so that the ship's women could finally do the laundry. As Eric Burns writes of their manners and their concern with propriety, "You would never have known it from their newspapers."

The colonial press, unrestrained by libel or copyright laws, seemed to thrive on the kind of scurrilous gossip easily collected in taverns, and to express its content in the angriest possible language. One paper accused another, for instance, of employing a collection of "incendiary, prostituted, hireling scribblers." Typically, an early colonist columnist wrote, "If ever a nation was debauched by a man, the American nation has been debauched by [George] Washington." When that writer died, a pro-Washington newspaper wrote that the "memory of this scoundrel cannot be too highly execrated."[18] In the meantime William Cobbett of the *Porcupine's Gazette* described his competitor, the contentious Benjamin Franklin Bache of the *Philadelphia Aurora*, as a "crafty and lecherous old hypocrite."[19]

George Washington, a wealthy Virginia aristocrat who loved parties and fox hunting, found out about the connection between drinking and voting for the American electorate the hard way. A rigorous military commander who drove his soldiers hard and expected much of them, he began to aspire to a government position after he did not get a command in the British military. While seeking a seat in the Virginia Assembly in 1755, he was roundly defeated.

Two years later he ran again, but this time he delivered 144 gallons of rum, punch, cider, and wine to the polling places distributed by election volunteers who urged the voters to drink up. At 307 votes, he got a return on his investment of almost two votes per gallon.[20] Most elections featured vats and barrels of free liquor as well as the candidate in hand to drink along with his constituency. Candidates showed off their generosity as well as their drinking capacity. Although voting while intoxicated was normal for the colonists, French traveler Ferdinand Bayard was horrified to notice, "Candidates offer drunkenness openly to anyone who is willing to give them his vote."[21]

A few years later the writer George Prentice described a Kentucky election that lasted three days. "During that period whiskey and apple toddy flow through our cities and villages like the Euphrates through ancient Babylon."[22] Later, after the Revolution, some of the Founding

Fathers objected to the American way of voting. James Madison, who drank a pint of whiskey daily to aid his digestion,[23] was also running for the Virginia Assembly in 1777. Madison decided that bribing the voters with alcohol was beneath his dignity and the dignity of the new nation. The influence of liquor at the polls was "inconsistent with the purity of moral and republican virtues," he announced. He lost.

Later, when he became Thomas Jefferson's secretary of state, Madison's ideas about democracy began to sharpen. A Virginia aristocrat who had grown up on a plantation, he did not believe in "excessive democracy"; democracy was too precious to waste on the common man. This belief, which may have begun with his horror at the way polling places were conducted, led him to favor a strong federal government, and he eventually helped Alexander Hamilton— another man who was disturbed by drunkenness—draft *The Federalist Papers*.

By the 1750s the stage was set for an explosion that would be "the shot heard round the world," as Ralph Waldo Emerson wrote. England was ruled by King George III, who took the British throne during the Seven Years' War (which included the French and Indian War) over the control of colonial lands in North America, India, Portugal, and other places. In North America, the campaign began with the seizure of a British encampment (later Fort Duquesne) by the French in the disputed Ohio Valley. This was followed by an attack led by George Washington, then a lieutenant colonel in the British colonial militia Virginia Regiment, at Jumonville Glen in 1754.

As this war on many fronts came to a close with a British victory, King George III was left with huge debts caused by expenditures during the war. His answer: tax and control the colonies he had fought to protect. In 1763, a Royal Proclamation put a boundary on the western expansion of the colonies, hoping to redirect colonial exploration of the north—Nova Scotia—and the south. In 1765, Whig party leader Sir George Grenville introduced the Stamp Act, which levied a tax on every document printed in America, including newspapers whose writers naturally lobbied against it in the most strenuous language.

In English minds, it was only fair for the American colonists to help pay for the armies that had already been deployed to defend them from the French and the Indians, and for other ways in which they had expected to be helped by Britain. In the colonial mind, taxes and regulations from England were unfair not because of their content, but because there were no Americans seated in Parliament. The colonies' fate was being decided by men who didn't have a chance to hear the colonies' story. "No taxation without representation," became the colonial battle cry.

Then in 1773, the British Parliament passed the Tea Act, taxing British tea sold in the colonies. Protestors kept tea from being unloaded all along the coast. If it was going to be taxed it would not be unloaded. Two of the tea ships returned to England with full cargoes of tea. But Governor Thomas Hutchinson refused to allow the tea slated for Boston to be returned to Britain. He would not be bullied by the colonists. As three ships filled with tea remained in Boston Harbor, on Hutchinson's orders, a mob swarmed up to his house and terrified the governor and his family, but he did not change his mind.

Many men knew that the Boston taverns were fermenting rebellion. John Adams, eavesdropping one night, heard drinkers rallying against the oppression of the new taxes. "Oppression will make wise men mad," one drinker, said while others cheered him on. In between hearing political speakers, men like Alexander Hamilton and Benjamin Franklin, drinkers heard a more incendiary type of exhortation.

One tavern in particular, the Green Dragon Tavern, a two-story brick building near the intersection of Union and Hanover Streets, had a basement room in which a powerful and violent revolutionary group first banded together in 1765. Joseph Warren, Paul Revere, Edward Proctor, as well as members of a secret antiloyalist society called the Loyal Nine regularly met there in the hope that they could enlist working-class men in their cause. Other taverns were also incubators of rebellion, but the Loyal Nine became the precursor of the Sons of Liberty, a group of dissidents including John Hancock and Benjamin Rush as well as Samuel and John Adams.

Meetings in the basement of the Green Dragon were planning sessions over beer and rum and occasional whiskey and the lethal house punch. Named for the copper dragon placard that hung over the door, the place was the center of Boston's North End and the center of the group of men who were to plan the American Revolution, which included Paul Revere's famous ride to warn the colonists that the British were on the way. Inside and downstairs the smell of beer mixed with the smell of sawdust, while out the high windows the land sloped down to a mill pond and finally the harbor. Conversations here led to the torching of the British customs ship *Gaspée* in Narragansett Bay, the burning of British officials in effigy, and the ransacking of Lieutenant Governor Andrew Oliver's home. The insurrectionary action that made them famous, tipping the scales from dissidence into war between the British and their colonies, occurred in December 1773 and included some shiploads of cheap black tea—Bohea—headed for Boston Harbor. Notes from a Green Dragon regular state that "we met to plan the consignment of a few shiploads of tea."

The plan, like most plans hatched in taverns, was a badly kept secret. A popular song, with rhymes enhanced by the blurring effects of drink, explained:

Rally, Mohawks!—bring out your axes!
And tell King George we'll pay no taxes
On his foreign tea!
His threats are vain—and vain to think
To force our girls and wives to drink
His vile Bohea!
Then rally boys, and hasten on
To meet our chiefs at the Green Dragon.

Our Warren's there, and bold Revere,
With hands to do and words to cheer
For Liberty and laws!
Our country's "braves" and firm defenders,
Shall neer be left by true North-Enders,
Fighting Freedom's cause!
Then rally boys, and hasten on
To meet our chiefs at the Green Dragon.[24]

The original plan for the night of December 16 was to block the unloading of the tea scheduled for the next day. British law required the return of cargo that had not been unloaded in twenty days. Unloaded tea could not be taxed. The tea ships would be forced to ignominiously return their cargo to England as other tea ships had been forced to do. Of course that was not what happened. That afternoon, crowds of citizens gathered at the Old South Church to determine a course of action. A more effective meeting was taking place at the Green Dragon Tavern.

On the night of December 16, 1773, just nineteen days after the *Dartmouth* arrived in Boston Harbor, a group of men dressed as Mohawk Indians to hide their identity illegally boarded the tea ships— the *Dartmouth*, the *Eleanor*, and the *Beaver*. Using a canoe they paddled out to the three ships, boarded them and took control from their captains. Then, under the influence of the drinking they had done while planning and perfecting their disguises at the Green Dragon, they jettisoned the original plan and got carried away. Perhaps if they had been sober the night would have been different; they were not sober. They were drunk enough to change history and change it for the better. Instead of securing the tea to the ships, they dumped the tea into Boston Harbor.

"Last night 3 cargoes of Bohea tea were emptied into the sea," John Adams wrote in his diary.[25] "This morning a man of war sails. This is the most magnificent movement of all. There is a dignity, a majesty, a sublimity, in this last effort of the patriots that I greatly admire. The people should never rise, without doing something to be remembered—something notable and striking. This destruction of the tea is so bold, so daring, so firm, intrepid and inflexible, and it must have so important consequences, and so lasting, that I can't but consider it as an epocha in history."

The British Parliament responded to the rebellion in 1774 by trying to make an example of Massachusetts with the punitive Coercive Acts, or Intolerable Acts, which ended local self-government in Massachusetts. Colonists throughout the thirteen colonies in turn responded with additional acts of protest, and by convening the First Continental Congress. Within two years the country would be at war with England.

CHAPTER 3

PAUL REVERE: "THE BRITISH ARE COMING!"

If the Pilgrims and Puritans started out as prodigious beer drinkers, the New World soon reshaped their drinking habits. The first settlers in New England had hoped to become farmers as they had been in England's pleasantly mild climate. It quickly became clear that this was not a possibility. Although England is on a latitude with Nova Scotia, the heated water in the Gulf Stream provides it with a long growing season and a short, rainy winter. Massachusetts, Vermont, and New Hampshire, although farther south, have short growing seasons and brutal, freezing, snowbound winters.

Plymouth Colony was founded on sand—not good growing soil. Even in Boston where the Puritans began to build, the growing season was short and the earth unwelcoming for the crops that had sustained them in England. Slowly, as slowly as traditions and convictions can change, the colonists turned to fishing, hunting, and woodcutting. Using these abundant resources they were eventually able to feed themselves and begin to reap profits.

They resisted the change. It wasn't just that they didn't know how to fish; they didn't want to fish. In the stratified society from which they came, fishermen were far below farmers. Even as fishermen became indispensable in the New World, they stayed low on the social totem pole. The Puritans drank a great deal; the fishermen drank even more.

As the colonists turned from an agricultural society to a society of skilled laborers, their liquor tastes turned as well. The early 1600s had been formed by the Pilgrims' need for beer, beer, and more beer. Beer is an agricultural product.

By the 1650s, because of a number of factors, their thirst had turned toward a liquid far more delicious and deadly—rum. Barley and corn and all the other plants that the early colonists had used to make beer became increasingly scarce, while molasses imported from the West Indies to make rum became increasingly available and cheap. The manufacture of rum began in New England with the first rum distillery in 1667, almost forty years after the arrival of the Pilgrims. By 1770, New England boasted 159 rum distilleries, imported 6 million gallons of Caribbean molasses a year, and consumed more rum than beer.[1] By the turn of the century, rum production was the largest and most prosperous industry in New England.[2]

New England rum, made through a double process including both fermentation (like beer) and distillation (like whiskey), was based on molasses—the brown, sweet sludge left at the bottom of the pot when sugar cane is boiled to make sugar. Rum, as the people of Massachusetts certainly understood, was both a gift from God and an invitation to dance with the devil. Unfortunately, the rum trade developed a dreadful dimension over time. Shrewd Yankee sailors soon saw that they could earn more substantial profits if they stopped in two ports of call rather than one—something that created what came to be known as the infamous triangle trade.

The ease of sailing with different winds and currents had already established many thriving trade routes. The voyages took about a year of sailing back and forth across the Atlantic from England and Africa to New England and the Caribbean. For instance on one route, sailors ferried New England rum from England to Africa, where it was traded for slaves captured from villages in West Africa. The slaves were taken to the West Indies over the often-fatal "middle passage" and sold or traded for a cargo of molasses. The molasses was then sailed to New England to be made into rum. The West Indians then sold many of their slaves to the American South, so the triangle trade that made the Yankee Captains of Boston and Newport wealthy also built up the institution of slavery in the south.

One of the first attempts by the British Crown to curtail the profits and wealth being generated in their new colonies of New England was the Molasses Act of 1733. This act, which imposed a tax on every gallon of foreign molasses imported to America from Africa or the Caribbean, was one of what would come to be dozens of laws controlling trade in and out of colonial harbors. These excise laws would eventually ignite the American Revolution. For the moment, the colonists ignored the Molasses Act. "Far from being considered a crime, smuggling became an act of patriotism, and New England's sea captains became artists at sneaking their cargoes past British customs inspectors," writes Alice Fleming in *Alcohol: The Delightful Poison*. Narragansett Bay in Rhode Island, with its three-fingered harbor and dozens of islands, was ideal for smugglers; Boston Harbor is also a warren of passages and islands. In one year alone, fifteen thousand hogsheads[3] of molasses were imported into Massachusetts; taxes were paid on only one thousand.

By the eighteenth century the colonists were less focused on God and more focused on profits. Gone was their piety as well as their distaste for local fish—a distaste which had led dozens of them to starve to death. Gone was their high-minded religiosity. Drinking had been part of what changed them along with adversity, rage at authority, and the tremendous abundance of the New World. They were no longer men and women wedded to freedom of belief. Now they were a community devoted to trade, eating, and drinking. In a poem about the residents of Derryfield, New Hampshire, one William Stark wrote: "It was often said, that their only care, / And their only wish, and their only prayer, / For the present world, and the world to come, / Was a string of eels and a jug of rum."

In American history drinking has sometimes caused disasters—the Pilgrims' landing—but has sometimes caused great triumphs. During the American Revolution especially, drinking seems to have gone hand in hand with heroism. A few drafts of rum could make a man powerfully convincing no matter what the odds. Rum can also make you brave, confident, and scornful of conventional obstacles. Conceived in the taverns of New England, the American Revolution continued to be fueled by rum.

It has been said that God watches over children and drunks. This seems to have been the case for both Ethan Allen, who sauntered into the bedroom of a commandant and ordered him to surrender, and for Paul Revere, who, after being captured by the British, talked them into letting him go and persuaded them that the small, ragged militia waiting for them on Lexington Green was actually a few hundred well-trained and well-armed men.

"Paul Revere's Ride" by Henry Wadsworth Longfellow and "Concord Hymn" by Ralph Waldo Emerson are both poems that sacrifice the actual facts to the constraints of rhyme and the possibility of entertainment. This is just as well, since liquor figures in both stories. Historical poems by men like Longfellow and Emerson were the movies of the nineteenth century. They were amusing, and a lot more fun than reading dry old history books, but extremely inaccurate and often embellished. Longfellow memorializes a ride that never happened and mistakenly writes that the lantern signals from Old North Church Tower—one if by land and two if by sea—were *for* Revere when in fact they were signals *from* Revere. The shots that were heralded by Emerson as the first shots of the American Revolution near Concord's North Bridge on the morning of April 19, 1775, were not the first shots of the armed conflict between England and her American colony. Those actual first shots were fired probably by accident, probably from the window of Buckman Tavern earlier the same morning on Lexington Green.

By April 1775 the colonists and the British were at war, although they had not yet begun shooting at each other in an official battle. Psychologically the colonies had been at war with the British since the Boston Massacre, in which British soldiers shot into an unruly crowd in March 1770 and killed five unarmed citizens. Since the Boston Tea Party, physical violence had become part of the angry disagreement between the colonists and their faraway British government. Still, until 1775 there had been no military engagement between the colonial militia, mostly recruited farmers, and the well-trained British Regulars.

While tensions boiled, the British and the colonial government each failed to understand the seriousness of their opponent's intentions. "Congress was bluffing, confident that Britain would again back down, as in 1766 and 1770…This time Britain did not do so, and called the colonial bluff," writes Peter Thomas in *Tea Party to Independence.* "The War of Independence was not a heroic enterprise but the result of a political miscalculation."[4] This cynical view skips over the passionate defiance and the ardent love of individual freedom that had somehow grown up in the New England colonies—defiance fueled by alcohol, but also embedded in the Yankee soul. The founders of New England came from a tradition of separatism and reform and the adversities of the New World had set their feisty character in local granite. "We always had been free, and we meant to be free always," said one veteran of April 18 in Concord, "[Those redcoats] didn't mean we should."[5]

On the night of April 18 a British force under Lt. Col. Francis Smith and Gen. Thomas Gage, walking in strict formation with their red uniforms, crossed bandoliers, and high bearskin hats, were given orders to march north from Boston where they were headquartered. Although the soldiers did not know it, their plans were to march north to the village of Concord and destroy military supplies hidden in houses there. They were also supposed to capture patriot leaders John Hancock and Samuel Adams, who were in hiding near Lexington, six miles east of Concord. The march was supposed to be a secret, and the British hoped to take the colonists by surprise.

Before the British began marching, however, the patriots had learned their intentions. Many people noticed the British call to arms and the ferrying of troops from the British warships in the harbor. General Gage's American wife, Margaret, who was friends with the colonial leader Dr. Joseph Warren, may also have given away the secret. News spread fast. By the time a breathless messenger arrived to tell Paul Revere at his house in Boston's North End that the British were marching, Revere had already heard it from three other sources.

Paul Revere was a silversmith by trade and a rebel by inclination. He had become an express rider for the colonists, and he had undertaken at least two other trips from Boston to warn villages of the British plans. On the night of April 18, he was one of at least three riders—with William Dawes and Dr. Samuel Prescott—sent from Boston by the Sons of Liberty to warn the populace. Like Revere, William Dawes left Boston late that night, riding both to let the colonial militia know that the British were coming and to urge Adams and Hancock to escape. Each of the riders took a different route.

Revere had huge advantages over the British, including but not limited to a few inspiriting glasses of rum. He was a guerilla, helped across Boston Harbor to Charlestown by local boatmen whose oars were hastily muffled by a willing female colonist's underwear. Even nature seemed to be on his side. The British had seized all the harbor ferries and moored the HMS *Somerset*—a ship of the line with sixty-four guns—in the middle of the harbor, where she swayed back and forth with the current like a tiger pacing in her cage. The moon was nearly full and on a normal April night would have cast sharp shadows of every boat on the water. Miraculously, a lunar anomaly on April 18, 1775, kept the moon low in the sky and to the south over the city of Boston. Revere's boat passed a few feet east of the great warship's bowsprit without being seen.[6]

The British Regulars had no such luck. They, too, left Boston at about ten p.m., but their harbor crossing was badly planned. Their navy's longboats were too big for the crossing, and the soldiers were forced to wade in and march their first long miles through the marshy swamps of Lechmere Point. British soldiers wore uniforms that "might have been designed by some demonic tailor who had sworn sartorial vengeance upon the human frame," writes David Hackett Fischer.[7] Their high bearskin hats were balky and heavy, their weighty red coats restricted any action, and were decorated with lace, buttons, loops, knots, and heart-shaped badges. Their heavy, thick leather boots fitted so badly that there was no distinction between left and right feet. The heavy leather clodhoppers were awkward and quickly filled with water and mud. The British troops marched in regimental formation, and were loaded down with supplies, muskets, bayonets, and ammunition boxes. Furthermore, their boots made a thunderous noise as they tramped north on a so-called secret mission—so secret that the soldiers did not know where they were going although, as they marched, it became clear that everyone else in the countryside was expecting them.

While the British floundered around in Lechmere, Revere, who had borrowed a fleet horse named Brown Beauty chosen for him by his fellow rebels, was already in Medford, having a drink with his friend Capt. Isaac Hall. In Medford, about halfway between Cambridge and Lexington on the road to Concord, Paul Revere had halted at Hall's house and tavern. Hall, a captain in the colonial minutemen and a rum distiller, provided Revere with two draughts—tall glasses—of rum to fortify him for the rest of his night ride.[8]

By midnight, while the British soldiers were still trying to get out of the swamps near Boston, Revere had reached the Clarke House in Lexington, where Hancock and Adams were staying. Here he found Hancock about to make dinner of a fresh salmon. Unperturbed by Revere's warning, Hancock and Adams reluctantly agreed to move. Hancock wanted to bring the salmon. Revere, Dawes, and Prescott joined Adams and Hancock for a few drinks and finally got them into

Hancock's heavy carriage without the salmon, then headed for nearby Woburn and relative safety. Hancock had told Revere that his trunk—filled with dispatches from the rebels and the militia—was safely in the attic of Buckman Tavern in Lexington. Later, Hancock sent a carriage back to get the salmon.

When Revere arrived at the Lexington Green, he woke everyone up. Soon the bell in the belfry of the Lexington Meetinghouse was ringing, and by two a.m. about 130 members of the Lexington militia had assembled on the green under the leadership of Capt. John Parker. These were men who knew each other intimately; many of them were related. They had built the town where they lived, and now they were happy to defend it. "Their sense of self-worth was determined not by ancient notions or protocols of class but by their ability to farm, hunt, and fight," writes Nathaniel Philbrick.[9]

Their sense of community was also entwined with their ability to drink. Across from the Lexington Meetinghouse on the lumpy triangular Lexington Green was the equally prominent Buckman Tavern. The citizens of Lexington worshipped on one side of the green and drank on the other. Once assembled, the militia realized that there was no threat…yet. The British were not coming—at least not for a while. Captain Parker sent scouts down the road toward Cambridge, and they reported no activity. Parker dismissed his men and told them to be ready to reassemble at any time. Parker and many of his militia retired to the warm, cozy, and boozy interior of Buckman Tavern. For three hours they drank, talked, and waited, and drank some more.

In the meantime Revere turned Brown Beauty toward Concord. There he reunited with Dawes and Prescott, but also ran into a roving group of British cavalry led by Maj. Edward Mitchell. It may have been the rum that caused Revere to let down his guard enough to be captured by a British scouting party. It was certainly the rum that allowed him to bluster his way out of trouble, telling Mitchell that the whole countryside had been alerted to the British plans, and convincing him that five hundred colonial militiamen were waiting for the

British on the Lexington Green with muskets loaded. Astonishingly, Mitchell let Revere go, but they took his horse. Weighted down by boots and spurs, Revere walked back in the direction of Lexington. About this time the thoroughly sodden, miserable British regiments finally began their march from Boston Harbor.

As they clomped north, the British soldiers could see that they were expected. They had hoped to surprise the rebels, but it was too late for that. The woods were filled with men running and they could see signal fires and hear warning shots as they passed through small towns where the houses were dark and shuttered. As they finally approached the Lexington Green at about five o'clock in the morning, the word raced through the small town and reached the militia drinking in Buckman Tavern. The British were arriving! The colonial drummer put down his rum and picked up his drum. The call to arms started to beat, and Parker lined up his militia at the other end of the green from the meetinghouse and the road to Cambridge. In the dim light, the British thought they were facing two or three hundred men.

In fact there were only about seventy militiamen on Lexington Green. After three hours of drinking and no sleep they were far from battle worthy. "They had assembled in a poorly organized, possibly alcohol-debilitated rush," writes Philbrick.[10] In the early light, things were so disorganized that both Paul Revere and John Hancock's secretary, John Lowell, who was carrying John Hancock's important trunk filled with confidential dispatches, staggered between the militia and the British unnoticed. As they stumbled with the trunk past the militia, Revere heard Parker order: "Let the troops pass by. Don't molest them, without they being first."[11]

Both the British and the militia had been ordered not to fire the first shot. All the anger felt by the British who had been betrayed by the leaking of their plans, humiliated by the rough farm boys who outflanked them, and frustrated by months of taunting and harassment, seemed to surface in the dawn light on the Lexington Green. The British, told not to shoot, began running toward the ragtag, hungover militia while shouting. One officer, perhaps the seething Mitchell, shouted, "Damn them! We will have them!" The British then formed a line of battle, still yelling. Captain Parker ordered his minutemen to retreat and disperse, but many of them just stood there, seemingly a little under the weather. The first shot may have come from a British officer on a horse, or it may have come from a window in Buckman Tavern.

"The real question," Philbrick writes, "was not who fired the first shot, but why were Parker and his men on the Lexington Green in the first place? Seventy or so militiamen had no chance of stopping an advance guard of more than two hundred British regulars. Instead of spending much of the early morning hours drinking at Buckman Tavern and then stubbornly lingering on the green, the Lexington militia should have already been in Concord." The answer is in the tankards of rum served to excited men at Buckman Tavern.

It wasn't just the militia who were out of line in this melee. The British soldiers, who had loaded their muskets as they approached Lexington Green, were out of control. Some formed a battle line, but others raced ahead as if they would grab the militiamen and tear them limb from limb. There were three officers on horses at the head of the British troops and "at least one of them was having a virtual tantrum," writes Philbrick, "shouting 'Throw down your arms, you villains, you rebels, damn you, disperse!'"[12] The infuriating colonial forces—out of formation, not even in uniform, appearing and disappearing into the woods they knew so well—were aggravating for the British. Now on the Lexington Green they had had enough. They didn't just shoot back at the windows of Buckman Tavern; they charged and screamed and stamped their feet. They huzzahed and howled. As a few shots now came from the houses around the green, the British anger became too much to bear. The Regulars prepared to raid the houses, guns drawn. "The men were so wild they could hear no orders," wrote John Barker in his diary.[13]

This encounter on the Lexington Green at dawn on April 19 was the real beginning of the Revolutionary War. Here the first shots were fired and the first soldiers killed. The British Regulars sustained one wound; the militia lost eight men and had ten wounded. But it was also something else: a classic encounter between guerrilla warriors and uniformed soldiers, and an equally classic encounter between those who drink too much and those who have to deal with them. Alcohol is closely associated with rage. The drunk rages, of course. But the drunk's family and friends will often be even more eaten up with rage. Nothing is more infuriating than a drunk—apologetic and contrite one moment and savage the next.

Colonel Smith, by beating the drum that called them into formation, was slowly able to reassert his command over the British troops. Their orders were to march to Concord. As morning broke, Colonel Smith and his officers and their men headed west leaving the scene of a deadly battle behind them. Colonel Smith had the fife and drums play during the six-mile march to Concord, where they were stopped by the mass of armed and well-prepared militia facing them across the span of the Old North Bridge over the Concord River. It was early in the morning, and the soldiers were sharp-eyed and sober. Here, as we are taught in American History classes, the British fired the first shots killing Isaac Davis and Abner Hosmer and fatally wounding James Hayward. The colonial militia drove the British troops back, back away from the bridge, back over the six miles they had marched so cockily earlier in the day, back to the Lexington Green where, injured and depleted, they were rescued by another British brigade that had come from Boston to help. The Revolutionary War had begun.

Because of the importance of the events of the years between 1750 and 1800, or because Americans are great storytellers, or because the combination of wild imaginations and plenty of rum made for tall tales, the mythologizing of the early colonists and the bold men who opposed the British in the Revolutionary War is rich historical territory. During the early years of the United States, it seemed all men were larger than life and vibrating with fierce courage and a wild desire for freedom. With Homeric tones and epic sagas, the historians who have written and spoken about these men have definitely let their feelings embroider their facts.

When news of the encounter on Lexington Green and at Concord's North Bridge reached the Catamount Tavern in Bennington, Vermont, it thrilled the group headquartered there—the Green Mountain Boys and their leader, Ethan Allen. Of all the characters in the American Revolution story, none embodies the courage and devilish style which drink can provide as well as Ethan Allen. Born to an aristocratic family in Litchfield, Connecticut, Allen had won and lost a fortune before he was thirty. He had prepared to go to Yale as many men in his family had before him, but he stopped at a tavern on the way to New Haven and never made it to college. He was a successful iron foundry owner, a tannery owner, a real estate speculator, and a professional hunter.

Allen was a controversial leader who had been banned from many towns in Massachusetts and Connecticut for his rowdy language and his disrespect for the clergy and town elders. He would become one of the best-selling writers of the new colony with his memoir about being held as a prisoner of war by the British and escaping. A large, rough-looking man who sometimes spent the winter alone trapping in the great New England forests, he had nothing but contempt for the rules and regulations from England that were slowly squeezing the profits out of the American trade. Men followed him, and by 1775 the Green Mountain Boys were one of the largest forces in the colonial army.

Ethan Allen was the kind of loner who was tailor-made for myth-making. A Robin Hood who bought land and then granted it to his personal soldiers, his larger-than-life quality and his almost supernatural courage enabled him to push back the landholders who had previously claimed the western part of New Hampshire and the eastern part of New York and create the new state where he is still worshipped as a secular saint—Vermont.

Rum was the drink of the colonies, and no one stood for rum consumption the way Ethan Allen did. Many of the stories about Ethan Allen, some true and some apocryphal, are centered on his prodigious appetite for booze and his almost godlike courage when under the influence. "Stories of his drinking prowess are without end," writes B. A. Botkin in *A Treasury of New England Folklore*.[14]

Of the dozens of Ethan Allen drinking stories, the most famous is the story of how he and his friend, Remember Baker, had been drinking and walking all night and lay down for a nap in a rocky glen. "Sometime later Baker was roused by a noise and woke to gaze horrified at the spectacle of Colonel Allen asleep while on his broad chest was coiled a huge rattler, all of five feet long."[15] As Baker watched, the rattlesnake repeatedly bit his friend. Baker pushed the snake off Allen and then noticed the snake's head weaving strangely. The snake released a huge burp, and Baker understood—the snake was drunk. When Allen woke up he complained about the mosquitoes.

Allen was married twice—once unhappily and once happily—and fathered eight children. Once, during his unhappy first marriage, a group of friends hoping to scare him out of drinking dressed up as ghosts and accosted him at a bridge on the outskirts of Arlington. When they rose up and hooted, Allen laughed. "If you are angels, welcome," he slurred out. "If you are devils come home with me—I married your sister."

An inspired woodsman and a man who put a simple notion of honesty and fairness above any laws of the king, Allen was inspired to attempt the exploit that made him famous—the taking of Fort Ticonderoga from the British—by the April 1775 news that the war between the British and the colonial forces had finally begun on the green at Lexington and the North Bridge of Concord.

Two weeks after the historic events at Lexington and Concord, Allen planned a May 9 attack on a British stronghold in his own territory: Fort Ticonderoga at the head of Lake Champlain. Ticonderoga, held by a skeleton force of fewer than fifty men, would be valuable for the cannons and ordnance it protected rather than for possession of the fort. At the same time, a colonial commander from Connecticut named Benedict Arnold was making plans to take the fort.

Arnold, too, had been headed for Yale until drinking intervened—but it wasn't Arnold's drinking; it was his father's drinking that led his family into bankruptcy. A fastidious man with a brilliant strategic mind, Arnold would become so disillusioned with the colonial militia and the colonial leaders that a few years after Ticonderoga, after the surrender at Yorktown, he would betray his country. He felt he didn't get credit for his role as a Revolutionary general. He planned to turn himself over to the British Army complete with the plans for West Point, the colonial army's principal fortification on the Hudson River, which commanded the Hudson highlands with a chain across the water to keep British boats from proceeding upstream. Arnold's spy, Maj. John André, was captured with the plans for West Point hidden in his boot and hung. Arnold barely escaped and later joined the British Army as a brigadier general.

Ticonderoga, on the strategically important narrow spit of land between the bottom of Lake Champlain and the top of Lake George, was a French-built, star-shaped fort that had been used during the French and Indian War. Designed by the Marquis de Lotbinière, it was finished in 1758, and with its red tile roofs, gray turrets, stone gables, and magnificent water views, it looked as much like a Loire Valley chateau as a military fort. Built at a critical portage across the turbulent La Chute River, it was also famously impregnable. During the Battle of Carillon four thousand French soldiers had been able to repel a force of sixteen thousand British soldiers.

Arnold, who always wore a scarlet uniform even as a colonial general, appeared at the Catamount Tavern to investigate his rival and, he thought, to enlist the Green Mountain Boys. A rowdy crowd of drinkers explained to Arnold in no uncertain terms that Allen was already on his way to the fort, and Arnold and his men set off to the north. When Allen and Arnold met near the promontory at Hand's Cove opposite the fort, the two men decided to work together. The attack date was set for May 9.

But waiting for his militia was making Allen nervous. It was planting season in Vermont. British patrols were everywhere, and many men wanted to be home to protect their families and farms. To follow Ethan Allen was to be half drunk a lot of the time, but many of the men selected to storm Ticonderoga had become too drunk to participate. "Some of the boys…had been distracted by a cellar stocked with choice liquors," Willard Randall wrote in his biography of Ethan Allen.[16] Near midnight the combined forces of Allen and Arnold—three hundred men—waited on shore for boats that never came. Finally, as the sky was beginning to lighten, two boats arrived, and Allen and Arnold were able to ferry more than eighty men across the choppy, icy water to New York. Like Paul Revere on the night of April 18, less than a month earlier, Allen was drinking constantly to keep up his courage and his energy levels as well as his optimism in the face of discouraging circumstances. It worked.

Undeterred, with a force of fewer than a hundred men, Allen gave the three-owl hoot, a signal to advance on the fort, at four o'clock in the morning on May 10. Allen and Arnold crept up the side of the fort with their ragtag group of soldiers. Everything went wrong. Allen had been told that the great iron gates of the fort were open, but they were shut. A sentry stood at the small door to one side. But the sentry was asleep. Awakened and taken into custody by Allen, he was forced to lead the Green Mountain Boys into the fort and toward the sleeping commandant. As Allen, Arnold, and their men clattered up the stairs, they were stopped by British lieutenant Jocelyn Feltham. Allen swung at Feltham and hit one of the prominent hair combs that British officers used to keep their powdered wigs in place under their hats—and the lieutenant was knocked out rather than killed.

After a few more fits and starts, Allen found himself face to face with Capt. William Delaplace of His Majesty's Twenty-Sixth, the fort's commandant who, having heard the commotion, was starting to get dressed. British soldiers wore elaborate uniforms, and Delaplace had barely got his pants on when Allen burst into his bedroom. When Delaplace asked on what authority he had entered the fort, most history books state that Ethan Allen bellowed out, "In the name of the great Jehovah and the Continental Congress." In fact, according to the men who were there, he yelled out: "Come out of there you goddam old rat!"[17]

Captain Delaplace emerged and handed over one of the most important British forts to a band of nonuniformed guerrillas. Allen's triumph was so swift and decisive that it took even the American leaders by surprise. Arnold was horrified when Allen gave his men permission to loot the liquor stores of the fort. Although the taking of the fort itself may have been a small victory in terms of soldiers captured, Allen's actions were critical to the success of the revolution. Taking the fort by surprise and guile meant that it did not have to be taken by force. The superior British army with its endless supplies and ammunition could be outsmarted. Perhaps more important, the captured cannons from Ticonderoga were transported overland to Boston by Allen and his men. There they were one of the factors that enabled the patriots to win the Battle of Bunker Hill.

Later, after he had been captured by the British, Ethan Allen waited out the war in a prison camp, then returned to his home in Burlington. Allen died on a cold night in 1789 after a night of drinking at his cousin Ebenezer's Tavern on South Hero at the north end of Lake Champlain. When Yale president Ezra Stiles heard that Allen was dead, he wrote one of the final angry assessments of the man who created Vermont: "13th Instant died in Vermont the profane and impious Deist General Ethan Allen, author of the *Oracles of Reason*, a book replete with scurrilous reflexions on Revelation."[18]

The first man who proposed a different way of looking at drinking in colonial life was Dr. Benjamin Rush, a Philadelphia aristocrat who was the doctor of the Continental Congress and the founding fathers—among his patients were Washington, Adams, Hancock, and Franklin, and their families. Before Dr. Rush there had been two clearly defined attitudes toward drinking in the colonies: drinking was a gift from God, and/or drunkenness was a curse from the devil. Rush understood the powerlessness of the alcoholic and the oversimplification many people brought to bear on the problem of liquor. In a way that was as prophetic as it was ignored, Benjamin Rush understood that alcoholism is a disease.

Dr. Benjamin Rush had great credentials. He was a signer of the Declaration of Independence and an early abolitionist, and during the Revolution he treated the soldiers of the colonial army. His great cause was community health, and he urged the city of Philadelphia to clean the streets and dispose of sewage properly. Born in 1746, he was the first United States surgeon general. A man who has had too much to drink, Rush wrote, is "in folly...a calf—in stupidity, an ass—in roaring, a mad bull—in quarreling and fighting, a dog—in cruelty, a tiger—in fetor, a skunk—in filthiness, a hog—and in obscenity, a he-goat."[19]

As his ideas developed, Benjamin Rush became much more than just another temperance crusader. He was fascinated by alcoholism and addiction. In his 1805 treatise *An Inquiry into the Effects of Ardent Spirits on the Human Body and Mind*, he put forward the idea that alcoholism was an affliction, a physical disorder, and not a moral failing or a lack of willpower. He understood that when an alcoholic drinks, he or she loses control. The alcohol was the problem, Rush believed, not the alcoholic. His solution to the problem was to wean alcoholics off hard liquor with less potent substances like beer or wine sometimes mixed with laudanum or opium.

Alternatively, Rush wrote that alcoholics with craving might try a drink called Switchel, made from sugar, vinegar, and water. Indeed more than a hundred years later, Alcoholics Anonymous cofounders Bill Wilson and Bob Smith weaned men off of alcohol with a diet of Karo corn syrup and sauerkraut. Called the "father of psychiatry," Rush also advocated compassionate treatment for the mentally ill—men and women who were at that time generally locked up in appalling conditions.

But Rush's ideas about addiction were a glimmer of brilliance in a seething mass of ignorance typical of the practitioners of nineteenth-century medicine. The early nineteenth-century doctors were often proponents of what they called "heroic" medicine, meaning that they depended on drastic measures to drive illness out of the body.[20] Emetics such as mercury, which poisoned entire generations of patients (including George Washington and Louisa May Alcott) were popular—as the body was purged, it was thought the disease would also be purged. Leeches and bloodletting were also popular. Rush was a proponent of bleeding patients and believed that the human body could lose 80 percent of its blood and still heal—he is sometimes accused of killing his patient Benjamin Franklin, who was eighty-four and had severe health problems including gout, with excess bleeding.

In some ways, Benjamin Rush was ahead of his times, in other ways he was just plain crazy. Rush, for instance, believed that drinking too much could cause spontaneous combustion. He wrote that he had once seen a hard-drinking man belch near the flames of a candle and become destroyed by flames. Out of ignorance, other medical men agreed. Union College president, Presbyterian minister Dr. Eliphalet Nott, whose student William James went on to write about a different kind of spiritual conflagration, also believed that too much drinking could cause a man to be burned alive from within.[21] As Eric Burns has pointed out, incidents of spontaneous combustion, which were also taken up by Charles Dickens a century later and used to comic effect in *Bleak House*, were the UFOs of the eighteenth century. Spontaneous combustion seems absurd in 2015, but so do many of the things that early American colonists believed: witchcraft, the inferiority of women, and the animal nature of slaves, to name a few.

In spite of his many illusions, Benjamin Rush had released a new idea into the world—the idea of a different attitude toward drunkenness, a kind of combination of forgiveness and temperance. He made temperance respectable. Soon after his last treatise was published at the beginning of the nineteenth century, the very first temperance societies began to be formed. Since the Pilgrims, the colonists had conflicted attitudes toward alcohol. It was so good, but it was so bad. With the idea that alcoholism was involuntary, the latter belief—that alcoholism was so bad—gained power.

CHAPTER 4

ALEXANDER HAMILTON AND THE WHISKEY REBELLION, JOHN AND ABIGAIL ADAMS'S SONS AND GRANDSONS

Many things in our country's history begin with the great George Washington. From our fierceness for the truth to our independence, our nature is embodied in the stories we are taught about our country's first president and founding father. What we aren't taught as often is that George Washington and most of our other founding fathers had close connections to alcohol—in politics, in business, and in their families. Washington's introduction to the intersection of alcohol and politics happened during his first election to the Virginia House of Burgesses—the one he lost because he failed to provide enough to drink at polling places.

It was a lesson he learned well. Awareness of alcohol's effects on other people's behavior became one of the cornerstones of Washington's leadership abilities. As a military man, he helped his soldiers fight by getting them a little drunk. "The benefits arising from the moderate use of strong liquor have been experienced in all armies and are not to be disputed," he explained.[1] From the drunken militia on Lexington Green on April 19, 1775, right through the Revolutionary War, liquor was used in the American military to embolden soldiers, to inspire military men, and, of course, to numb the pain of the wounded and dying.[2] Washington, himself an enthusiastic drinker who favored rum from Barbados, knew what to do for his men during the grueling winter of 1777 at Valley Forge—he doubled their rum ration. By the time the Revolutionary War ended, there were 2,579 registered distilleries in the thirteen states[3] for fewer than three million people.

It was in the years after his service as president, when he had retired to the elegant, eight-thousand-acre Mount Vernon in Virginia, that George Washington's connection to liquor became profitable. At the suggestion of a Scottish estate manager, James Anderson, Washington agreed to put some of his acres into rye and corn with an eye to building a distillery at the edge of Dogue Creek, about two miles from the columned mansion. Rum had become expensive to produce, because the molasses trade had been interrupted by the war. Although Washington himself favored imported port, which may have contributed to his dental problems, Anderson persuaded Washington that homegrown liquor could be just as good.

By 1798, with its five stills going, the newly built distillery—about seventy-five feet by thirty feet—was one of the largest structures in a young America, producing eleven thousand gallons of whiskey. It was the most profitable of Washington's Mount Vernon ventures. The process created a great deal of slop and mash that was fed to some very happy Mount Vernon hogs. In 1798, Polish visitor Julian Niemcewicz toured the site and noted: "If this distillery produces poison for men, it offers in return the most delicate and the most succulent feed for pigs. They keep 150 of them of the Guinea type, short feet, hollow backs and so excessively bulky that they can hardly drag their big bellies on the ground. Their venerable and corpulent appearance recalled to me our Dominican convents, like so many priors."[4]

Expanding his distilleries, Washington began producing brandy, fermenting his own grapes into wine and then distilling the wine. He also built a brewery to make beer. His final years were spent strolling through his prosperous estates and sitting on the veranda drinking with friends while looking out over the city that had already been named after him. A typical Currier and Ives print of 1848 showed

Washington, glass in hand, toasting his officers while a carafe of the same Madeira stood waiting on the table. (Thirty years later, when the country was swept with temperance fever, the engraving was redone, with the glass removed from Washington's hand and the carafe transformed into his habitual tricorne hat.)[5]

Yet Washington's principal aide, one of his bravest soldiers and the man who would shape his sense of the right way to govern, was a man who despised excessive drinking—Alexander Hamilton. Hamilton came from the small Caribbean Island of Nevis in the Leeward Islands, where he was born out of wedlock to Rachel Faucette, a French Huguenot, and James A. Hamilton, the fourth son of the Scottish laird Alexander Hamilton of Kerelaw Castle, Ayrshire. Despite his fancy lineage, James Hamilton was a drunk who abandoned Rachel and her two sons; Rachel died when Alexander was thirteen. James Hamilton never reappeared. This complicated family history left Alexander with a hatred of disorder and a contempt for drunkenness. "The consumption of ardent spirits…is carried to an extreme which is truly to be regretted, as well in regard to the health and morals as to the economy of the community," he wrote.[6]

By the end of the eighteenth century, many farmers in the fledgling United States had realized, along with their president, that there were profits to be made in creating liquor out of their excess corn and rye. Whiskey was easy to make, easy to transport, and easy to sell. A horse that could carry four bushels of grain could carry the whiskey made from twenty-four bushels of grain.[7] Stills began to spring up on farms everywhere. This struck Hamilton as a great opportunity to levy taxes and, perhaps, punish drinkers.

In 1791, Hamilton, who was Washington's secretary of the treasury, decided to add a heavy tax on whiskey to already existing taxes on molasses and rum. Taxation was unpopular with the citizens of the new republic, especially those who had recently fought in a war that seemed to guarantee an end to taxes—a war that had been provoked by unjust taxation. This was different, Hamilton argued. Here, where there was taxation, there was also representation. Hamilton brought a bill before Congress and was granted the ability to tax liquor at seven and a half cents a gallon for domestic products, a tax which rose to nine cents or eleven cents a gallon if the liquor was made from an imported substance like molasses. In addition, sixty cents a year had to be paid for every gallon of liquor a still could produce.

The farmers who produced liquor were outraged. Too late they wrote letters to Congress in protest. Not only was the tax unjust, but it was intrusive. Federal agents looking for stills could snoop in houses, barns, and cellars. In western Pennsylvania, which housed 25 percent of the nation's stills, the citizens swore resistance to the tax inspectors. Federal marshals were intimidated and their houses burned. They were threatened with tarring and feathering—the old treatment for British collaborators. When one colonist offered his house to be a headquarters for the federal agents, his neighbors tied him up and shaved his head.[8]

Soon, both sides were enraged. To Hamilton it seemed that the farmers were refusing to pay their fair share. Drunken irresponsibility! What made it worse was that the federal government, through its massive purchases of liquor for the military, was actually the biggest single customer of the Pennsylvania whiskey distillers. How could the farmers compare the U.S. Treasury to the British? They had representation now, each able-bodied man had a vote, and the people's wishes were reflected in the new democracy.

To the farmers the new tax was an example of another oppressor telling them what to do and then charging them for it. The British had been defeated at great cost. Were they expected to yield to their own federal government, which behaved as the British had? Taxation had started one war. Would it start another?

In 1794 Hamilton tried to bring the Pennsylvania and Kentucky distillers to heel by serving papers that required them to appear in court in Philadelphia. A federal marshal served the seventy-five distillers who were alleged to be breaking the law. The last farmer of the

seventy-five organized a protest that ended in gunfire at a federal inspector's house the next day. A Revolutionary War veteran became
the leader of the insurgents, who then marched ahead of five hundred
men to another inspector's house. More shots were fired, one of the
insurgents was killed, and the farmers set fire to the barn and out-
buildings, smoking out the soldiers whom they took as prisoners and
then released.

Two weeks later the farmers had a larger meeting at Mingo Creek
to address their biggest problem: apathy. Most of the distillers in
Pennsylvania did not want to fight with their government. A few decided to agitate for the many. Four insurgents from the Mingo Creek
meeting were sent to tell the inhabitants of Pittsburgh that if they
did not side with the farmers the whole city would be burned down.
Women wept. People hid their valuables. Fear radiated through the
city. For safety, residents left their homes and assembled in Braddock's
Field.

The response was violent. The group of rebels calling themselves
"the whisky boys" increased their violent resistance, burning down the
home of the new tax inspector, and then fanning out across the countryside taking more retribution against anyone who had collaborated
with the tax inspectors. If Hamilton had not taken them seriously before, they now demanded to be recognized as a serious threat. They
formed an army of irate men to march on the city of Pittsburgh,
which they claimed as their own. They wrote letters to the governments of Britain and Spain proposing an alliance against Washington
and Hamilton.[9] Hamilton obliged by taking their threats seriously.

Finally, at Hamilton's insistence—a passionate insistence that
combined his hatred of drinking with his contempt for the common
people and their idiotic ideas about individual freedom—President
Washington committed one of the greatest overreactions of his years
of leadership.

To quash what came to be called the Whiskey Rebellion, a rebellion of a few hundred farmers and distillers in a remote part of

the United States, Washington sent a force of fifteen thousand uniformed, trained, and armed militiamen to Pennsylvania. Fifteen thousand men! This was more troops than had fought in any single battle of the Revolutionary War. The militia was as reluctant to muster against their own former comrades as the comrades were to fight. The troops marched, and Hamilton and Washington both joined them as military leaders in Carlisle, Pennsylvania. The troops were also led by Robert E. Lee's father, Gen. Henry Lee, who was eager for a fight. "To his disappointment the rebels vanished like rye mash when the heat was applied," writes George Tindall, "and the troops met with little more opposition than a few liberty poles."[10]

At a meeting at Parkinson's Ferry on the Monongahela River, the cowed delegates for the insurgents voted to comply with the new laws. Under Hamilton, the reluctant militia took much of their frustration out on the farmers anyway. "Much violence and abuse was vented on the captives by the ill-disciplined militia," writes Page Smith. "Stories of people dragged from their beds, reviled, and beaten were numerous, as were tales of the hardships suffered by those who had to march back to Philadelphia as prisoners to be tried for treason in federal courts."[11] Twenty leaders of what was now being called rebellion were rounded up and walked through Philadelphia as prisoners of war.

At trial, two men were found guilty of treason. President Washington, who had apparently come to his senses, quickly pardoned them. In spite of Hamilton's tantrum politics, the story had a happy ending except for those who had been killed or wounded or permanently traumatized by fear. "The new government had displayed both its resolution and its capacity for mercy," writes Smith.[12] Other historians are not so forgiving about the Whiskey Rebellion and its aftermath. "We see then," writes historian Howard Zinn, "in the first years of the Constitution, that some of its provisions—even those paraded most flamboyantly (like the First Amendment)—might be treated lightly. Others (like the power to tax) would be powerfully enforced."[13]

Thomas Jefferson, who ran for election in 1800 using the repeal of the whiskey tax as a campaign platform, was slightly more scathing in a letter to James Monroe. "An insurrection was announced and proclaimed and armed against, but could never be found," he said.[14]

Whiskey, even taxed as it was, became the drink of the future. Although whiskey is an ancient liquor, distilled in Ireland and Scotland for over 500 years, it suited the colonists well. The great victory of the glorious American Revolution, itself fueled by rum, did not diminish colonial America's enthusiasm for drinking. After the war, taxes on imports like molasses as well as a more thriving agriculture for growing corn shifted the new nation's drinking habits. The early settlers were dependent on beer. The American Revolution was instigated and carried on with energy provided by rum made from Caribbean molasses and with Caribbean distilling techniques. The eighteenth century in America, beginning with the Whiskey Rebellion, was all about whiskey. Whiskey did not require foreign ingredients. It could be made at home by anyone with a still and some corn.

"The Revolution wrought no transformation in virtue in respect to drinking habits," writes David W. Conroy. "The number of public houses continued to multiply according to population growth. In Middlesex County the number rose from 242 in 1776 to 289 in 1791. In the 1790s farmers on the New York and Pennsylvania frontiers began to inundate the eastern seaboard with cheap corn whiskey. The per capita consumption of hard liquor in the new nation rose…But governments did not act to repress consumption, because it was still entwined with political discourse. Not only had Americans refused to forswear rum, but they now supplemented it with whiskey…In contradiction to every republican precept, intemperance and democracy seemed to proceed and deepen hand in hand after 1790."[15]

The taverns, which had once been the center of every colonial village, which had served as news centers and courthouses and civic buildings and inns, were now thought by some citizens to be depraved and a bad influence. John Adams had warned, "It would be well worth the attention of our legislature to confine the number of and retrieve the character of licensed houses." Otherwise their influence might "arise at length to a degree of strength that even the legislature will not be able to control."[16]

"Drunkenness was, indeed, America's national malady," writes Page Smith in a thoughtful attempt to understand why even as it was founded our country floundered. "…From the days of the earliest settlers in colonial America, drunkenness had been a problem. Even in the records of Puritan ministerial associations we find strong expression of concern over intemperate clergymen…What are the roots of this national disease?" There are many answers to this question. Smith's answer is complicated and based on class. "The fact is that each class and section of the United States had its own incentive to drink to excess," he writes. "The upper classes because of the pressure on them to preserve their privileged status…; the middle classes because they were spurred on by ambition…; the laboring classes because of the instability, the hardship, the often pinched and dreary quality of their lives."[17]

Hamilton and Washington diverged in their attitudes toward drinking—one abhorred it while the other was happy to enjoy it and make money from it. Another one of their founding fathers had a more complicated relationship with alcohol.

John Adams, although he was not killed or disabled by alcohol as others in his family were, was an ardent drinker. He downed a tankard of cider before breakfast every morning just to get started. In his frequent travels to France and England, Adams drank with gusto whatever was being served. When liquor wasn't available, he whined about that in letters to his stalwart, intelligent wife, Abigail. She had attracted Adams because of her straightforward manner, and she was already well acquainted with what her grandson Charles Francis Adams would later call "the scourge of intemperance."

A member of the Continental Congress, Adams had been one of the voices persuading congress to declare independence. He helped his friend Thomas Jefferson draft the Declaration of Independence in

1776 and signed it. He nominated George Washington to be commander of the Continental Army. As a philosopher and writer, Adams understood the role of drinking in the defiance and bravery that had caused the American Revolution. "I know not why we should blush to confess that molasses was an essential ingredient in American independence," he wrote. "Many great events have proceeded from much smaller causes."[18]

Adams had a passionate and opinionated connection to drinking, but it is in the sad history of his family over at least three generations that the effects of alcohol are most obvious. Alcoholism is a family disease. Whether through genetic components or through environmental components or both, it is passed from parents to children. Drinking is as much part of a family tree as other inherited traits like hair color and height. Because of the family aspect of alcoholism, innocent spouses and children are drawn into a cycle of damage and heartbreak.

The Cheevers, for instance, are a family with all the distinction, myth, talent, and destruction that alcoholism entails. The founder of the family, a Boston schoolmaster in the seventeenth century named Ezekiel Cheever, was famous for misbehaving in church and for, as his friend Samuel Sewall wrote, "abominating periwigs." This phrase thrilled my father with its antiauthoritarian overtones. Ezekiel apparently loved to grab wigs off the heads of the Plymouth Bay Colony lawyers and political leaders. His legacy—as the head of the Boston Latin School and a colleague of Cotton Mather—was tinged with the playful attitudes and hatred of authority that often follow a few glasses of whiskey.

"Many skeletons in family closet," writes Leander Wapshot, the protagonist of my father's National Book Award–winning novel *The Wapshot Chronicle*. His diary, written in a personal shorthand, continues, "Dark secrets, mostly carnal." This diary, which includes a great deal of Yankee advice about women and drinking ("Rye on whiskey, mighty frisky") was based on journals kept by my grandfather

Frederick Cheever, a man whose drinking reduced him from a prosperous shoe manufacturer to a penniless old man whose wife supported him with her gift shop earnings.

Frederick's father, Aaron, was an alcoholic whose death certificate cites morphine as a cause. William Liley, my father's grandfather on his mother's side, was a British "remittance man," a man who was paid to stay away from England and his family of origin. My father and his brother were both alcoholics, and the disease has been passed along to my generation as well.

Like the Adamses, the Cheevers were often successful and talented until their drinking caught up with them. One symptom of an alcoholic family is the myths that grow up around family members, myths which immortalize the fun around drinking and drape the horrors of drinking in romantic, delightful storytelling.

Yes, Bill Liley was a remittance man whose mother, Sarah Devereaux, had disowned him, but my father liked to speculate that because the family tree had been obscured he, my father, was in fact the Lost Earl of Devereaux. Frederick Cheever was a drunk, but my father liked to say that when he was found dead, there was a bottle of gin and an ashtray filled with lipstick-stained cigarettes on the table next to him.

My father loved to talk about his own mother's courage in the face of death. When the doctors told her she was a diabetic and had to stop drinking, she sat down at her loom—she loved to hook rugs—with a bottle of whiskey and controlled her own fate. What a family!

I was dazzled by these stories and by the radiance of the idea that—because I was a Cheever—I had some special role to play in a universe of ordinary people. No surprise that I ended up being brought to my knees by alcoholism and stopped drinking as my father did before me.

One of the sad things about alcoholic families—and there is plenty of sadness underlying these fancy stories—is the way in which the swashbuckling, derring-do, glamour, and mischief of the family stories (he pulled the wigs right off the barrister's heads!) actually hides or mitigates the truth. Whether they are Cheevers or Adamses or whoever else, alcoholic families are nightmarish places, heartbreak machines in which the innocent fare worse than the guilty.

John and Abigail Adams had three sons and a daughter. One of the sons became the sixth president of the United States, following in the footsteps of his father, who had been the second president. The other two sons died of alcoholism at a time when ignorance and lack of experience made alcoholism a very rare diagnosis. The hard-drinking members of the Continental Congress, for instance, were never thought of as alcoholics. Thomas Jefferson's personal brewery, his obsession with fine wine, and the fact that he wrote the Declaration of Independence in a tavern attracted little notice. Even Benjamin Franklin's *Drinker's Dictionary*, with its two hundred phrases for *drunkenness*, seemed good fun.

The John Adams family, for the three generations during which they played important parts in the formation of the United States, is a textbook case of an alcoholic family. The family nature of the disease works in two ways. First, there is clearly a genetic component to alcoholism, although many studies have failed to determine exactly which genetic features create an alcoholic. In the case of the Adams family, the alcoholic gene seems to have come from the Smith line through Abigail Smith Adams. John Adams was not an alcoholic. Abigail was not an alcoholic, either, but her brother William Smith was.

Billy Smith, who was referred to in Abigail's letters to her sisters as "our unhappy connection," was the family shame—a kind of shame that would become common for the Adamses. He failed in business, became estranged from his family, desperately begged for money, and died of liver disease in September 1787, when he was less than forty years old. Tut-tutting over the possible overindulgent parenting that she guesses might have caused Billy's fall, Abigail sounds very innocent in her letter to her sister Mary on Billy's death. "I say this to you who will not consider it as any reflection upon the memory of our dear parents, but only as a proof of how much the best and worthiest may err, and as some mitigation for the conduct of our deceased relatives."[19]

Billy's upbringing probably had nothing to do with his drinking—as Abigail found out the hard way. Two of her own beloved sons and two of her grandsons—John Quincy Adams's sons—died alcoholic deaths by liver disease, suicide, and unexplained illnesses. Her sister Elizabeth's son, William Shaw, also succumbed to alcoholism in 1826 at the age of forty-eight.

But alcoholism works in families at a level deeper than genes. Living with an alcoholic, whether the drinker is a child or a spouse, can have a dramatic effect on family members who are not alcoholic. Alcoholics are inspired liars, and soon enough in an alcoholic family no one knows exactly what is true and what is not true. Alcoholics are charming and loving when they need to be, so their families suffer a kind of emotional whiplash. "Years of living with an alcoholic are almost sure to make any wife or child neurotic. The entire family is, to some extent, ill," a doctor tells Alcoholics Anonymous cofounder William Griffith Wilson in the book *Alcoholics Anonymous*.[20] Wilson's wife, Lois, who found herself in a rage after her husband got sober, started a twelve-step program for the families of alcoholics called Al-Anon.

In alcoholic families, addiction can skip around and take different forms—overeating, gambling, and sexual acting out, as well as drinking. Not everyone in an alcoholic family is an alcoholic, but everyone is influenced by alcoholism. John and his son John Quincy, the two Adams men who were presidents of the United States, were not alcoholic. Yet they were deeply affected by the alcoholism of those they loved dearly and could not understand. The drinkers in the Adams family were almost always in trouble. This had a huge effect on the men who were spared the actual addiction—John Adams, John Quincy Adams in the next generation, and Henry Adams two generations later—who became some of our greatest and angriest statesmen.

There are generally two kinds of people in an alcoholic family:

the alcoholics who are sloppy, unreliable, infuriating, yet sometimes charming; and the nonalcoholics who in response can become hyper-competent, compulsive, and often furious. They are rarely charming. Rage runs in alcoholic families. Depression and sadness also run deep in families—especially alcoholic families. When Ralph Waldo Emerson wrote that the gloomy misanthropist John Quincy Adams was so difficult and angry that he seemed to have put sulfuric acid in his tea,[21] he was describing a classic reaction of the nonalcoholic in an alcoholic family. John Adams himself suffered from sharp spells of melancholy.

Although John Adams's friend and colleague Benjamin Rush, with astonishing prescience, had written that alcoholism was a disease and not a failure of willpower, John and Abigail Adams were baffled by their sons' alcoholic behavior, by Abigail's brother William's behavior, and later by their grandson John Adams's behavior, which was so heinous that his letters were removed from the family archives.

Benjamin Rush was unable to communicate his new understanding of alcoholism to his friends; nevertheless the Adams family slowly changed from accepting the conventional wisdom that drinking was a necessary and benevolent way to make life more pleasurable to hating drinking because of the behavior of their own family members—and coming to hate the family members themselves.

Later, after the deaths of his sons and grandsons from alcoholism, John Adams came to a more bitter understanding of the passionate connection between alcohol and the new country he had helped to found. "(I am) grieved to the heart by the losses sustained because of alcoholism," Adams wrote his friend Benjamin Rush. "If I should then in my will, my dying legacy, my posthumous exhortation, ... recommend heavy, prohibitory taxes upon spirituous liquors, which I believe to be the only remedy against their deleterious qualities in society, every one of your brother Republicans and nine-tenths of the Federalists would say that I was a canting Puritan, a profound hypocrite, setting up standards of morality, frugality, economy, temperance, simplicity, and sobriety that I know the age was incapable of."[22]

John Adams's son Charles was born in 1770. "Charles wins the heart, as usual, and is the most gentleman of them all," his father wrote. The charming Charles was educated in schools in Paris and Holland as he and his brother Thomas followed their father on diplomatic missions around Europe, and he was sometimes farmed out to some cousins while his parents traveled. Before his entry into Harvard at the age of fifteen, his father had written him a few throat-clearing letters filled with Polonius-like advice to a son. "What subject do your thoughts run upon these times," he wrote in 1777, when Charles was a little boy and the United States was just a year old. "You are a thoughtful child you know, always meditating upon some deep thing or other. Your sensibility is exquisite too. Pray how are your nice feelings affected by the times? Don't you wish for peace—or do you wish to take a part in the war?"

It was a privileged but difficult childhood. Both parents traveled, and being pushed to go along with them was often rigorous and lonely. Sent home from France at the age of eleven on a ship with a sketchy chaperone, Charles actually disappeared for a few months as one ship was exchanged for another—he was being looked after by friends of the family, as it turned out, but for a while his parents lost track of him. Her husband's incessant traveling put Abigail Adams in a painful quandary. Would her boys grow up with an absent father, or would she risk their safety by having them travel with him?

"I have felt anxious some times lest the long separation should estrange the affections of my children from their parent, and this was a powerful inducement with me; for my two sons to accompany their father. Charles was a careful observer of his father's sentiments, many of which he has treasured up. He is called here the man in miniature. His manners are pleasing and agreeable," she wrote to her friend John Thaxter in 1782, when Charles was twelve. (Being abandoned by parents who took their civic duties more seriously than their family duties became an Adams characteristic. When John Quincy Adams spent six years in Europe on diplomatic missions, he needed his wife Louisa by his side. Without telling her, he decided to leave their sons at home with relatives. Louisa was distraught, but she went with her husband.)

Sent to Harvard in the Adams tradition, Charles was almost immediately in trouble. The exact details of Charles's misadventures are not recorded, although he and some friends were apparently reprimanded—and one expelled—for running naked through Harvard Yard after some drinking escapades. Since running naked through campus is a time-honored Ivy League sport (Princeton suspended their naked Olympics just over a decade ago), and since getting drunk was also expected of every adventurous college underclassman in the 1700s as it is today, it is hard to know what Charles may have actually done to merit punishment.

Other documentation shows that after Thanksgiving dinner in the Hollis Hall dining room, some students staged a disturbance in which they broke windows and furniture.[23] Charles may or may not have been a perpetrator, but he was one of the students who later refused to say who was guilty in order to protect his classmates.

Was he exceedingly principled? Was he drunk? Or both? At any rate, within the Adams family closeness and mutual praise and protection were always the rule. "I am persuaded that Charles did not deserve the suspicions which were raised against him; and I have great hopes that his future conduct, will convince the governors of the University that he was innocent," wrote his brother John Quincy Adams in his journal.[24] Still, his father and mother were mildly alarmed. "You have in your nature a sociability, Charles, which is amiable, but may mislead you," Adams wrote to Charles.[25]

After Harvard, Charles decided to go to law school, and he seemed to settle down. He moved to New York and with his father's financial help set himself up as a lawyer with offices in Hanover Square. His sister Abigail, called Nabby, had married William Stephens Smith, who worked with her father in London where John Adams was U.S.

minister. The couple moved to New York and while visiting them, Charles met his brother-in-law's sister Sarah. Soon they were married and had two daughters, Sarah and Abigail.

When the good, nondrinking brother, John Quincy Adams, left for his first diplomatic mission at the age of twenty-six at the behest of an admiring President Washington, he decided to leave his life's savings—some $2,500—in the care of his brother Charles. Anyone who has ever left money in the care of an alcoholic knows what happened. Charles lost the money and didn't tell anyone. When asked, he lied about it. When the truth finally came out, both John and Abigail Adams were distraught—but no one is ever more distraught about an alcoholic's behavior than the alcoholic himself. Alcoholics often see themselves as victims, even in situations where they have victimized others by lying or stealing. "I have not enjoyed one moment's comfort for upwards of two years on this account," Charles wrote self-pityingly to his mother. "My sleep has been disturbed, and my waking hours embittered."[26]

The discovery of the loss of John Quincy Adams's money prompted visits from Charles's creditors who told a dreadful story of "the sordid details of a double life," writes Joseph Ellis in his biography of John and Abigail. "Respectable lawyer and family man by day; barhopping drunk, drug addict, and adulterer by night."[27]

In the fall of 1799, John Adams—who was near the end of his first and only term as president of the United States—stopped in East Chester to visit his daughter Nabby and her family. He found a tragedy. Nabby and her husband had bought twenty-three acres there and built a fancy house that looked south down the East River toward New York Harbor. Unfortunately they could not afford the house, which was built on debt, and now they were losing it to creditors. It would be sold in the next year. Now John Adams had what, McCullough speculates, "could only have been one of the most dreadful moments of his life." When John Adams arrived, he found that Charles's wife Sally Smith Adams and her two girls were staying with

Nabby in East Chester because they had been deserted by Charles, who had disappeared. Adams's son was, McCullough writes, "bankrupt, faithless and an alcoholic."[28]

Finally John Adams had had enough of his feckless son. He seems to have been surprised and horrified and to have had little understanding of what was happening to his formerly beloved Charles. Charles is "a mere rake, buck, blood, and beast," he wrote to his wife about the son he had once loved so much. Charles is "a madman possessed of the devil...I renounce him."[29] On his next trip south to Washington, John Adams avoided stopping in New York to see his son for what would have been the last time.

John Adams had a lot to be angry about that terrible autumn. In spite of his courageous role in joining the Continental Congress, negotiating with the French, and establishing the United States, the electorate turned on him and refused him the second term as president that he desperately wanted. News of his treaty, which made an ally of Napoleon, arrived nine days too late to sway the election. He lost the 1800 election to a man he considered a second-rate alternative— Thomas Jefferson. Since 1774, when he became a delegate to the Continental Congress, John Adams had been in some kind of public office. His business had been leading his new country, a country that now rejected him without even providing a financial stipend. When Adams got to Washington from New York, he moved into the White House. He was the first president to move into that iconic structure, but he would soon have to relinquish the house to Jefferson.

On her way south to Washington, Abigail stopped in New York. It was a difficult time for all of them, and she hoped to comfort herself with a visit to her daughter Nabby and her family, and to her son Charles and his family. The situation for both families was grim. Charles had finally reappeared and temporarily moved in with Nabby because his own wife wouldn't have him. By the time Abigail arrived, Nabby had kicked Charles out. He was living with a friend in a sordid basement. "His Physician says he is past recovery," Abigail wrote to her sister Mary Cranch. She was not too heartbroken to make an excuse for her husband's preoccupation. "I shall carry a melancholy report to the president who, passing through New York without stopping, knew not his situation."[30]

Charles, Abigail wrote to her husband, was "laid upon a bed of sickness, destitute of a home. The kindness of a friend afforded him an asylum. A distressing cough, an affection of the liver and a dropsy will soon terminate a life."[31] His face was red and bloated and his body shriveled and useless. His liver had stopped working. Charles would die of cirrhosis of the liver a few days after his mother's last visit.

He was buried with military honors as befitted the son of the sitting president, but he was banned from the Adams family burial ground and was laid to rest in New York in the old Presbyterian burying ground.[32] In December John Adams wrote to his friend François Adriaan van der Kemp, "The affliction in my family from the melancholy death of a once beloved son, has been very great, and has required the consolation of religion, as well as philosophy, to enable us to support it. The prospects of that unfortunate youth were very pleasing and promising, but have been cut off."

Some historians seem baffled by the story of Charles Adams. As Princeton PhD Jeremy Stern has pointed out, the depiction of Charles Adams in the much-praised PBS special on John Adams, based on the biography by David McCullough, is inaccurate—and also improbable. The moviemakers tie Charles Adams's destruction to his abandonment as a child because his father was often away from home. Yet as Stern points out, beginning when he was nine, Charles was often taken along with his parents even to Europe, and when he did suffer from homesickness at age eleven, he was promptly sent home. Although alcoholism can sometimes be tied to early trauma, this connection is always tenuous. From what we do know, alcoholism seems to be caused by a perfect storm of experiential and genetic components.

At the time that John Adams's son Charles was dying, the word *alcoholism* was not in common use. In the eighteenth and early nineteenth centuries, alcoholism was still referred to as "drunkenness" or "excessive drinking" or "intemperance." In the beginning of the nineteenth century the medical community begin to refer to it as dipsomania. The words *alcoholic* and *alcoholism* were not used until the mid-nineteenth century when, as we shall see, they were alarmingly apt for a great deal of the population of the United States.

Many historians have theories about the misfortunes that mysteriously visited the Adams family. To Page Smith, the Adamses' problems are a slipping away from the family life of privilege because of a "lack of self-discipline." "The family of John Adams is a case in point," he writes. "Of John and Abigail's three sons only John Quincy sustained the tradition established by his father. Charles, married too young to a woman of lower social standing, found it impossible to make a living, took to drink, and drank himself to death in his late twenties. His brother Thomas Boylston, a Harvard graduate and a lawyer, also married 'beneath' him…Thomas Boylston, like his brother Charles, was an intemperate drinker, and [his nephew] Charles Francis [Adams] described him as 'one of the most unpleasant characters in the world, in his present degradation, being a brute in manners and a bully in his family.'"[33]

The heartbreak of the two Adams sons, and the two Adams grandsons, boys who were educated all over Europe and ended up at Harvard, defies explanation even by modern historians. Or perhaps it gets short shrift because the obvious explanation—alcoholism—still carries a stigma that doesn't seem to fit with our noble portraits of the founding father John Adams.

For a while Thomas Boylston Adams seemed to have escaped the family curse. A successful businessman, he took charge of his brother John Quincy's finances, and instead of stealing the money as his brother had done years before, he made John Quincy Adams into a moderately wealthy man through wise investments. But by 1818,

Thomas's gambling habits had estranged the two brothers. Thomas and his family had moved back to the village of Quincy to live with Thomas's parents in the Adams family house. Begging his brother to stop gambling, John Quincy Adams wrote a letter urging him to seek "the spirit of truth and self-knowledge."[34]

By the time Thomas Boylston Adams died in 1832, few mourned. His nephew Charles Francis Adams, who had inherited the obligation of supporting him, his wife, and two children with the dwindling Adams inheritance, wrote that Thomas had paid a "bitter penance" for his follies. Brooks Adams, John Quincy Adams's grandson, summed up the situation more bluntly years later. "There never was harm in poor Tom except that he would drink. He nearly drove John Adams and J.Q.A. into insanity with it."[35]

Yet alcoholism had worse in store for John Quincy Adams. His son George at first seemed to be nothing more than a gambler and a spender. By the time he was in his twenties, he had run up enough debt that he could not pay his own rent and faced angry creditors. His father, infuriated, nevertheless offered help. In a typical family maneuver, he offered to pay off the debts by pretending to buy George's library, but George would keep the books. Soon, though, there were more debts. Worse, George had a secret. He had an illegitimate child with a servant girl—not the kind of thing that the Adamses welcomed, although he was unmarried. By the time he was twenty-eight, George's fear of his family's censure, increased by the necessity of going to live with them, came to a head. On his way to Washington on the steamboat *Benjamin Franklin*, he appeared to have an attack of nerves and jumped or fell to his death from the upper deck.

John Quincy Adams's second son, John, followed the same sad, predictable path. Married with two children, he also tried managing the family finances. Living in Washington, D.C., in 1834 he began drinking heavily and became gravely ill—probably with cirrhosis of the liver. He was hardly coherent by the time his father got to his bedside. John Quincy Adams had already lost two brothers and a son.

Sitting at his son John's bedside, the old statesman broke down, hovering over the corpse and kissing his beloved son. "My child, my child," John Quincy Adams prayed over the body, "in the bosom of your God, may never-ending joys, joys unspeakable and full of glory, cancel all the sufferings of which your portion was so great here below."[36] He was almost seventy years old, the son of a president, whose own presidency had been magnificently successful in shaping foreign policy and paying down the national debt, but no worldly accomplishments could protect him from the awful death of his children. John Quincy helplessly "hovered over the corpse, kissing John's lifeless brow."[37]

Although the doctors in attendance had no explanation for John's death, his brother Charles Francis had a clear-eyed view of his family problem. "In both brothers he saw a terrible lesson he knew he could not ignore, and it made him remember the time when the 'scourge of intemperance' had afflicted his grandmother Abigail's brother," writes Paul C. Nagel. "Vices are hereditary in families," Charles Francis wrote, and "our family has been so severely scourged by this vice that every member of it is constantly on his trial."[38] Alcohol, as biographer Joseph Ellis has written, had turned the distinguished Adams family into "a menagerie of wounded animals."[39]

Fourteen years after the death of his second son, John Quincy Adams collapsed on the floor of the House of Representatives, where he represented his beloved Massachusetts. At the age of eighty, John Quincy Adams was hard-working and law-abiding, with his broad face fixed in a permanent scowl. It was an early winter afternoon in Washington, D.C., with its muddy streets, dank alleys reeking of horse manure, and two great but unfinished monuments—the Capitol and the Washington Monument. The vote before the House was on whether or not to suspend the rules in order to award gold medals to generals who had fought in the war with Mexico. Adams had been against the war from the beginning. His last public word was...*no.* [40]

A few moments later, as he struggled to say something else his face reddened; he grabbed for the corner of his desk and then slumped to the floor. He had had a stroke. Someone brought a sofa, and the aging statesman was carried lying down and slowly losing consciousness to the East Portico. By the time his wife got there, he no longer recognized her. He died two days later.

More than a dozen of the Adams men over four generations were enrolled at Harvard College. One of the turning points for many of them seemed to be their departure from home to the dormitories of Harvard Yard. Charles and his brother and nephews all got in trouble at Harvard, or perhaps they got in trouble because of Harvard. Like most colleges then and now, Harvard was an incubator for alcoholism. The first president of the college had been fired because he let the students run out of beer. More recently, a 1992 to 2004 study from Dr. Henry Wechsler at Harvard's School of Public Health, based on interviews with thousands of students at 140 colleges, showed that drinking was at an all-time high.

Although college has always been a place where students drink whether or not they are Adamses, recent studies show alarming increases. These days, four out of five students drink during their college years, many of them heavily. Wechsler's study showed that drinkers who drank to get drunk had increased from 10 percent of the student body in 1977 to 34 percent of the student body. A recent National Institutes of Health study showed that almost 2,000 college students a year die from alcohol-related causes, and more than 690,000 students a year are assaulted in drinking-related incidents. What's even more heartbreaking are the students affected by others' drinking. In an atmosphere of why-the-hell-not, it is hard to become a serious student—harder than it was in the twentieth or the nineteenth centuries in this country. Joseph A. Califano Jr. at Columbia University writes, "College presidents, deans and trustees have facilitated or tolerated a college culture of alcohol and drug abuse that is linked to poor student academic performance, depression, anxiety, suicide, property damage, vandalism, fights and a host of medical problems.

By failing to become part of the solution, these presidents, deans and trustees have become part of the problem."[41]

Still, the effects of alcoholism can be inspiring as well as heartbreaking. Adversity is often a source of strength. The Adams men who escaped alcohol's direct effects became some of the most distinguished and effective statesmen in our country's history. Perhaps, by ignoring what was really happening to his family and instead hewing to his own myth of the perfect marriage and the talented sons, John Adams may have been doing his writing a favor. Great writing is often based on a longing for what might have been, a yearning for a kind of dream, a pushing away of reality. Adams's most famous writing about his sons is an eloquent encapsulation of American history in a few lines: "I must study politics and war that my sons may have liberty to study mathematics and philosophy. My sons ought to study mathematics and philosophy...in order to give their children a right to study paintings, poetry, music, architecture, statuary, tapestry and porcelain."[42]

CHAPTER 5

JOHNNY APPLESEED, THE AMERICAN DIONYSUS

Although they sometimes claim objectivity, historians are the most subjective of all writers. Hidden behind the thousands of facts unearthed by research, they safely arrange the world to reflect their own vision. Drunkenness is glossed over in many accounts, and alcoholism is obscured. Even now, the press hesitates to call anyone an alcoholic, and they treat the word like a wild animal—dangerous and to be kept far away. Flagrant alcoholic acts—like the accident in which Diane Schuler killed eight people driving the wrong way on the Taconic Parkway—are often chalked up to other problems. Schuler's family is still adamant that she was not an alcoholic. After all, she had a good job, and she took care of her children...until she didn't.

One of the most smoothed-over stories in American history has to be that of the itinerant, animal loving, humbly dressed John Chapman, who planted frontier nurseries that grew into apple orchards in Pennsylvania and up and down the Ohio Valley. Chapman came to be universally loved and known as Johnny Appleseed. Although children's books and Disney drawings often feature Chapman literally sowing apples out of a hand-sewn burlap bag, he was far more organized than that—luckily for his crops and for his very happy customers.

An American Saint Francis of Assisi (according to one story he put out a cooking fire rather than hurt some mosquitoes) crossed with Paul Bunyan and Henry David Thoreau, he strode into the national consciousness as smoothly as apple cider. There he stayed, enshrined in our most sentimental frontier myths, the subject of dozens of sanctified children's books and depictions, like *The Legend of Johnny Appleseed*, the 1948 film from Walt Disney Studios that tells the story of a skunk-loving apple farmer led west by an angel who sings an apple song.

In Hugh Nissenson's National Book Award–nominated *The Tree of Life*, Chapman appears in a more serious role. The novel, which purports to be the nineteenth-century Ohio frontier journal of the masturbating, hard-drinking ex-Congregational minister Thomas Keene, hinges on Keene's troubled friendship with Chapman. "Chapman is famous in these parts for his eccentric appearance: shaggy black beard, bare feet, pasteboard visor, and ragged pantaloons," Keene writes. "Sometimes he wears a tin saucepan on his head, which serves as hat and mushpot. He thinks of himself as a messenger sent into the wilderness, like John the Baptist, to prepare the way for the Revelations of Emanuel Swedenborg." In Nissenson's book, Chapman is sowing religious tracts as well as orchards. Chapman was more like Robert Crumb's Mr. Natural than Saint Francis, but his fictional image survived well until the twenty-first century when the writer Michael Pollan, writing about food in a book that would be called *The Botany of Desire*, took a fresh look at the lovable Johnny.

Chapman, born in 1774 in Massachusetts, was indeed a devout student of the popular teachings of Emanuel Swedenborg, whose many American followers embraced a secular humanist creed. He had a system for growing apple trees. He would find seeds from the leavings of cider mills and plant them to become nurseries for orchards. He seemed to have an instinct about where people would want to settle—on riverbanks, at the confluence of the primitive roads beginning to be built—and it was in those places that he planted. By the time a community had grown up, Chapman had apple trees to sell. Then he would leave the plantings in the care of local farmers and return every two years to oversee the crop.

In general, seeds like those that Johnny Appleseed carried did not grow edible apples. Most edible apples are grown from grafts in which pieces of trees that bear a certain kind of apple are grafted onto other trees to create the best eating apples. Apples grown from seeds are usually small and sour. They are called spitters for obvious reasons. They are "sour enough," Henry David Thoreau wrote, "to set a squirrel's teeth on edge and make a jay scream."[1] But apples grown from seeds are very good for one thing—making hard cider. Furthermore, apple cider was almost the only way the settlers could experience sweetness. Sugar was rare. Honey was hard to get.

Johnny Appleseed was not carrying the possibility of eating apples; his mission was something quite different and more mature than Disney's 1948 movie version. Far from being the American Saint Francis, John Chapman turned out to be the American Dionysus. No wonder everyone was glad to see him coming down the western roads! "The reason people…wanted John Chapman to stay and plant a nursery was the same reason he would soon be welcome in every cabin in Ohio," Pollan writes. "Johnny Appleseed was bringing the gift of alcohol to the frontier."[2]

Until Prohibition, most apples were used to make cider, which was always fermented to create a healthy drink with a healthy punch— about 10 percent alcohol. By freezing cider and siphoning off the alcoholic content, which did not freeze, farmers made the more powerful applejack—often as high as 66 proof. "It takes a leap of the historical imagination to appreciate just how much the apple meant to people living two hundred years ago," Pollan writes. "By comparison, the apple in our eye is a fairly inconsequential thing—a popular fruit (second only to the banana) but nothing we can't imagine living without. It is much harder for us to imagine living without the experience of *sweetness*, however, and sweetness, in the widest, oldest sense, is what the apple offered an American in Chapman's time, the desire it helped gratify."[3]

Digging further into his research, Pollan became even more convinced that, although Chapman did not frolic in the orchards with naked maidens, he was very much like the mythical Greco-Roman God of drunkenness, Dionysus. By teaching man how to ferment grapes, Dionysius had given men the gift of wine. American grapes were too sour to be fermented successfully, so the grape was replaced with the apple. In his book *The Golden Bough*, Sir James Frazer writes that Dionysus was also the patron of cultivated trees and the discoverer of the apple. Although, as Pollan points out, Chapman's sexual experimentation was limited to trees in orchards, in many other ways he came to represent the twining together of man and the natural world symbolized by the earlier god. "As I delved deeper into the myth of Dionysus, I realized there was much more to his story, and the strangely changeable god who began to come into focus bore a remarkable resemblance to John Chapman. Or at least to 'Johnny Appleseed,' who, I became convinced, is Dionysus's American son."[4] The success of Johnny Appleseed was just one of many factors contributing to drinking in nineteenth-century America. As Chapman was floating down the Ohio River carrying his seedlings in a hollowed-out log, or headed farther west for Indiana, the United States had reached a crisis in the amount of drinking that was done on a routine and daily basis by almost everyone.

Until the early nineteenth century, two centuries of American drinking had passed without being examined carefully. The country had floated together on beer, switched to rum, and finally converted to corn whiskey with a side of cider, but drinking was just a fact of life. Not many people thought twice about it. Benjamin Rush, as we have seen, wrote about intemperance and proposed the idea that drinking too much was a disease, but few people listened. Not even Rush's good friend and patient John Adams was able to see his own sons' drinking as anything but an infuriating moral failing. Rush's version of temperance, typically, also allowed beer and wine, which seemed entirely harmless. Beer and wine were not powerful enough to cause spontaneous combustion no matter how much the patient had been drinking.

By the 1820s American drinking was out of control. Children drank before school, during school at recess, and after school. Farmers had jugs stashed at the end of every row in their fields. Factories featured frequent drinking breaks. Meals were washed down with applejack. Workers invariably headed for the bar on payday long before they thought of going home to spend the money on their families' needs. The whole country was more or less living under the influence, farming under the influence, and even studying under the influence. In 1820, the average amount an individual drank in one day was more than three times the average today.[5]

Although all this drinking clearly generated a certain amount of happiness, it also generated sharp disapproval of alcohol and its effects beyond common drunkards. One of the first voices to be raised in opposition was that of Lyman Beecher, a Presbyterian minister who launched the nineteenth-century temperance movement with his sermons, reprinted as *Six Sermons on Intemperance*. Beecher, who was the father of Harriet Beecher Stowe, took the unprecedented position that only total abstinence could help drunkards—men who could not control their drinking. Historian Katherine Chavigny wrote of Beecher, "Intemperance was a 'sin so deceitful,' he warned, gaining such 'physical and moral influence…upon its victims,' that to advise moderation was disastrous: 'if we cannot stop men in the beginning, we cannot separate between that and the end.'"[6] In 1829 there were about 1,000 temperance societies. By 1834 there were 5,000 local societies claiming a total of 11,000,000 members.

With the development of a temperance movement, drinking in America began to slow down. Maybe it wasn't the best thing in the world to have everyone passed out after dark. Perhaps drinking was responsible for some of the inefficiency in the factory system. By 1830, American drinking had reached its highest point since the landing of the Pilgrims on Cape Cod; the highest point it had ever reached.

One of the earliest and most powerful temperance reform movements came from a Baltimore group of workers who called themselves the Washingtonians. Started by six men who had managed to get sober together after meeting at Chase's Tavern on Liberty Street in 1840, the Washingtonians addressed themselves to the individual drunk rather than the broad scope of temperance. In fact the Washingtonians were formed at a temperance meeting during which men from Chase's Tavern were disgusted by the speaker's wild threats and admonitions. A few men managed to talk each other into staying sober and going to their own meetings to share their problems and solutions. More and more gathered. The men came to understand that helping other men get sober actually helped them stay sober themselves.

In Washingtonian meetings, reformed drunks told their detailed stories in a call to get more men to take the pledge. The Washingtonians were the first group to understand that an alcoholic cannot be scared or scolded into sobriety. They attracted many orators, including John Hawkins, whose rousing story of how his little daughter Hannah's innocence had inspired him to take the pledge was a hit throughout the United States. Stories of drunkards' redemption through their childrens' intervention were wildly popular. Hawkins's story, written by John Marsh and published as *Hannah Hawkins, the Reformed Drunkard's Daughter*, told the tale of "his rescue from the fangs of the rumseller, through his own child." The Washingtonians were also the basis for the novel by T. S. Arthur *Ten Nights in a Bar-Room*, which became a temperance play and later a movie.

Working with the observation of Benjamin Rush that alcoholism is a disease, they used sympathy rather than coercion to get their points across to those who were still drinking. Coercion did not work, and as a result the group refused to endorse any kind of temperance legislation.[7] "It was a pragmatic discourse, intended to motivate listeners to sign the total abstinence pledge," historian Katherine Chavigny writes. "In the course of their speeches, however, many... Washingtonians admitted to a progressive inability to control their drinking habits."

Even Abraham Lincoln approved. At a speech in Springfield to the Washingtonians, Lincoln revealed a more than tolerant attitude toward drunks. Although he said he had promised his mother on her deathbed that he would never drink, he clearly never took the moral high ground so universally favored when it came to those who preached against the evils of alcohol.

"Although the temperance cause has been in progress for near twenty years, it is apparent to all that it is just now being crowned with a degree of success hitherto unparalleled," Lincoln told the Washingtonians in 1842. The speech is a study in tolerance and praise for the Washingtonian idea that sympathy will succeed where punishment had failed. In conclusion, Lincoln went even further in praise of drunks. "I believe if we take habitual drunkards as a class," he said, "their heads and their hearts will bear an advantageous comparison to those of any other class. There seems ever to have been a proneness in the brilliant and warm-blooded to fall into this vice—the demon of intemperance ever seems to have delighted in sucking the blood of genius and of generosity."[8]

But the Washingtonians' enlightened approach to drinking was part of the group's splashy downfall. Political issues like Prohibition and abolition split the membership into factions, which quickly became bitter. Attacked for refusing to admit that drunkenness was a moral failing and a sin, hounded by some of its members publicly drinking again in spite of their pledge, and split by the issue of laws against drinking, the movement that had once boasted as many as five hundred thousand members sputtered to a halt before the Civil War.

Alcoholics Anonymous literature uses the story of the rise and fall of the Washingtonians to illustrate the importance of keeping temperance separate from politics. In the AA version of the Washingtonians' story, which appears in *Twelve Steps and Twelve Traditions*, the book written by Bill Wilson and coeditors in 1953, the Washingtonian story is used as an example of how a political issue can tear apart an organization from within. Politics destroyed the Washingtonians; Alcoholics Anonymous avoids politics.

One of the most delightful and effective temperance crusaders in the country was a man who by some accounts was never a "real" alcoholic, but who managed to be almost everything else—a showman, a friend to Abraham Lincoln and to Queen Victoria, a celebrity in the age before celebrity, the inventor of the circus, and a consummate wordsmith—Phineas Taylor Barnum. After he died, it was said that he was more alive than anyone still living.[9]

Born in Connecticut in 1810, Barnum eventually became shopkeeper. A friend mentioned that he had purchased an ancient slave, Joice Heth, who had been George Washington's nurse—she was said to be more than a hundred years old. Fascinated, Barnum traveled to Philadelphia to see the woman, an ancient-looking creature who reminisced about taking care of her "little Georgie." At that moment he had a vision of what Americans wanted: exhibits that would be both sensational and educational. He bought Heth and began immediately showing her off for a fee—Heth was the opening act in what would be a lifetime of exuberant theatrical performances, from General Tom Thumb to the Swedish Nightingale Jenny Lind. Barnum was the epitome of American individualism, the America reveling in self, and the wild American curiosity. He was, Brenda Wineapple has written, the Walt Whitman of the stage: "cocky, optimistic, self-centered, a purveyor of the American scene and in a way its singer. He celebrated the variety, the innocence, the agitations that Whitman declared quintessentially American."[10]

Barnum loved to eat and drink. By the time he married, settled in Bridgeport, Connecticut, and built Iranistan, an extravagant pavilion on his property (inspired by the Royal Pavilion in Brighton, which he had seen in England), Barnum's appetites were exceeded only by his fortune. At lunch he invariably downed a bottle of champagne, or brandy if he was in a different mood, and by afternoon he was almost invariably drunk.

On a trip to the New York State Fair in Saratoga Springs to show off the diminutive General Tom Thumb, Barnum was shocked by the way his own drinking was put in the shade by the wealthy and high-class swells he met. If men of substance and intelligence could be drunkards, and they obviously could, then where did that leave him? "I saw so much intoxication among men of wealth and intellect, filling the highest positions in society, that I began to ask myself the question, what guarantee is there that I may not become a drunkard?" he wrote in his autobiography.[11]

Frightened and shocked, Barnum destroyed his beloved wine cellar and decided to abstain from hard liquor. Soon after that he attended a temperance lecture by a Reverend E. H. Chapin that focused on "the moderate drinker"—the man who had not yet bankrupted himself physically and mentally through drinking. This hit home for Barnum, who hired Chapin to lecture in Bridgeport, signed an abstinence pledge, and devoted himself to converting other drinkers to pledge abstinence—it's said he had gotten twenty friends to sign pledges in his first day.

In the second half of the nineteenth century, Barnum became one of the country's most effective temperance speakers. "I now felt that I had a great duty to perform," he wrote in his autobiography. "I had been groping in darkness, was rescued, and I knew it was my duty to try and save others."[12] Thundering from stages around the country, the eloquent Barnum explained the evils of drink. During the question-and-answer period, one man asked if the effects of alcohol were external or internal. "They are e-ternal!" yelled Barnum at his audience.

At the Metropolitan Hall in New York City, for instance, he told the crowd that there were seven thousand grog shops in the city costing drinking residents an aggregate of $25,550,000 a year. On top of that, he made the very modern point that drinking was costing the nation $250 million a year in health expenses and lost work. As the ladies in bonnets and long dresses fanned themselves in the heat and the gentlemen consulted their pocket watches, Barnum upped the ante. If the city would declare Prohibition for a year and give him the money spent in taverns, Barnum offered, he would pay all the city taxes, send every child to school, and present every family with a library and three barrels of flour as well as providing a silk dress for every lady and a broadcloth suit for every man.[13] The city was apparently unimpressed.

Barnum's American Museum, a worldwide success, was also devoted to temperance and featured performances of a play titled *The Drunkard; or, the Fallen Saved: A Moral Domestic Drama in Five Acts.* The play became a huge hit, playing to crowded houses and endorsed by newspapermen like Horace Greeley, who praised it in his *New York Tribune*. In 1881 when Barnum got together with James Anthony Bailey—who had his own museum and circus—to form the Barnum & Bailey Circus, the first rule they agreed on was temperance for everyone who worked for them. The greatest show on earth was also the most sober show on earth.

Later Walt Whitman interviewed Barnum on the subject of America. They were both fervent Yankees and both, as it happened, temperance men. Whitman's first novel—*Franklin Evans*, published in 1842—was a temperance tract. Whitman rarely drank and quietly espoused temperance his entire life.

From Henry Hudson's 1609 voyage on the *Half Moon* up the river named for him to Samoset's first beer shared with the Pilgrims on Cape Cod a decade later, the three-way relationship between the colonists, the Indians, and liquor in all forms was disastrous for the Native Americans. Hudson had heard such wild stories about the level of drinking among the American natives that he brought plenty of liquor to bribe the residents of what was called *manahactanienk*— or in some translations, "the island of general intoxication."[14] The whiskey he gave the Delaware tribes was just the beginning of what has been called a "holocaust" for the Native Americans who dared to be friends with the settlers.

Whether it was because the Native American physiognomy was particularly vulnerable to the effects of liquor—a possibility that has been argued over for hundreds of years—or whether getting drunk was more dangerous to Native Americans for other reasons, the colonists' liquor was bad for Native Americans. "Liquor addiction went hand in hand with mortal disease," writes Edward Behr.[15] But drunkenness also goes hand in hand with violence. Soon enough the Native Americans, who had seemed friendly when they were first encountered by the Pilgrims, split into warring factions. The Plymouth Colony surrounded its houses with a protective dike. They needed it.

The brutality of the occupying colonists was met by brutality from the Native Americans. The colonists had shown genocidal disregard for the people living in Massachusetts when they arrived. Now colonial villages were laid waste, all residents mutilated and killed. Women and children were kidnapped. Men were tortured in ways that seemed truly inhuman. In taking on the white settlers, the Native Americans had started a war they could only lose, but many forces, including liquor, seemed to blind them to that reality.

As Eric Burns has pointed out, the Native Americans did not need the explorers or the colonists to introduce them to the concept of mind-altering drugs. With a variety of intoxicating beverages made from the plentiful plants of North America, each tribe had found a different way of attaining an altered consciousness. "They drank…not to raise hell but to avoid it," Burns notes.[16] In the dreadful story of the North American indigenous peoples and their genocide at the hands of the colonists from England, France, and Spain— colonists who decided that North America was a rich wilderness that was theirs for the taking—alcohol plays a big part. Burns points out that the colonists were not innocent in this awful saga. "[The white man] contributed to the stereotype of indigenous peoples as victims of alcohol in ways that were indefensible…and he did so by converting the original settlers from the alcoholic beverages they made themselves to products of European origin, which were in almost all cases stronger and less pure. The natives were not used to this stuff…They consumed the booze that the white man provided and the booze consumed them."[17]

Pequot memoirist William Apess agrees with Burns's indictment. "My sufferings were through the white man's measure," he wrote in 1833, "for they most certainly brought spirituous liquors first among my people."[18] Worse, Native American historians blame drinking for much of what happened to the once strong and noble tribes who wandered the North American continent. As recently as 1975, American Indian Movement chairman John Trudell explained that the conquest of the continent had depended on the Native Americans being drunk. "This is how our land has been taken from us," he declared, "because every time an inhuman act has been committed against our people, we have been disoriented with the madness of alcohol."[19]

Many of the colonists took the Native Americans' drunkenness as a symptom of their savagery. The colonists believed that the Native Americans did not understand the art of drinking; they just got drunk. In the captivity narratives—memoirs written by men and women who had lived with the Indians after being captured and who had escaped or been rescued—the colonists used the Indians' relationship to alcohol to diminish them. What was the cause of the Native American's problem with the liquor that was brought by the colonists? Are Native Americans genetically prone to drunkenness as some nationalities seem to be, so much so that alcoholism is sometimes called the Irish disease? Or was their untenable situation what led them to court oblivion? Or was liquor just another form of oppression by the invading colonists? "To understand alcohol use in Indian country, present-day observers would do well to recognize that tragedies associated with such use have no single cause," writes Peter C. Mancall. "Alcohol problems among Native Americans, like those experienced by other Americans, need to be understood in their complexity, and understood as well as the product of specific historic circumstances."[20]

As the nineteenth century reached its midpoint, colonial values began to shift in a heartening way. In what is called by historians the flowering of New England, and the American Renaissance, the country from Massachusetts to Missouri began to relax and enjoy itself— oddly enough, by drinking less. For its first two centuries, the American colonies retained the philosophy engendered by their survival in the difficult 1600s. Even as the huge amount of drinking had gone unnoticed, Yankee character had been formed as frightened, frigid, angry, and averse to anything surprising or creative. The world was a hostile place, and that adversity bred good character. "Downy beds make drowsy persons," wrote the colonial poet Anne Bradstreet, "but hard lodging keeps the eyes open. A prosperous state makes a secure Christian, but adversity makes him consider."[21]

All that began to change in the 1840s, and suddenly America was the land of great experiments and eventually great art. Downy beds were in, hard lodging was out. The middle of the nineteenth century was the time when America began to search out an identity, and when Americans became thoughtful about their own experiences and their own character.

The colonists had been suspicious of any kind of foreign influences—Britain was not their friend. They did not much like Germany, France, or Italy. In the 1840s, increased ease in travel began to chip away at the wall of xenophobia that isolated New England's intellectuals. With what seemed unusual suddenness, Margaret Fuller brought German literature to the attention of Ralph Waldo Emerson and his friends. Emerson himself spent a year in England, where he became an admirer of Thomas Carlyle. Influences from European literature flooded into the simplicity of the classic New England reader.

The colonists had been more or less at war with nature since the bleak months of the winter after the Pilgrims' landing. If pummeled and plowed, nature could give up crops. If planted and fertilized, nature could grow orchards. But in her wild and uncivilized state, nature was dangerous and not to be trusted. She was red in tooth and claw, as Alfred, Lord Tennyson wrote in 1850: "Who trusted God was love indeed / And love Creation's final law / Tho' Nature, red in tooth and claw / With ravine, shriek'd against his creed." Slowly, instead of seeing nature as an enemy, New Englanders began to see it as a friend. Naturalists like Henry David Thoreau began to sing the praises of nature as if she was a goddess. Nature went from being the mindless and evil force to being a fruitful and gorgeous source of food.

Nature's beauty from the sparkling landscapes of the lakes and mountains of New England to the thrilling waterfalls of upstate New York, from the glorious S curves of the wide Mississippi to the great vistas of the American West, was suddenly a favorite subject of painting and poetry as well. In the flowering of New England, the colonists seemed to have relaxed enough to embrace the world they lived in, and they stopped seeing enemies behind every apple tree and rosebush. Life was no longer a desperate, painful journey to the better world they expected to find after death. They began to wonder if natural beauty and the glories of the world at large might not be healthier intoxicants than the rum at the Green Dragon or the whiskey from a flask on the factory floor. More content with the world around them, they began to drink less.

The new flowering also changed the American attitude toward all things foreign. The despised British Empire had been the colonies' number one enemy in the eighteenth century. Colonists who were struggling to set up educational facilities tried to teach Greek and Latin—they had little use for German poetry, Italian literature, or the poems of Omar Khayyam. This huge shift toward appreciation and away from rigidity and fear was very much like the shift that happened in the 1960s, when the old rules were overthrown and a younger generation embraced the world. With this shift came different ways of thinking about drinking and the role it played in the lives of men, women, and even children.

Although the Flowering of New England (as the philosopher Van Wyck Brooks called it) in the 1850s was to parallel the Swinging Sixties a hundred years later, there was one sharp and telling difference, and that was civil rights. There were already angry protests at the passage of the Fugitive Slave Act in 1850—the law that made every citizen responsible for the return of a slave to his or her "rightful" owner even if that slave had escaped to a free state like Massachusetts. The idea that it was wrong for one man to own another had already taken root, but most people were blind to another group of people with almost as few rights as the African Americans who were used to chop cotton below the Mason-Dixon line, a group of people with no right to own property, a group who were not allowed to hold most jobs, or give speeches in public, or conduct their private lives as they saw fit—women.

By the 1850s many liberals had come to understand the wrongs visited on African Americans and even the wrongs visited on the Native Americans who had been driven out of their own lands by the colonists. Few, however, were ready to face the treatment of women. Women, it was thought, were as weak mentally and emotionally as they were physically. They could not and should not function without the guidance of the man who owned them—either a father or a husband. The nineteenth century was a century that saw the worst war in American history to that point, but the gender wars had not yet begun. The connection between temperance crusaders and crusaders for women's rights—a connection that would change American history for good and for evil—had not yet been made in the minds of the countries' philosophers or in the minds of the countries' housewives.

Temperance, first as an idea and then as a crusade, had a wildfirelike quality to the way it spread—even as beer and rum had a wildfirelike spread in other centuries. Alexander Hamilton's overreaction to the Whiskey Rebellion had begun to draw the lines that would bisect the colonies. Jefferson and Hamilton stood for temperance and taxes on liquor. The federal law should control and protect the people; the people should pay for the federal law. Anti-Jeffersonians and Federalists stood for the freedom to drink and, indeed, the freedom to ferment and distill without government interference. Jefferson himself had been slowly veering toward a belief in temperance. He wrote a friend that he hoped Americans would drink plenty of beer, "instead of the whiskey which now kills one third of our citizens and ruins their families."[22] Americans had gone from beer to rum to whiskey to temperance in a little more than a century. Once Jefferson had served his second term as president in 1809, the temperance movement had to find another power source, one that equaled the power of having a friend in the White House. They soon did, and it came from the Christian Church. The American Temperance Society was started by the minister Lyman Beecher with Justin Edwards in 1826. "Within a decade after Lyman Beecher began denouncing alcohol, the war against drinking had grown into a national conflict," writes Alice Fleming.[23]

The American way of drinking began to change, again. Prudence replaced profligacy. Employers no longer provided two breaks a day for factory workers to drink. Jugs of rum were no longer left at the end of each row when farmers were planting or plowing. Even the military discontinued their liquor rations. The early temperance movement left wine and beer and other light drinks out of their prohibitions. "Taking the pledge," as more than a million people did in the 1830s under the aegis of the American temperance movement, meant a kind of moderation, an abstaining from certain kinds of hard liquor, and more than anything a new and less cozy relationship with drunkenness.

By 1840 the temperance movement was thriving. Most doctors and ministers took the pledge and exhorted the new temperance to their patients and to their parishes. "The essential source of the cause's dynamism was its accordance with two impulses of the era," writes W. J. Rorabaugh, "an appetite for material gain and a fervent desire for religious salvation...Materialism and devotion to religion were two contrasting sides of American culture, the former a cool, detached rationalism, the latter a highly charged emotionalism."[24]

Americans loved money. Rorabaugh quotes a mythic Scot as saying that Americans would skin a flea for the profits to be made of the hide and tallow. Men who had taken the pledge were better workers and better earners. What they earned was no longer automatically spent in the bars and taverns that were still at the center of the new United States.

The first temperance groups were secular and calm. Their purpose was to help men hang on to their paychecks and their dignity. But America is not a calm nation. Before long the fervor of temperance crusaders more than equaled the fervor of hard drinkers. Temperance meetings became more and more like prayer meetings. American Protestantism began to take on the prissy, pious, uptight character that would serve it so poorly in the twentieth century. Before, the Church had been a great support; now it became a scold, especially for those who didn't want to give up their liquor.

As the pendulum moved away from the stupendous levels of alcohol consumption in the 1830s, a complex web of causes and effects radiated out from each beer that didn't get drunk, each whiskey not ordered. The fervor of the temperance missionaries to "convert" their drunken brethren to the new religion of abstinence was as heated as the fervor of missionaries to the Pacific Islands and China in their attempt to convert the "heathens" to Christianity. In both cases, the missionaries offered a reprieve from the fires of Hell—in the case of alcoholics, however, their subjects had already experienced the fires of Hell.

One of the most marked directions this temperance conversion fervor took was based on the nineteenth-century idea of womanhood. Women, in this worldview, were never drunks; they were always victims of drinking along with their innocent children. Men would spend their money, beat their wives, and neglect their families, all because they drank. Slowly the move to reform America's drinking habits became a move to give America's women some of the power they had sorely lacked for a century.

Another group of oppressed citizens who were drastically affected by liquor were the slaves. Slave owners used free liquor, especially on holidays, to keep their slaves "happy" and obedient. "It was deemed a disgrace not to get drunk at Christmas," writes Frederick Douglass in his memoir, *Narrative of the Life of Frederick Douglass, An American Slave, Written by Himself.* "From what I know of the effect of these holidays upon the slave, I believe them to be the most effective means in the hands of the slaveholder in keeping down the spirit of insurrection."[25]

Douglass, born into slavery in Maryland, was sent to famous "negro breaker" Edward Covey after he was caught teaching other slaves to read and write by his owners Hugh and Thomas Auld. Covey tortured the slaves who worked for him with a combination of surprise, sadism, and physical pain, and his beatings often left his subjects close to death. It was while he was being "broken" by Covey that Douglass experienced his own worst moments of drinking. On Saturday nights Covey gave his field hands whiskey, and whiskey made Douglass feel the confidence of a president. His life was unbearable, and the only thing that seemed to ease his psychic, spiritual, and physical pain was whiskey. He spent his Sundays in a "beast-like" drunken stupor. One night he got so drunk that he passed out in the slops and filth of Covey's pigsty. When he came to, he found himself fighting for space with a sow and her litter.

While still a teenager, Douglass was sent to a better master, one William Freeland. As he points out, a slave who has a bad master dreams of a good master, but a slave who has a good master dreams of freedom. Douglass finally stopped drinking and began to focus on getting away from his situation more literally than he could by drinking—through an escape to the north. Finally, by disguising himself as a sailor and getting on a train to Philadelphia in 1838, he was able to get away. He was twenty.

As a free man, Douglass married and had children, became a key member of the abolitionists, visited President Lincoln in the White House, ran for Congress, and was appointed U.S. Marshal of the District of Columbia. Even now there are dozens of studies and theories on slavery, from repulsive practice to its economic effects, to its effects on our country today. Douglass, a man who knew this issue from every angle, connected slavery to whiskey. Slaveholders' "object seems to be to disgust their slaves with freedom by plunging them into the lowest depths of dissipation," he writes. "For instance the slaveholders not only like to see the slave drink of his own accord, but will adopt various plans to make him drunk." Slaveholders would make bets on which slave could drink more with the object of getting their slaves drunk. "The most of us used to drink it down, and the result was just what might be supposed; many of us were led to think that there was little to choose between liberty and slavery. We felt…that we had almost as well be slaves to man as to rum."[26]

CHAPTER 6

THE CIVIL WAR

At many of our country's crossroads, alcohol—beer and whiskey or rum and applejack—was an important factor in the direction taken. When George Washington issued rum to his troops, it seemed so natural that no one noticed. Generals who did not drink or use liquor to lubricate their troops' difficulties and buttress their courage were far more noteworthy than those who did. The history of the American military is a drunken one, but there is no correlation between generals who drank and generals who lost battles. One general who abstained, George Armstrong Custer, lost everything, and his name has become synonymous with massive defeat. Not drinking, Custer was routed and killed. Gen. Ulysses S. Grant, a heavy drinker, was the greatest general of the Civil War.

Of course our military leaders drank—the birth and early years of the great United States were cradled in taverns with a beer tap as a wet nurse, and by the 1830s American history was soaked in a local brand of liquid courage. After almost two hundred years of increasing bibulousness, from William Bradford's concerns about beer to the booming molasses trade that flooded the colonies with rum, Americans began to wake up to some new realities. Foreigners were not enemies. There was a possibility of connecting with the formerly hated British as well as European and Eastern counterparts on the other side of the great Atlantic and Pacific Oceans.

As the nineteenth century began to build to the great creative energies and apocalyptic war that defined it, the American people began to feel a different way about drinking. It was no longer understood that one's scant free time was spent drinking, or that one got through life's difficulties with a bottle. Drinking recreationally began to be frowned upon. It was women and their children who paid the price of a drunken husband—a man who left most of his paycheck at the bar on payday and had little left over, financially or emotionally, for his family. The two strands of American character—the drunk and the puritan, the tavern keeper and the temperance crusader—weave around each other as the centuries come and go. By the 1850s the pendulum was swinging sharply toward temperance.

No one thought the Civil War would happen. Its generals on both sides had been a bunch of kids at West Point together. Lee and Grant, Beauregard and Longstreet, Jefferson Davis and McClellan, had all shared dorms and classrooms on the heights above the Hudson River, drilled together at the Point's parade grounds, endured hazings, and shared epiphanies. When newly elected president Abraham Lincoln understood that there was going to be a war, the first thing he did was pass a new tax on whiskey to pay for the supplies, ordnance, and uniforms he would need for his volunteer army. Then he asked the best commander he knew to lead the Union troops—Robert E. Lee. Lee declined with respect. He would be honored to lead Lincoln's troops, but he was a Virginian born and raised and felt that he was more needed by Jefferson Davis and the Confederacy. It was a war between gentlemen. A war between the Union armies who named battles after natural settings—Bull Run, the Wilderness—and their Confederate brothers, some of whom were their actual brothers and cousins, who named battles after the nearest town—Manassas, Spotsylvania, Gettysburg. How could they kill each other? It seemed impossible.

The first shots of the war were fired by Confederate general P. G. T. Beauregard at Fort Sumter, which was held by Gen. Robert Anderson, who had been his artillery instructor at West Point. In the first battle, the Union was ignominiously routed at Bull Run, a battle that turned ugly when retreating Union soldiers trampled the Sunday picnickers who had come out from Washington to make a day of it and see the war be won by their brave soldiers in blue. Still, no one seemed to believe what was happening. Eighteenth-century attitudes persisted. War was a spectator sport, a gentleman's folly, an organized matching of talents to settle a dispute. But instead of sabers and cavalry, the Union and Confederate armies were armed with muskets and cannons. These guns could kill a man who was invisible to the shooter. Cannons obliterated everything, and left huge craters scattered with the remains of buildings and men.

Especially to northerners whose lives went on as usual—except the interruptions for parades as their boys went off to war—the battle seemed far, far away. Southerners were equally innocent; former South Carolina senator James Chestnut facetiously promised to drink all the blood that was shed, since he thought the war woudn't amount to anything serious. "Southern secessionists believed northerners would never mobilize to halt national division or that they would mount nothing more than brief and ineffective resistance," writes Drew Gilpin Faust in her book on the Civil War, *This Republic of Suffering*. "Neither side could have imagined the magnitude and length of the conflict that unfolded, nor the death tolls that proved its terrible cost." Between 1861 and 1865 when the war ended, three million men went to war—two million on the Union side and a million on the Confederate side. Recent estimates have increased the number of dead in the Civil War from 650,000 to 750,000[1]—even the lower number is almost as high as American losses in all other wars combined.

Two-thirds of those killed during the war lost their lives not to muskets but to disease, which was often fatal because of the high incidence of drunken incompetence and drug-addled lack of judgment in both Union and Confederate physicians. As George Worthington Adams famously wrote, "The Civil War was fought in the very last years of the medical middle ages."[2] The weapons were modern; the medical practices were ancient.

Many of the Civil War medics, often self-appointed docs who used alcohol as their principal means of anesthetic, were drinking too much themselves. "Our most valued medicament was the alcoholic liquors," wrote the Confederate doctor William Henry Taylor, who worked in Richmond, Virginia. "As alcoholic liquors were indispensable on a battlefield, it is conceivable that the sudden and complete vanishing to which they were liable might at some time prove to be a serious matter. And so it would have been but that one of our staff, being in tolerably constant communication with his own home, where there was a distillery, was able to keep on hand a full keg of his own."[3]

Addiction to alcohol and other narcotics was common among the Civil War doctors, according to David Williams in *A People's History of the Civil War*. "Our regimental doctor has no more respect for a sick soldier than I would have for a good dog, no not near so much," wrote one Tennessean.[4] Some surgeons were dismissed for drunkenness, but stories of their incompetence and abuse continued. One Ohio surgeon became so intoxicated that "he went staggering through the camp…with one man on each side of him," before absconding altogether.[5] Other soldiers refused treatment from inebriated medics, writing home that they would rather die by rebel bullets than by Union quackery.

Among the men, the drinking usually began as soon as they were out of sight of home—or even during the riotous send-offs many towns provided for the young men heading off to war. "Once the train or ship was under way, the soldiers' spirits took an upward turn," writes Bell Irvin Wiley. "In many instances the festive bent was helped along by drinking."[6] Sometimes too much whiskey caused accidents even before the soldiers reached the battle lines. Once the soldiers reached camp, the drinking continued, often along with gambling and prostitution.

After reviewing a case of insubordination in the division of Gen. Joseph Hooker—a famously hard-drinking division led by a famously hard-drinking general—in February 1862, Gen. George McClellan wrote disgustedly, "No one evil agent so much obstructs this army…as the degrading vice of drunkenness. It is the cause of by far the greater part of the disorders which are examined by courts-martial. It is impossible to estimate the benefits that would ac-crue…from the adoption of a resolution on the part of officers to set their men an example of total abstinence from intoxicating liquors."[7]

General McClellan, who had organized the Army of the Potomac, was not a drinker. A fastidious leader who was great at marshaling de-tails, he ended the war with a reputation for being too indecisive on the battlefield—in other words, sane. His colleagues who succeeded on the battlefield—Grant, Meagher, and Hooker, for example—were drinkers whose performance was often affected by their whiskey intake.

Hooker was falsely thought to be the origin of the word for "pros-titute," because his camp was so rowdy. "Of Hooker I saw but little during the war," Gen. Ulysses S. Grant wrote in his autobiography. "I had known him very well before, however. Where I did see him, at Chattanooga, his achievement in bringing his command around the point of Lookout Mountain and into Chattanooga Valley was bril-liant. I nevertheless regarded him as a dangerous man. He was not subordinate to his superiors. He was ambitious to the extent of caring nothing for the rights of others."[8]

Hooker was not alone in being often drunk and even more often defiant. Gen. Thomas Meagher famously fell off his horse because he was drunk while leading his men into battle at Antietam. Confederate general Benjamin Franklin Cheatham of Tennessee also apparently rode while intoxicated at the Battle of Stones River.[9] Cheatham sur-vived the war, and his portrait was put on the label of an early Jack Daniel's bottle.

Camp soldiers were allowed rations of almost everything—hardtack, meat, soap, coffee, and whiskey measured out from a barrel. Officers helped themselves before the precious stuff was funneled down to their troops. A lot of war was waiting, and whiskey made the time go faster. Many officers were unable to time their drunkenness and were impaired—either drunk or in the grip of dreadful hangovers—at the moment of battle. "Doesn't it seem strange that the enforcement of the rules of war was so lax as to allow the lives of a hundred, a thousand, or perhaps fifty or a hundred thousand sober men to be jeopardized, as they so often were, by holding them rigidly obedient to the orders of a man whose head…might be crazed with commissary whiskey?" asks John D. Billings, a soldier in the Army of the Potomac, in his 1887 account *Hardtack and Coffee: The Unwritten Story of Army Life*.[10] Commissary whiskey was as low as a soldier could go on the scale of drinking, and it was mocked as much as it was desired. One soldier guessed at its contents as being made from bark-juice, tar-water, turpentine, brown sugar, lamp oil, and alcohol.

Gen. Thomas Meagher, who had been an Irish freedom fighter in his home country during the uprising of 1848, was arrested after the Battle of Ballingarry and—instead of being executed—was exiled to what is now Tasmania, an island off Australia, which was then a penal colony for Great Britain. In exile, Meagher married. In 1852, while his wife was pregnant, Meagher escaped and made his way to New York City, where he went to law school and became a popular lecturer on behalf of the cause of Ireland—he could lecture in a clipped, upper-class British accent or in a thick Irish brogue. Waves of Irish immigrants rushed to hear him. This articulate, glamorous leader, who had left family and death sentence behind, decided to support the cause of the Union. When the Civil War began he recruited a company of infantry for the New York volunteers, which was attached to Gen. Irvin McDowell's Army of Northeastern Virginia. After the First Battle of Bull Run, a rousing defeat of such humiliation for the Union that it obscured some reports that Meagher had been drunk on the field, he returned to New York and formed another company—the Irish Brigade of the Union Army, which, during the Peninsula Campaign, developed a reputation for fierce fighting as well as fierce drinking.

Meagher was singled out for his wild behavior by many of his colleagues, particularly Army of the Potomac provost marshal Gen. Marsena Patrick. Patrick, a sober Presbyterian, was asked by General Hooker to join Meagher's Brigade in March 1863. When he joined the men, Patrick found them in the middle of drunken games, including a cavalry steeplechase. "The crowd soon adjourned to drink punch at Meagher's Head Quarters," Patrick wrote. "Everybody got tight and I found it was no place for me."[11] Patrick later complained that he had observed Meagher being drunk for days.

But the general from Ireland fought as hard as he partied. Called Meagher of the Sword, he impressed President Lincoln with his courage at Antietam, and at Fredericksburg the Irish Brigade charged furiously into the enemy ranks and took huge losses. Wild bravery during Civil War battles often led to being wounded or killed. Within a year Meagher went from commanding four thousand soldiers to the command of a few hundred. After the war Meagher became governor of the territory of Montana, and he died in 1867 when he drunkenly fell off a riverboat into fast-moving, deep water near Fort Benton.[12]

"A frequent accompaniment of swearing and gambling was the drinking of intoxicating beverages," writes Wiley about camp life. "Whiskey was the usual tipple, but gin, brandy, wine and—among German troops especially—beer were also consumed in large quantities. The cider stocked by sutlers [civilian merchants who followed the army] sometimes had sufficient potency to make imbibers of a few glasses limber and joyful."[13]

Meagher was not the only Irishman who was drunk in the Union army. With the thoroughness that characterizes obsession with the Civil War, researchers Thomas and Beverly Lowry spent years in the National Archives in Washington, D.C., examining the records of every court-martial in the Union Army during the war. Of the 75,964 courts-martial of which there are records (the Confederate records were destroyed) alcohol was a factor in more than 14, 000, or almost 19 percent. The court-martial records yield many stories of drunkenness. The records are rich with stories of drunken soldiers falling off horses, wandering into enemy lines, going unintentionally AWOL, and knifing and cursing at their superior officers. Maj. John Moriarty was so drunk that one day while riding up Pennsylvania Avenue, he crashed into a horse and buggy and cursed out the occupants. Priv. Peter Kreutz got drunk, wandered off the base to a nearby saloon, and tried to knife the corporal of the guard who came to get him.

The Lowrys then analyzed their court-martial data by nationality—using definitions based on the soldiers' names. Many, many soldiers were drunk, they concluded, but the court-martial records analyzed by the Lowrys show that the Irish soldiers were drunk far more often than their comrades.[14]

How did all this drinking change American history? There are a few incidents where whiskey actually seemed to turn the tide of battle. In 1862 at Middletown, Virginia, Confederate general Turner Ashby's men were able to stop and plunder the Union supply trains of Gen. Nathaniel P. Banks. The wagons contained barrels of whiskey and other liquor, and the soldiers apparently forgot all about fighting the Union enemy and abandoned themselves to partying while the trapped Union forces quietly escaped. Ashby's superior, Gen. Stonewall Jackson, who did not drink, was outraged and accused the men of "abandon[ing] themselves to pillage."[15]

There are many Civil War battles where one side or the other seemed to have lost their good judgment with or without a drink. In a disastrous battle for the Union army, Gen. Ambrose Burnside attacked the heights above Fredericksburg where General Robert E. Lee's men were immovably entrenched—fourteen times. Burnside's many delays allowed Lee to fortify his lines. Burnside couldn't seem to decide when to attack, and when he did, he seemed to be unable to understand what was happening to his men. "General Burnside was an officer who was generally liked and respected," Grant wrote later. "He was not, however, fitted to command an army. No one knew this better than himself."[16]

Another example is Gen. Robert E. Lee's seeming miscalculation, after a night of waiting for information from Jeb Stuart, when he ordered Gen. George E. Pickett to charge uphill into Union lines commanded by General George G. Meade at Gettysburg, an action that may have lost him the war. Then there is the example of McDowell's fatal arrogance on the July Sunday when the first Battle of Bull Run was fought and lost. Like drinking, lapses in judgment seem to have occurred with equal frequency—often—among the leadership of the Union and the Confederacy. In a war awash with liquor, it is difficult to separate the sober mistakes from the mistakes made under the influence. Some of the deadly energy that created a war, where no one had expected a war, may well have come from the barrels of whiskey and crocks of cider and bottles of gin that were as much a part of soldiers' diets as hardtack and dried beef.

Thousands of books have been written about the Civil War. There are books about individual generals and books about camp life. There are books about each battle and books that track the war year by year. There are books about the Civil War strategies that both the Union and the Confederacy learned in the classrooms of West Point and which only sometimes worked on the ground. There are books about the elaborate uniforms both sides wore, and books about Lincoln's first inaugural address—in which he made it clear that his goal was to prevent secession, not slavery—and about his second inaugural in which he had seen the light of civil rights and come to understand that the war had to be the end of one race being the chattel of another.

Many great writers—Bruce Catton, David Williams, Robert Penn Warren—have written about the four years of war that became our homegrown holocaust. Even Ulysses S. Grant, in his last years and as he was dying of throat cancer, wrote a powerful two-volume memoir with accounts of each of his battles. Yet in all these histories there is scant or no mention of the effect drinking had on the troops, the generals, or the progress of the war. Although Bell Irvin Wiley, writing in 1952, describes the role of drinking in the battles of the Civil War, only one or two books since then even mention Civil War drinking, much less the ubiquitous barrels of whiskey, the level of intoxication among the army doctors, and even the drinking among the itinerant chaplains who went from camp to camp. Even books about what the soldiers ate and what they wore ignore what they drank.

Why do historians leave out this interesting aspect of life in the nineteenth century? Although hearty drinking was almost universal in 1830, by the start of the war thirty years later, the subject of drinking had become surrounded by shame. Temperance had done its work. Instead of being a hard-drinking country, we had become a hard-drinking country whose residents often felt guilty about their hard drinking. Already our ambivalence about drinking—the kind that makes us deny it in our families, in our communities, and in our government—had taken root.

One general had so many public problems with his alcohol intake that even our bowdlerized historical accounts take note of his drinking. Of all the drunken generals who fought during the Civil War, the one who most famously battled the bottle as well as his enemies was Ulysses S. Grant. Born the son of a leather goods producer in Ohio, Grant was sent to West Point, where he graduated in the bottom half of his class. At West Point he fell in love with his roommate's sister, Julia Boggs Dent. He proposed, she demurred. He proposed, she asked for more time. His father disapproved of Julia. Her parents disapproved of Grant. After a four-year courtship he finally won her over, and was married to the sensible, loving woman in 1848. The couple adored each other in war and peace, in sobriety and drunkenness. They had four children. Almost forty years later, Grant's dying act was to finish his great autobiography—*Personal Memoirs of Ulysses S. Grant*—which he hoped would help support them for their lives after his death.

A soldier's life is not his own, and Grant was posted from camp to camp, finally ending up in Fort Humboldt in Eureka, California. Here, with his beloved wife and family far away, Grant's drinking began to catch up with him. There was plenty of tolerance for drinking in the military, but less tolerance for a drunk. Grant was a small man—five foot two—who became famous for being unable to hold his liquor. He would sometimes get drunk on what appeared to be one glass, and at other times would drink a great deal. Grant's commander at Fort Humboldt, Col. Robert Buchanan, took offense at Grant's behavior. Grant was lonely in northern California and missed his family. One day when he was drunk and his company was receiving their pay, his inebriation was reported to Buchanan, who was furious. Buchanan had previously warned Grant about binge drinking, and this time he had had too much. Buchanan gave Grant the choice of resigning his post and his military career or having charges pressed against him.[17] Grant resigned.

Suddenly, at the age of thirty-two and with a family to support, Grant had no profession. His father, who still disapproved of Julia and even of his own grandchildren, offered him a job in the leather business if his wife and children would leave and go home to her family; the couple refused. Instead Grant tried farming land given to him by Julia's father, but with scant success. Inspired by love, he felled trees and built a log cabin for his family, which Julia hated, and which he jokingly referred to as "Hardscrabble."

When his father again offered a tannery job with no conditions, Grant moved his family back to Galena, Illinois, and joined his father's store. But what of the alcoholism and the binge drinking that had gotten him booted out of the army? Under Julia's gentle influence, Grant—who thought she was much too good for him—was able to moderate his drinking. Half afraid, half eager to be the husband he felt she deserved, he was apparently able to drink less when he was at home than he almost inevitably drank as a soldier. Like many alcoholics, he struggled to control his drinking—a struggle that was sometimes more successful than others. In his memoir, he tells a sweet autobiographical story about an Illinois Irishman who was promising and well liked but had a "habit of drinking." The man's friends determined to save him, and they drew up a pledge to "abstain from all alcoholic drinks." They asked Pat to join them by signing the pledge, and he consented. He had been so long out of the habit of using plain water as a beverage that he resorted to soda water as a substitute. After a few days this began to grow distasteful to him. So holding the glass behind him he said: "Doctor, couldn't you drop a bit of brandy in that unbeknownst to myself."[18]

When the war began in April 1861, Grant acted decisively. Soon he was the head of a company of Illinois volunteers, who launched an attack from Cairo, Illinois, on the Confederate armies near the important junction of the Ohio and Mississippi Rivers. At this point, Grant did not drink and he did not tolerate drinking among his men. Grant's forces won, and this early victory for the Union after the demoralizing and frightening defeat of Bull Run made him famous. Grant's next engagement was more complicated and perilous but equally victorious. Now a major general, Grant led his forces south to Corinth, Mississippi, on the Tennessee River, where the Confederate army was massed.

On the morning of April 6, 1862, the Confederate army launched a surprise attack with the aim of wiping out the main Union army once and for all. The first day of the battle at Shiloh was disastrous for the Union, but Grant's troops held on, fighting desperately in the mud although Grant himself was not there to lead, but was visiting troops across the river. Night fell without a retreat from the Union, although many of the men were two miles closer to the Tennessee River, and defeat, from where they had begun the day. The troops were exhausted. Many people thought the Union was beaten, including the Union general and Grant's friend William Tecumseh Sherman (his friends called him Cump) who had been in the thick of the battle all day and slowly losing ground. Grant had been absent during the first day of battle. His men thought he had been drinking. Sherman, who had his own struggles with reputation when he had been treated for a nervous condition earlier in the war, was ready to quit. Perhaps the war was over.

Then during the night Grant reappeared with a vengeance. First, he was reinforced by another Union army. It was raining hard, and Grant set up camp under a tree, ignoring the pain from an ankle injury caused when he had fallen off his horse the evening before.

"During the night rain fell in torrents and our troops were exposed to the storm without shelter," he wrote in his memoir:

> I made my headquarters under a tree a few hundred yards back from the river bank. My ankle was so much swollen from the fall of my horse the Friday night preceding, and the bruise was so painful, that I could get no rest. The drenching rain would have precluded the possibility of sleep without this additional cause. Some time after midnight, growing restive under the storm and the continuous pain, I moved back to the log house under the bank. This had been taken as a hospital, and all night wounded men were being brought in, their wounds dressed, a leg or an arm amputated as the case might require, and everything being done to save life or alleviate suffering. The sight was more unendurable than encountering the enemy's fire, and I returned to my tree in the rain.

Gen. William Sherman found him under his large oak tree just before dawn, smoking a large cigar. The rain was heavier, and thunder and lightning had begun to flash through the trees. Sherman was coming to talk about the details of what seemed inevitable—a Union retreat. The trees were dripping water, the battlefields were a sea of mud, but Grant was placidly puffing away as if he were in a gentleman's club with a snifter of brandy. As the storm passed away to the south, the two men stood quietly looking toward the rolling hills beyond the battlefield in the darkness. Standing there, Sherman found he couldn't bear to talk about retreat, although he believed it was necessary. "Well, Grant we've had the devil's own day, haven't we?" he said.

"Yes," Grant replied. "Lick 'em tomorrow, though."[19]

Grant was right. Instead of being finished off the next day, the Union launched a furious counterattack and drove the Confederate army back to its original position. "The endeavor of the enemy on the first day was simply to hurl their men against ours—first at one point, then at another, sometimes at several points at once," Grant wrote in his memoir. "This they did with daring and energy, until at night the rebel troops were worn out…The object of the Confederates on the second day was to get away with as much of their army and material as possible."[20]

Later in the war, Sherman summed up his friendship with Grant for a reporter. "General Grant is a great general," he said. "I know him well. He stood by me when I was crazy, and I stood by him when he was drunk; and now, sir, we stand by each other always."[21]

Because of the intimate nature of the fighting, which had gone on all one day and most of the next, the casualties at Shiloh were the worst of the war to that date—almost twenty-three thousand men from both armies. The casualty numbers shocked people, and some called for Grant's removal. There were also rumors that seemed to follow Grant wherever he went that he had been drinking in camp, and that the Confederates had been able to surprise the Union army because he was drunk. "There was no more preparation by General Grant for an attack than if he had been at a Fourth of July frolic," wrote Horace Greeley angrily in his *New York Tribune*. For those who found Grant's behavior disturbing, there was an object of blame ready for use—his drinking.

But to those who brought their complaints to President Lincoln, he answered, "I need this man. He fights." Lincoln always made an exception for Grant and with good reason. "What if Abraham Lincoln had not gotten around to replacing the sober General McClellan with the heavy-drinking General Grant?" asks Strobe Talbott in *The Great Experiment.* "Would the Union have lost to the Confederacy, and would some distant cousins of mine in Texas be living in a separate country?"[22]

Lincoln's affection for Grant was based on his simplicity and his bravery. Lincoln, who abstained because he had seen the effects of alcohol in his own family, seemed a little in love with Grant both on and off the battlefield. "Well...I hardly know what to think of him, altogether," he told his secretary, William Stoddard. "He's the quietest little fellow you ever saw. Why, he makes the least fuss of any man you ever knew. I believe two or three times he has been in this room a minute or so before I knew he was here. It's about so all around. The only evidence you have that he's in any place is that he makes things git! Wherever he is, things move!"

The president elaborated that, unlike other generals, Grant did not look for excuses to avoid an advance. "When General Grant took hold, I was waiting to see what his pet impossibility would be, and I reckoned it would be cavalry, as a matter of course, for we hadn't horses enough to mount even what men we had. There were fifteen thousand, or thereabouts, up near Harper's Ferry, and no horses to put them on. Well, the other day, just as I expected, Grant sent to me about those very men; but what he wanted to know was whether he should disband 'em or turn 'em into infantry. He doesn't ask me to do impossibilities for him, and he's the first general I've had that didn't."[23]

History has not been quite so forgiving. "Grant was what we would call today a binge drinker," National Military Park historian Jim Ogden told a reporter from the *Chattanooga Times Free Press.* Grant's chief of staff, Brig. Gen. John Rawlins, was actually a sober coach, as they are called today—a man whose only job was to keep Grant from getting drunk. In early June 1863, during the siege of Vicksburg, Rawlins's job became impossible. Anyone who has ever tried to keep another person from drinking can sympathize. No one is cannier or more charming than the drunk who needs a drink. Grant had decided to travel up the Mississippi to reconnoiter, but apparently during the voyage he fell ill and was confined to his cabin. The steamer was warned of Confederate activity by two Union gunboats, but nothing could wake General Grant.

In a letter Rawlins let his employer know that he had not been fooled. Rawlins had seen the box of wine and the empties that Grant's binge had left behind when he retired to his room. But Rawlins, brilliantly, didn't scold Grant. "You have full control of your appetite, and can let drinking alone," he wrote. "Had you not pledged me the sincerity of your honor early last March, that you would drink no more during the war, and kept that pledge during your recent campaign, you would not today have stood first in the world's history as a military leader. Your only salvation depends on your strict adherence to that pledge. You cannot succeed in any other way."[24]

Whether or not he was drinking his favorite Old Crow whiskey on any given occasion, Grant was clearly a man with a drinking problem. Julia and his children seemed to help him control his drinking, but under the pressures of war he had hired a shadow and sworn to that shadow that he would not drink. Grant's grandfather had been a drinker, and enough of a problem so that his father, Jesse, had the strict sense of rules and order that are characteristic of children of alcoholics. Jesse didn't drink and he had no tolerance for his son's drinking. Perhaps the last word on Grant's drinking goes to Lincoln who, when his aides complained about Grant, famously replied that they should find him one hundred barrels of whatever Grant was drinking so that he could give it to the rest of his officers.

Whether alcoholics are drinking or not, they often have certain character traits that are shared by other alcoholics. Recovering alcoholics call this "the ism" as in *alcoholism*. A drunk can put down the alcohol, they say, but they can't get rid of the "ism." Grant certainly had it. "Underlying our failure to place the personality of Grant into clearer perspective is the problem of his drinking," writes biographer Lyle W. Dorsett. Although Grant had tried to give up drinking entirely, and even joined the Sons of Temperance at one point, there are many reports of his being drunk during the war. Furthermore, Dorsett argues, his ability to command was markedly influenced by his alcoholism.

Indeed, there is no evidence that drinking made Grant a lesser general or a less effective leader; quite the opposite. Grant had courage where none was called for; he had confidence in the face of what a sober man might have thought of as defeat. Grant's understanding of weakness and his quicksilver ability to inspire his men with his own hard-won brass, combined with his fearlessness and his understanding that winning the war would require the sacrifice of a generation of men, might have made him a more effective fighter. Lincoln certainly thought so.

Grant's drinking was also part of a larger problem that has plagued American military forces since 1776. American soldiers drink. This can have very good effects; being a little drunk can make a man or woman more courageous and more focused. It can also have very bad effects. World War II was fought by American troops at a time when heavy drinking was accepted in and out of the Army. Our modern wars, in which our troops may be seriously impaired when they engage with the enemy, are not so forgiving. Although it is difficult to measure the effects of drinking financially, a 2009 study showed that alcohol abuse was costing the military $1.12 billion a year, with 34,400 military arrests for drinking and drinking-related crimes. Frequent heavy drinking, defined as five or more drinks at a time on more than one occasion a week, is higher in the military than it is in the civilian population. A substantial portion of the military, especially younger men, is impaired by drinking.

Alarmed by drinking in the military, the Defense Department commissioned an Institute of Medicine report that called drinking in the military a "public health crisis." Not only did 20 percent of soldiers drink heavily, according to the 2012 report, but binge drinking—five or more drinks at a sitting—had increased among male soldiers from 35 percent in 1998 to 47 percent in 2008. Many soldiers suffering from stress, trauma, and PTSD try to self-medicate with alcohol rather than ask for help, the report says. Help is often not available. "Better care for service members…is hampered by inadequate prevention strategies, staffing shortages, lack of coverage for services…and stigma associated with these disorders," wrote the University of Pennsylvania Center for Studies of Addiction vice-chairman Charles P. O'Brien, the chair of the committee which produced the report. O'Brien noted that in the entire U.S. Army, only one doctor was trained as an addiction specialist.

CHAPTER 7

THE GREAT AMERICAN WEST

By the end of the Civil War, when Robert E. Lee surrendered to Ulysses S. Grant at Appomattox Court House on April 9, 1865, the westward expansion that created today's United States was well under way. Five days after Appomattox, Abraham Lincoln was assassinated by the actor John Wilkes Booth while he sat with his wife at Ford's Theatre in Washington, D.C., watching a play. Together these two events—a surrender and a murder—jolted the country westward again with a burst of energy.[1]

Westward expansion wasn't a new idea. It had already done its part to form the American character: the lust for wide-open spaces where anyone could start over, the emphasis on self-reliance, and the religion of the individual and his family. The exploration and exploitation of the American West started with Thomas Jefferson's presidency and with one of the most intriguing characters in American history: Meriwether Lewis.

Lewis, who grew up in the woods of Albemarle County, Virginia, and went to Washington and Lee University, became Jefferson's secretary at the age of twenty-six and soon integrated himself into the affections of the new president—Jefferson had just been elected the country's third president after the one term served by John Adams. Generous, voluble, an accomplished woodsman and an experienced soldier, Lewis had served among the troops who put down the Whiskey Rebellion in Pittsburgh and was a captain in the United States Army.

Jefferson had recently overseen the Louisiana Purchase, a negotiation that would create the American West as we know it. Jefferson's representative, James Monroe, hoping to buy the port of New Orleans for $10 million so that trade could move freely on the Mississippi River, was offered the entire bulk of French Louisiana for an extra $5 million. The purchase doubled the size of the United States and opened up huge territories that had previously been claimed by the French or the Spanish, although they already had many residents— the Native Americans.

Jefferson had often dreamed of westward expansion, and now he had the opportunity. He also had Meriwether Lewis, a young man who was shaping up to be a diplomat and leader. He spent two years preparing Lewis, including a year of the study of natural medicines with none other than Dr. Benjamin Rush. For a companion Lewis chose another soldier who had impressed him with calm and competence: William Clark. "Dispatched by Jefferson to seal the greatest achievement of his administration, the Louisiana Purchase, the Lewis and Clark expedition ranks as one of the greatest explorations in history," writes historian Page Smith.[2]

As long as there were physical hardships to endure and dangers to survive, Lewis was a magnificent leader. Although there was plenty of whiskey in the stores carried by Lewis and Clark from Saint Louis to the Pacific Ocean, there is no record of Lewis being drunk during the twenty-six months of the expedition, which set off from Saint Charles, Missouri, just north of Saint Louis by boat in May 1804. It was a trip with many difficulties, as the boats traveled north on the Missouri River, through what is now Nebraska, and west past the Yellowstone River toward the Pacific. Although the explorers were searching for the mythic Northwest Passage, they never found it. Instead they managed to find a serviceable way to go by water in their twenty-two-oar keelboat from Saint Louis to the Pacific and back again. Lewis and Clark were careful with their men. Only one member of the expedition died, his death caused by a burst appendix.

There were difficulties as the men got sick, were chased by Native Americans and bears, nearly drowned, and survived Lewis's accidental shooting in the leg by a hunting partner. Lewis and Clark, who called themselves the Corps of Discovery, managed to move peaceably among the Native American tribes west of the Mississippi—the Pawnee, the Sioux, and the Arikara among others. Among the Arikara, the "gift" of Indian women who willingly had sex with the explorers was a welcome exchange. "Women were not, as Clark imagined, merely a way to return a favor," writes Ted Morgan. "The real benefit was a perceived transfer of power. With their boats and cannon and compasses, these white men had potent magic. Some of that magic could be passed to the tribe via the squaws. The Indians regarded sex as a conduit for the passage of spiritual capabilities, a way of gaining access to the white man's skills, in much the same way that by eating the heart of a brave enemy you could gain his courage."[3]

Lewis's drinking problem, as well as his possible mental illnesses, did not surface until after his great adventure, when he had little to do but rest on his laurels. After returning from the expedition, Lewis received a reward of 1,600 acres of land. He made arrangements to publish the Corps of Discovery journals based on his own diaries, but he had difficulty completing his writing.

In 1807, after Jefferson appointed him governor of the Louisiana Territory, Lewis settled in Saint Louis. He found the governor's job thoroughly demoralizing. It was a glorified desk job with enemies. Lewis was generally hated as being a representative of Jefferson's. Washington writers attacked him as a man with no governing experience. Off the trail, ordinary political life seemed difficult for Lewis and drinking continued to be one of his principal respites. He did not seem to want to get married. He did not want to continue as an explorer.[4]

Once a great American hero, he slid into debt and was pursued by his creditors. He was so depressed that his friends became concerned. Jefferson suggested he come back to Washington. He finally decided to head north, taking with him the parts of the journals he had completed for publication. He left Saint Louis and headed east through Tennessee, following the explorer's trail called the Natchez Trace for part of the journey. The 450-mile-long Natchez Trace, originally used by prehistoric people, had become a Native American trail. By 1800 it was a popular route from north to south, running from Nashville, Tennessee, to Natchez, Mississippi.

At Fort Pickering in Memphis, Tennessee, Lewis's condition was so critical that the fort's captain, Gilbert Russell, kept him for two weeks trying to wean him off alcohol. "The free use he made of liquor…he acknowledged very candidly to me after his recovery and expressed a firm determination never to drink any more spirits…again…But after leaving this place by some means or other his resolution left him."[5] Later, in the introduction to the journals when they were finally published, Jefferson hedged his views on Lewis, writing that when Lewis had lived with him, the younger man had suffered from "depressions of mind."

Historian Ted Morgan speculates that the pressure of being governor was too much for Lewis. On the expedition, his nerves had been perfect, but they may have been damaged by the pressures of politics in which he was not a hero but a scapegoat. "He must have felt a terrible injustice in having his Washington bosses treat him like a malefactor when he had repeatedly risked his life in his country's service, without the slightest thought of gain," Morgan writes.[6] In any case, the thirty-five-year-old Lewis snapped.

At an overnight stop at an inn called Grinder's Stand farther north and east near the end of the Trace, Lewis was either shot by robbers or shot himself in the head with his own pistol. He died the next day. "The symbolism is almost too pat," writes Smith. "America was a land that could drive its best to madness, the greatest achievements shadowed by tragedy." For Lewis, as for Charles Adams before him and Ulysses S. Grant after him, the American madness had a particular trajectory and a particular set of circumstances. "At the end of his life he was a horrible drunk, terribly depressed, who could never even finish his [expedition] journals," says Paul Douglas Newman, a professor of history who teaches a course in Lewis and Clark at the University of Pittsburgh.

Almost two hundred years later, historians are still arguing over what happened to Meriwether Lewis that night at Grinder's Stand. Requests to exhume the body have been rejected by the state and by the National Park Service. But the result of Meriwether Lewis's untimely death, as well as his history of mental illness, is that he is rarely mentioned in American history books. He is, as Vardis Fisher has argued, "the most neglected American hero." No wonder. Lewis's story in both its positive aspects—his charm, his intelligence, his endurance—and its negative aspects—his depression, his inability to lead a normal life, his drinking—is all too familiar to many Americans who have lived with alcoholism, their own or others.

Many of the paths Lewis and Clark followed west had originally been blazed by a rough kind of new American, a man who traveled light and trapped beaver furs, which were easy to find and very easy to sell. American fur traders were the explorers who opened up the American West, not out of a belief in American expansion but rather out of a desire to make money. These mountain men lived off the land, slept on the ground, hunted for food, and trapped for a living. Some of these men were educated, some had moved west a few steps ahead of the law, and some were escaped slaves. The West was a place where no one cared who you were or who you had been; they only cared what you could accomplish.

The effect of these men, who were able to roam the West and discover mountain passes and pathways and navigable rivers that would later make the great migration possible, is hard to estimate. They chose their lives because of solitude and other benefits of living off the grid.

Their year was measured by a single social event, an annual drunken blowout called the rendezvous.

In these wild, commercial, and social gatherings, first arranged by the eastern fur companies to centralize the trade of furs, men who lived and hunted alone for eleven months were thrown together with the money, whiskey, and tobacco they received for the furs they had trapped during the year—there was little stable currency west of the Mississippi. The rendezvous was a tradition begun by William Henry Ashley, who had a string of failures in the fur trade before hitting on a very good idea: He invited a group of fur trappers to meet at Henry's Fork on the Green River to exchange the furs they had trapped for wagonloads of goods, which Ashley would drive in from Saint Louis.

Soon the annual rendezvous were weeklong parties of trappers with their piles of "hairy bank notes"—beaver pelts—as well as wagonloads of traders from the East with all the things the forest did not provide—ammunition, traps, knives, tobacco, and alcohol. Whole tribes of Native Americans camped at the rendezvous sites. Historian Ray Allen Billington argues it was because the rendezvous system was so much like the fairs held by the Indians that it worked. "A comparable trade fair had been staged annually by the Shoshoni Indians as a means of attracting white traders to their villages," Billington writes. "Indeed Ashley may well have known of the success of this venture when he planned his own gathering."[7]

Within two years of swapping furs for goods, Ashley became a wealthy man as the head of the Rocky Mountain Fur Company. John Jacob Astor with his American Fur Company also made his first fortune. According to some accounts, Astor's traders discovered the South Pass—the wide valley that was the easiest and soon the most popular way to cross the Continental Divide on the way from Missouri to California.

According to Morgan, however, it was Ashley's men who discovered the pass. "The way through this wall of mountains was the South Pass," he writes, "a broad and flattened cavity on the continent's spine at 7,500 feet. Shivering like aspen leaves, it took them two weeks to traverse the pass. The wind blew so fiercely it blew the trapper's fires out, and they had to eat their meat raw, while the horses ate snow." In spite of the hardships they suffered, the men who discovered the South Pass had found a navigable way across the impassable wall of snow and ice and rocks that reared up in front of them as they crossed the prairies of Kansas and Nebraska—the Rocky Mountains.[8] It wasn't the Northwest Passage, but it was just as important.

The annual rendezvous grew into a great Rocky Mountain gathering, "combining aspects of a carnival, a souk, a hoedown, and a rodeo…The proceedings reached their climax when the whiskey kegs were bunged and a saloon was improvised under a tent," writes Morgan. These rugged individuals who spent most of their time alone in the wilderness were the forgers of the American character. Although the phrase was not yet in common usage, these were the point men for the driving eighteenth-century force of manifest destiny.

Manifest destiny was the term coined by journalist John L. O'Sullivan in 1845 in the *Democratic Review*. He used the phrase to refer to the God-given right of the United States and its people to expand across the American continent. First he urged the annexation of the Republic of Texas, and in a later article he explained that because of "manifest destiny" the United States should also claim Oregon. Manifest destiny had a religious overtone, as well; it suggested that American imperialism was somehow God's mandate. Later, President Woodrow Wilson echoed the idea when he spoke about making the world safe for democracy.

The reign of the mountain men and the wildness of the frontier, as well as the roaring good cheer of the gatherings, were brought to an end by waves of immigrants from the East and their attendant preachers and clergymen. Still, the legacy of individual accomplishment and the possibility of anyone making a fortune remained the promise of the unsettled West and remained—in the American myth—the thing that separated the new United States from the Old World. In Europe and Great Britain, citizens were born into a class and a profession, and they stayed there—in this new world anyone could get rich, anyone could own land, and anyone could be a leader.

"The trapper believed in the myth of perfect, natural freedom," writes W. J. Rorabaugh in his thoroughly documented account of how drinking shaped the American West. "The independent man needed no one, for he was complete in and of himself. He lived in Rousseauian harmony with nature, coaxing her to yield up her trea-sures, making her do his bidding. He savored his freedom, which he jealously guarded."[9] But as Rorabaugh points out, these flagrantly free men were actually controlled by the owners of the fur companies, who provided for them every year at the rendezvous and who were happy to trade furs for liquor. In the 1850s when the European and eastern fashion for beaver hats was replaced by a fashion for silk top hats, the abundant fur trade sputtered and stalled. The freedom of the moun-tain men was over, but the myth of that freedom persists even today.

In order to make manifest destiny a reality for the millions of men, women, and children who headed west for almost a million reasons—the promise of land, gold, wealth, freedom, status—new and easier ways had to be found to transport goods and services. Back when Jefferson had been president, even he had dreamed of a network of railroads and canals that would open up the resources of the West to the East and provide ways for easterners to go west.

First, there was the Erie Canal, an idea that Jefferson had dreamed about but which was finally brought to reality in 1817 by New York State governor DeWitt Clinton. Without a canal, wagon trains had to cross the Appalachian Mountains to go west of Pennsylvania, or go by boat up the coast of Canada and through the Saint Lawrence River to the Great Lakes. A canal connecting the Hudson River at Al-bany to the new city of Buffalo on Lake Erie would cut transportation costs almost 95 percent. The canal, following the east-to-west Mo-hawk River watershed, which cut through both the Catskills and the

Appalachians, would be almost four hundred miles long and include thirty locks that would take up the slack between the height of the water in Lake Erie and the water at the head of the Hudson. An engineering miracle, few people thought that such a canal was practical or even possible. Even its supporters expected it would take decades to dig the forty-foot-wide, four-foot-deep trench across New York State.

The workers, primarily taken from the droves of Irish immigrants who had begun to pour into the Northeastern United States, were paid with fifty cents a day with room and board, and thirty-two ounces of whiskey a day. The canal foremen, called jigger bosses, woke the workers with a gunshot and two ounces of whiskey at six a.m. every morning. The canal was finished in eight years. "Could the Erie Canal have been built without whiskey?" asks one documentary.[10]

The huge success of the canal was one of the many inspirations for the generation of railroad builders who changed the United States from a vast wilderness to a settled place, and the distance from New York to California from a yearlong trip to a four-day jaunt in relative comfort. In Baltimore, wholesale grocer and liquor distributor Johns Hopkins would help finance the first railroad from Maryland to Ohio. In the years after the Civil War two competing railroad companies—the Union Pacific and the Central Pacific—were building competing tracks from California to Saint Louis and back. The workers for the western part of the line were thousands of immigrant Chinese displaced by poverty and revolution and originally attracted to the California gold mines. The eastern side of the line was built by Civil War veterans.

Eventually, as the railroad appeared to be a good idea, the federal government stepped in. In a rare, triumphant moment during his scandal-ridden presidency, President Grant decreed that the two lines of track would meet in Promontory, Utah, and that a "golden spike" would be the last spike driven to unite the two railroads and create a transcontinental track.[11] On the afternoon of May 10, 1869, crowds formed to watch the ceremony as railroad baron and former governor of California Leland Stanford prepared to drive in the last spike. Stanford missed, but no one seemed to care.

Millions of settlers now poured west. Each small town started with a saloon and ended with a schoolhouse. There were many discoveries along the way. In a small town near Sacramento, a settler named Sutter found some flakes of gold in a river he was crossing and set off the great gold rush of 1849—a gold rush that made some men rich and caused others to drown their sorrows in local saloons.

Virginia City, Nevada, built on the ridge that holds the rich silver of the Comstock Lode, was where a man named James Fennimore, who had traveled west to stay ahead of the law, found silver in 1859. In the twenty years of its boom, forty million dollars' worth of silver was pulled out of the Comstock Lode. Virginia City became the richest town in America. Its streets were lined with gorgeous Victorian houses filled with loads of European furniture, saloons that served platters of oysters along with their whiskey and champagne, the only elevators west of Chicago, and a printing press and newspaper. In its heyday the newspaper, the *Virginia City Territorial Enterprise*, was edited on and off by Samuel Clemens and in the 1950s boasted Ambrose Bierce and Lucius Beebe as reporters. The *Territorial Enterprise* was the paper where Sam Clemens first used his pseudonym—Mark Twain—and later he wrote about Virginia City in the autobiographical *Roughing It.*

As much as silver and gold, the treasure that seemed to thrive in the American West was mythmaking. "The most important effect of the frontier has been in the promotion of democracy," writes Frederick Jackson Turner in his *The Frontier in American History*. "The frontier is productive of individualism. Complex society is precipitated by the wilderness into a kind of primitive organization based on the family. The tendency is anti-social. It produces antipathy to control…The tax-gatherer is viewed as a representative of oppression."[12] The frontier character—defiant, solitary, and prone to binge drinking, storytelling, and gambling—was solid gold when it came to larger-than-life characters and almost-impossible feats of strength, goodness, or villainy.

One of the men who made gold out of the straw of his origins and character was Wyatt Earp, who became an embodiment of the glorious principles of the Wild West. Born in Illinois in 1848, when Illinois was still the frontier, Earp was one of a family of close-knit brothers: Virgil, Warren, Newton, James, and Morgan. There was a quiet sister, Adelia; two other sisters, Virginia and Martha, died in childhood. The Earp family moved west with the frontier, taking all kinds of jobs that were available in the small new towns of the west—they ran saloons, they staged gambling games, and they served as lawmen and occasionally as outlaws. By the time Wyatt Earp got to Dodge City, Kansas, he was the assistant to the city marshal. This didn't keep him from running a profitable card game and investing in the local silver mines.

Earp was a teetotaler. He had tried drinking when he was young and had a powerful adverse physical reaction. Because he didn't drink, his gambling games were well run and profitable for him, but he had his eye on immortality. Men who didn't drink stand out in the history of the formation of the American West. Sometimes, as was the case with General Custer, abstinence seems to feed their manic energy and their dreams of glory. At other times it gives them the ability to manipulate those around them. Just as the American character was shaped by the pressures and circumstances of the frontier, the idea that we have of the American frontier was shaped by a few creative characters—including Earp.

In Tombstone, Arizona, Earp and his brothers pursued some cowboys—the Clanton brothers—who had been robbing stagecoaches and terrorizing the population. The famous Gunfight at the O.K. Corral may have been a shootout between the white hats—the Earps—and the black hats, or it may have just been more slaughter inflicted on western low-lifes by other outlaws. At any rate two of the

Earp brothers were killed and, in revenge, Wyatt then sought out the Clantons and killed them. Was this a high-minded search for justice, a justice that he knew he had to take into his own hands? Or was it just frontier machismo? Earp continued as a murderous outlaw and a famous flim-flam man. He fixed a prize fight in Los Angeles and ran a traveling card game wherever he went.

By the turn of the century two events had catapulted Earp into being a legend in his own mind—and in all of our minds. One: He had read the 1901 novel *The Virginian* by Owen Wister. Two: He had moved to Hollywood. There, according to Andrew C. Isenberg's biography *Wyatt Earp: A Vigilante Life*, he sold the heroic version of his story, inspired by Wister's story of justice in the West, to an aspiring screenwriter named Stuart Lake. The Wyatt Earp who emerged from Lake's interviews with the aging, still handsome Earp was a noble man who sometimes found that he had to put himself against the law in the service of justice.

This myth—that justice is sometimes better served by an individual than it is by the law of the land—was one of the frontier's most appealing ideas. No wonder Lake sold the rights to Earp's story to Twentieth Century Fox, and no wonder Earp has been played in the movies by Burt Lancaster and Kevin Costner. Historian Andrew C. Isenberg writes that "having tried and failed to invent a better future for himself, in the end he invented a better past"[13]

CHAPTER 8

THE END OF THE NINETEENTH CENTURY AND THE NEW TEMPERANCE CRUSADERS

We all grew up saturated with the myths and stories of the old West, the Wild West, the television and movie West, and the West in our history books. One of the great stories featuring larger-than-life heroes is the story of Gen. George Armstrong Custer of Ohio, Michigan, and West Point, and his great adversary, the Lakota chief Sitting Bull.

Custer, along with Alexander Hamilton and Abraham Lincoln, is one of the few American heroes who did not drink. Like the others, he saw his father's drinking firsthand, was hurt by it, and detested it. As a young man he fell in love with a woman named Libbie—Elizabeth Bacon—who was his superior in social status and wealth. Libbie's father opposed Custer as a suitor, and by the time the two were married Custer had taken yet another vow to abstain from drinking, a vow that, according to most sources, he kept.

But like Hamilton, a nondrinking man with drinking genes, Custer seems to have had a preening arrogance, an inability to follow orders, and a sense of his own messianic rightness that is characteristic of dry drunks. Fearless in battle and the finest cavalryman of his generation, Custer came from a poor Ohio family. Born in 1839, he spent much of his childhood in Michigan with an aunt. Humans love stories about last stands—Horatius at the Bridge, Davy Crockett at the

Alamo—and although Custer is primarily remembered for his final, bloody failure, Custer's Last Stand, he had an astonishing and impressive military and civilian career before he ever rode west.

Custer, whose first jobs were carrying coal and working as an Ohio schoolteacher, by a combination of brashness and good luck, eventually secured a place as a student at West Point. There he cut classes and made trouble, but managed to rebound from the threat of expulsion a dozen times and graduate last in the class of 1861, just as the Civil War was becoming a certainty.

At Bull Run he was on the field as a messenger and quickly was promoted to brigadier general of the volunteers—a general at the age of twenty-three. He was already famous for his fearlessness, his arrogance, his wild howling and whooping as he rode into battle, his long, blond, ringletted hair, his self-proclaimed luck, his glorious war horses, and the fancy uniforms he had specially made for his slender body. But it was at the battle of Gettysburg that Custer made his name.

At Gettysburg, Confederate general Robert E. Lee had commissioned troops under Jeb Stuart to go east behind the Union lines that were entrenched under Gen. George Meade. The Confederates under Stuart would attack from behind. At the same time, Lee ordered Gen. Pickett to attack the Union lines from the front.

The clear-eyed, quick-thinking Union general Custer, whose troops were on the other side of the battlefield, saw exactly what was happening. This pincer motion was one of the maneuvers both he and Lee had studied in the classrooms of West Point. Wearing an outfit of black velvet and gold braid, of his own design, he commandeered a Michigan brigade. He led them whooping and galloping furiously against Stuart's men, heading off what almost surely would have been a disaster. The next day it was Lee's men who experienced disaster after Pickett's famous charge into Meade's entrenched troops.

When the Civil War ended, the well-respected Custer was sent west to colonize new territory and to neutralize the Native American tribes who were a hazard to exploration, homesteading, mining, and every other frontier endeavor.

As Nathaniel Philbrick points out in his biography of Custer, the battle of Little Bighorn was not just Custer's last stand—it was also the end of a Western myth and the end of freedom and dignity for the Native American tribes. It was the last stand of the Native American people. Because of the outrage of Custer's defeat, the administration of President U. S. Grant was able to get Congress to push through anti–Native American measures that it would not have agreed to months earlier. The Army increased its efforts and aggression. "Within a few years of the Little Bighorn, all the major tribal leaders had taken up residence on Indian Reservations," Philbrick writes.[1] Sitting Bull held out for another fourteen years, but he was killed by Indian Agency police in 1890.

Before the Civil War the three reform causes in the United States were abolition, temperance, and women's rights. As the war approached, abolition emerged as the most important. After the war, with the abolitionist cause supposedly victorious, reformers in the country turned to temperance—which quickly became tangled around the cause of women's suffrage. Until Prohibition, temperance was thought to be a women's issue. Women stayed home with the children and depended on wages brought home by their men. If the men drank, women's lives were difficult. Temperance was a cause worth voting for, except that women couldn't vote because they were still legally chattel of the men they married or the men who happened to be their fathers. Temperance became a women's cause in a way that it had not been before the Civil War.

Eliza Thompson, a temperance crusader who became Mother Thompson; Susan B. Anthony, who gave her first speech to the Daughters of Temperance, and became a crusader for women's rights when the Sons of Temperance refused to let her speak to them; and Amelia Bloomer, who was also barred from a men's temperance meeting—all ended up devoting their energies to women's suffrage. If women could not get the vote, they could not change the rules in general and the rules about drinking and barrooms in particular. "One could make the argument that without the 'liquor evil,' as it was commonly known to those who most despised it, the suffrage movement would not have drawn the talents and energies of these gifted women," writes Daniel Okrent.[2]

In 1874, a woman named Frances Willard from Wisconsin cofounded the Women's Christian Temperance Union, a 250,000-strong army of women who protested by going down on their knees in saloons and singing Christian hymns. After reading Edward Bellamy's *Looking Backward*, Willard called herself a "Christian Socialist," and she made the alliance between temperance and women's welfare even stronger.

CHAPTER 9

PROHIBITION

January 16, 1920, New York City. Freezing wind howled down Broadway and the air smelled of snow, but groups of already tipsy people wandered shivering from bar to bar to have what they assumed would be their very last legal drink. Prohibition! Black-bordered invitations had summoned the faithful to funerals all over town to perform "the last rites and ceremonies for our spirited friend John Barleycorn."[1] At the Park Avenue Hotel, black-robed girls wept and keened, and at the bar there was a last round of sad, slurred toasts.[2] At Healey's on Sixth Avenue, patrons tossed their empty glasses into a silk-lined coffin, and every customer was given a small casket as they left for the last time "to remember the fallen." Uptown, women in cloche hats and ermine coats chug-a-lugged their last drinks. At Maxim's the waiters hauled a coffin to the center of the dance floor.[3] Reporters on deadline tapped out eulogies, and the *Daily News* imagined John Barleycorn's final words: "I've had more friends in private and more foes in public than any other man in America." The Volstead Act, enacted to carry out the Eighteenth Amendment to the Constitution, would go into effect at midnight. The act was described as "an act to prohibit intoxicating beverages, and to regulate the manufacture, production, use, and sale of high-proof spirits for other than beverage purposes, and to ensure an ample supply of alcohol and promote its use in scientific research and in the development of fuel, dye, and other lawful industries."

As the deadline approached, flasks came out of pockets and brief-cases as word went around that the big hotels like the Waldorf had already run out of liquor. The day had been crowded with New York-ers stocking up for alcoholic Armageddon. Cars, trucks, taxis, wagons, and baby buggies were all employed to cart liquor from the closing liquor stores to the residents' private stores—thus carrying it from the land of illegality to the land of the legal. (It was legal to drink at home.) In Boston, saloons and bars were crowded right up to the deadline of midnight, but after that the city went quiet out of fear of the $1,000 fine or six months in jail that awaited first offenders.

Could this really be happening? The newly minted and trained men of the Internal Revenue Service's Prohibition Unit[4] were also overwhelmed. They told themselves that the new laws worked—enforcing them would be easy. But the United States has long borders, and even before the last call on the night of January 16, bootleggers were moving crates of whiskey throughout Canada and preparing to drive them up from Mexico. In Chicago the revenue agents were unable to stop the robbery of two boxcars with $100,000 worth of whiskey by six masked men just a few minutes after midnight.

Between the bootleggers' smuggling and the illegal brewers (both industrial distillers and brewers, and individuals making booze in ev-ery bathtub in the nation) the revenue agents became symbols of helplessness, especially in hard-drinking New York City. "Prohibi-tion…was a joke in most of urban America," writes Ann Douglas in her book about the 1920s, *Terrible Honesty*, "but in New York it was an all-out full-scale farce."[5] The level of ingenuity used by smugglers came to seem almost purposeful, as the level of corruption among the revenue agents became legendary. Stills sprang up in every household. A six-thousand-gallon pipeline of beer was run through the Yonkers sewer system to bring beer from boats on the Hudson River to local saloons. One Midwestern gang froze unmarked bottles in ice blocks bound across Lake Huron, a trick that worked well until the weather turned unseasonably warm. Another gang drove over the Canadian border dressed as priests and were waved through by customs without anyone looking under their robes—until the day one of them had a flat tire. Others carried bottles in carefully tailored loose clothing, in hoses wrapped around them with stoppers at each end, in hot water bottles, in barrels, and once in two dozen eggs that had been carefully emptied out and refilled with whiskey. All this smuggling made for great stories to be told over a spirit-warming hot toddy on the United States side of the border. In New England, liquor came from ships anchored beyond the three-mile limit and ferried to shore in small boats. Rum runners in everything from rowboats to yachts used the nation's beaches as their landing points—a boat loaded with four hundred cases of whiskey and 150 barrels of malt extract ran aground on Jones Beach, Long Island. In Chicago an Italian family ran hundreds of home stills all over the Near West Side and in Detroit, of course...Canada was just on the other side of town.

Struggling to stanch the flow of liquor, revenue agents dumped enough beer, wine, and whiskey into New York Harbor to float a drunken armada. Acres of ruined barrels lined the Brooklyn waterfront, where men in hats and suspenders and vests scavenged whatever had been left behind. Agents poured beer out of windows and hauled stills out of cellars, but the job was impossible. Isador Einstein and Moe Smith, a couple of brilliant agents who got fired when corruption became the rule rather than the exception in the revenue service, wrote memoirs about their ingenuity. They dressed as gravediggers, iron mongers, even saloon owners, and arrested almost five thousand miscreants.[6]

Altogether, few people took the new ban seriously. When the mayor of Berlin came on a state visit to New York for a week in the fall of 1929, he asked Mayor Jimmy Walker when the Prohibition laws were going into effect—because from what he could see they were clearly not yet being enforced. Nowhere was this attitude clearer than at the White House, where President Warren G. Harding, the whiskey loving successor to the sober-sided Presbyterian Woodrow Wilson, was not about to give up his evening highballs. Although the president was disturbed by the epidemic of law breaking created by Prohibition and called for an "awakened American conscience," he was not interested in a dry cabinet. At his famous parties, where even Alice Roosevelt got drunk, liquor sometimes was provided from the Prohibition Unit's confiscated stock.

Although even the president broke the law, legal Prohibition marked a sharp change in the way drinking was perceived in this country. As far back as the Pilgrims, we had an intense connection to alcohol—we embraced it and then we outlawed it; we floated great political and social movements on it and then we demonized it. Drinking caused wonderful things to happen, and it caused terrible things to happen. In our culture, drinking changed from "the good creature of God" to "the Demon Rum," and most of this transformation went on just below the level of written history.

With Prohibition, our love-hate relationship with alcohol burst out of the shadows and became—in all its craziness—a great public cause that swept forward, carrying women's suffrage along with it, and a great public failure that did not diminish drinking and created criminal opportunities that led to the formation of organized crime.

Before Prohibition, generations of Americans drank without thinking. Whether it was Governor-to-be William Bradford fighting with *Mayflower* captain Jones over beer, the sons of John Adams drinking themselves to death, or the blithe Johnny Appleseed's distributing hard cider, we drank because it tasted good and the effects were powerful and delicious. If a little drinking was good, a lot of drinking was better. The United States were Edenic when it came to alcohol, a country where innocence and mindlessness made drinking an uncomplicated pleasure. We did the drinking without the thinking until American drinking flooded the country with liquor in the 1830s.

Then just before the mid-nineteenth century, drinking began to have more negative effects. As more and more men went to work in factories and the industrial revolution came to the northeast, the clumsiness and sloppiness associated with drinking became less tolerable. A farmer who was drunk after a day of swigging from a bottle stashed at the end of each row couldn't do much damage. But a machinist taking mandatory breaks for a drink at eleven o'clock—elevenses—and again in the middle of the afternoon could make dangerous mistakes while handling heavy equipment. At the same time, as the industrial revolution rolled forward with its gender separation of wage-earning and domestic duties, drinking began to be associated with noxious male behavior. Men, finally let off from work on Friday nights, had their paychecks cashed by the local publican and got home broke in the early hours of the morning.

The taverns and saloons were still the center of social life in most villages. Many were owned by liquor companies who provided whiskey and beer as well as furnishings—the gleaming wooden bars and the florid, over-the-top murals of grand subjects like Custer's Last Stand. Manhattan Island alone had more than nine thousand bars for a population of less than a million, bars that not only served alcohol but that often provided for their customers' other hungers—sexual and otherwise. What came to be called "innocent syphilis" traveled from barrooms to bedrooms across New England, Virginia, and the West. "Bars appeared to invite family catastrophe," write historians Mark Edward Lender and James Kirby Martin. "They introduced children to drunkenness and vice and drove husbands to alcoholism; they also caused squandering of wages, wife beating, and child abuse; and, with the patron's inhibitions lowered through drink, the saloon led many men into the arms of prostitutes."[7]

This yoking together of Prohibition with women's rights, and of drunkenness with destructive male behavior, is one of the things that caused the unthinkable to happen in the form of Prohibition. No one dreamed that women would ever drink the way men did; no one dreamed that women would ever work the way men did. Prohibition was a gender-specific issue, a cause that promised to rein in the male propensity to drink, spend, and consort with prostitutes. If men were irresponsible, Prohibition came to be seen as the answer.

In this way, Prohibition was more than a series of laws. It was a new way to protect the American family. It was an amendment to the great Constitution that banned the manufacture and sale of the very liquids on which our nation floated into being. In many ways temperance, with its zealotry, its heroes (many of them women who had been sidetracked from the suffrage movement), its gatherings, and its feverish beliefs, became a perfect replacement for drinking.

Still, although Prohibition seems to make sense in the way that history always makes sense—it happened, therefore it could have happened—it's hard to imagine how unlikely it was at the time. As our current prohibitions of drugs have tragically shown, legally outlawing things does not work well, whether the outlawed thing is heroin or a giant mug of sugary soda. As a nation, Americans do not like being told what they can and cannot do. Gadsden's Revolutionary flag spelled it out in the motto over an American rattlesnake: "Don't Tread on Me." We are a nation founded on this kind of creative defiance, brought into being by our desire to do as we please without interference. Taxes on beverages—whether the beverage was tea or rum or molasses—were the instigation of the American Revolution on which our laws and assumptions are based. When our government had tried taxing liquor—not abolishing it, but just taxing it—there was a great deal of outcry. At the turn of the nineteenth century, liquor was the fifth largest industry in the country. Outlawing it seemed unthinkable.

"How did it happen?" Daniel Okrent asks in his book on Prohibition, *Last Call*. "How did a freedom-loving people decide to give up a private right that had been freely exercised by millions upon millions since the first European colonists arrived in the New World?" For one thing, there is the obvious observation: Those who don't drink often have an advantage in organizing and making things happen over those who do drink.[8] Okrent points out that the Constitution itself had only regulated the activities of government, not of the individual. As of January 1920 there were two exceptions: It was illegal to own slaves and it was illegal to buy a beer.

The Volstead Act, passed in 1919 to take effect on January 17, 1920, over President Woodrow Wilson's veto, became famous for the many ways it was circumvented, but there were also many loopholes in the act itself. Drinking was not prohibited—only the sale, manufacture, or transportation of alcohol was against the new law. Wealthy Americans had spent the previous year stockpiling cases to get them through the dry years. Cider and other homemade fruit brandies, as well as wines, were not covered under the Volstead Act. Synagogues and churches were both allowed a generous ration of wine for religious purposes. Medicinal alcohol—anything prescribed by a doctor—was also exempt from the new law. Even with its exceptions, it was a remarkable historic moment—the passage of a punitive, restrictive series of laws that made living in the United States more like life in a convent than in a free country—a country that had fought more than two wars to preserve that freedom.

To understand how this odd and unimaginable amendment came to be part of the United States Constitution, it's necessary to go back almost to the beginning of American history, at least to the hard-drinking days of the 1820s and '30s. "Religion is not simply a topic among topics but the driving force of American history," writes Page Smith.[9] American Protestantism after the Civil War had become a powerful force for temperance.

By the early 1910s a variety of historical and legal forces mixed together in the perfect cocktail for a very imperfect amendment. After the Civil War, our country turned toward the rampant, unbridled materialism that is still with us today. Although the Protestant Christian ideal was very much a guide for government and for living, all of a sudden it seemed that everyone wanted to make money. Tolerance for drunkenness and even tipsiness diminished radically. If the business of America was going to business, its practitioners had to be sober enough to work on assembly lines, run complex machinery and do mathematical projections and inventories.

Many of the women who led the suffrage movement were also temperance crusaders. Susan B. Anthony and Elizabeth Cady Stanton started off as temperance speakers. Drinking in the nineteenth century was primarily a man's sport—its public face was as masculine as a factory worker using his paycheck to drowning his sorrows in a local tavern at the end of the week. Even as abolition as a cause had pushed women's suffrage aside at the middle of the nineteenth century, now temperance threatened to once again push women's suffrage aside. By 1917, when the first Prohibition amendment was proposed to Congress, women's suffrage was an equally popular cause for which women had high hopes. Throughout the beginning years of the twentieth century the two causes, of temperance and women's suffrage, one absurd and the other essential, ran together in the public consciousness. Prohibition was the Eighteenth Amendment, and women's suffrage followed it as the Nineteenth Amendment, which was finally ratified in August 1920.

Another contributor to the passage of Prohibition was the Sixteenth Amendment—the government's declaration of the right to levy a federal income tax. This was ratified in 1913 just as the twin causes of Prohibition and suffrage were beginning to make their way toward Congress. Since Alexander Hamilton, an increasing percentage of the federal budget had been provided by taxing alcohol. In the early 1900s taxes on liquor made up almost 30 percent of the federal budget—a seemingly implacable obstacle to Prohibition. Now, with the passage of an amendment that allowed a broader tax, the government could give up the alcohol taxes for income taxes.

Even these few causes don't reflect the complexity of the situation around Prohibition—a kind of national penance, but for what sin?

The context of the passage of Prohibition was a knotty, confusing moment in American history. War broke out in Europe in 1914, and in 1917 President Woodrow Wilson finally and reluctantly declared war on Germany two years after the American liner *Housatonic* was sunk by a German submarine. (The sinking of the liner *Lusitania* in 1915, as Germany U-boats began patrolling the Atlantic shipping lanes, had outraged the American people, pushing many to think that the country should join the War in Europe; Wilson held back.) During that same year—1917—the Russian Revolution began, forcing Czar Nicholas II to abdicate.

The Russian Revolution may have been provoked by Czar Nicholas's own attempt at Prohibition. In the summer of 1914 he banned the sale of vodka throughout the Russian Empire. "He may as well have ordered fish to leave the ocean," writes Daniel Okrent. Czar Nicholas had good reasons for instating Prohibition; when the country declared war on Germany, a month after the assassination of Archduke Ferdinand in Sarajevo in June 1914, one of the Russian leaders' great tasks was how to keep Russian soldiers from being literally too drunk to fight as they had been in previous wars. In banning the sale of alcohol, Czar Nicholas also eliminated 25 percent of his own budget for running the country, which had come from exorbitant taxes on liquor.[10] Whatever the czar's intention, he may have helped cause his own overthrow, which had been coming for a while.

Count Leo Tolstoy had written the czar suggesting a peaceful transition a few summers before. "Autocracy...no longer answers to the needs of the Russian people," the novelist advised.[11] Aristocrats like Tolstoy were not affected by laws like the vodka prohibition—laws in the czar's Russia were not for the ruling class. Just like their American counterparts, wealthy Russians hoarded alcohol, bought it from others who had hoarded it, and had a steady flow from illegal brewers and bootleggers. Some historians have argued that a relatively clearheaded Russian proletariat was the engine behind the revolution itself.

"Religion is the opiate of the people," Karl Marx had written in the nineteenth century. (The final word in Marx's statement—*volkes*—is sometimes translated as "the masses.") Now it seemed that vodka had been the opiate of the people. Without it the people were both clearheaded and enraged. After the original cataclysm and the czar's abdication, Alexander Kerensky set up a moderate government, which was quickly overthrown by Bolshevik leaders and teetotalers Leon Trotsky and Vladimir Lenin. "No drinking, comrades!" John Reed has Trotsky exhorting in *Ten Days That Shook the World*. "No one must be on the streets after eight in the evening, except the regular guards. All places suspected of having stores of liquor should be searched, and the liquor destroyed. No mercy to the sellers of liquor…"

About the vodka prohibition of 1914, Russian expert Harrison Salisbury wrote, "There were those who later were to say that this was a major factor in the Revolution, since the poor could get no vodka…while the rich drank what they liked." The revolution swept out the old drunken rulers and swept in the new sober leaders. Lenin did not smoke or drink. In July 1918 the entire Romanov family, including Czar Nicholas and his wife, four daughters, and son, were murdered on Lenin's orders in the basement of the local merchant's house where they had been incarcerated by the Bolsheviks in Yekaterinburg.

World War I was another tremendous force that pushed the United States into the madness of Prohibition. "After such knowledge, what forgiveness?" T. S. Eliot wrote in his great World War I poem "Gerontion," published in 1920. The 50,000 American soldiers lost in combat during World War I were hardly comparable to the 750,000 men lost in combat during the Civil War—yet it was the deadliest war the world had ever seen with millions of soldiers killed. Many of the voters who might have voted against Prohibition were still overseas or enlisted in places where they were unable to vote.

The war, and his inability to pass a peace plan after it had ended, certainly broke President Woodrow Wilson's heart. Wilson, who had been a young boy in the American South during the Civil War, never forgot what war was like and never stopped hating it. Yet his own country, the United States, would not join the League of Nations, which he had thought might keep the next war from happening. By the time he tried to veto Prohibition in 1919, he was already a few months from the first of a series of debilitating strokes. A moderate drinker, Wilson objected not on the grounds that liquor was a good thing, but on constitutional grounds. "In all matters having to do with personal habits and customs of large numbers of our people, we must be certain that the established processes of legal change are followed."[12] No one listened to President Wilson anymore. "I am just a broken machine," he said before he died in 1924.

So the country was reeling from war, and vibrating with anxiety about the role of women who had stepped forward during the war to take men's jobs. Women had begun wearing short, bobbed hair and demanding the vote. We were led by a sad old man exhausted by fighting for what he had hoped would work—a peace treaty—and powerless to fight what he knew was not going to work—Prohibition. This situation, on top of the sudden alternative method of supporting the government through income taxes, set the stage. At the same time, the "wets," as anti-Prohibition forces were called in Congress, began opening loopholes in what would become the Eighteenth Amendment.

There were a few uglier, more private reasons for Prohibition as well. The waves of Italian and Irish and German immigrants that had transformed American society in the late nineteenth century were from cultures steeped in drinking. Many of the immigrants were thought to be alcoholics, and some conservatives thought that controlling alcohol would, perhaps, control the spread of foreigners on sacred American soil. Politicians, capitalizing on anti-German feeling generated by World War I, wisecracked that our principal German enemies were Pabst, Schlitz, and Anheuser-Busch.

In spite of hastily organized opposition and many dire predictions, the thirty-sixth state ratified the Prohibition amendment on January 16, 1919, to go into effect a year later. Backed by rural democrats and the Anti-Saloon League, the amendment was the result of almost fifty years of organization, scare tactics, and charismatic and somewhat crazy leadership—think of Carrie Nation and her hatchet. At the time of the amendment's passage, wartime prohibition was already in effect, banning all liquor with an alcohol content of more than 2.75 percent. Prohibition officially began in January of 1920. In August, the states ratified the amendment giving women the right to vote. The decade nicknamed "the Roaring Twenties," the decade of F. Scott Fitzgerald's wealthy, soulless heroes and Louis Armstrong's mellow trumpet, the decade of Eugene O'Neill's angry first plays and the Chicago White Sox scandal and a horse named Man O' War, began with an act of outrageous puritan hubris.

In June of 1923, Anti-Saloon League president Wayne Wheeler, known as the "dry boss" because of his political effectiveness in bringing about Prohibition, decided to have a bracing chat with the president. Harding had to set an example! Prohibition was not being taken seriously—Wheeler must have known that Washington, D.C., was the heart of the country's bootlegging and that many members of Congress patronized a drinking establishment on K Street. Worse, the Prohibition Unit under Roy Haynes was apparently a hotbed of corruption, with jobs being handed out as political rewards. Wheeler hoped to persuade the president, just two years into his first term of office, to pass a law forcing the dismissal of any federal employee who was guilty of a liquor violation.

By the time of Wheeler's visit, Harding had already weathered a few storms in the White House. A handsome Republican from Ohio, he wielded his political power as if it were a personal asset. Elected partly because of his support of women's suffrage, Harding had campaigned on the postwar promise that he would oversee a "return to normalcy." Whether he was referring to drinking is not known, but things were certainly very normal at the White House, where copious amounts of whiskey were served at wild parties. Harding was ahead of his time in some ways; he championed some civil rights bills, child welfare laws, and an antilynching legislation that failed to pass. In others he was an old-fashioned political operative who handed out jobs to friends and didn't watch them very carefully. The Teapot Dome scandal for which he would become famous was a result of this kind of behavior when it came to oil rights.

The mood in Harding's White House was relaxed and often tipsy. Harding was even part owner of a whiskey distillery—Kentucky's Old Overholt. He and his wife Flossie—called "the Duchess"—loved to entertain children. They fed their Airedale Laddie Boy scraps from the table and entertained their guests with fierce card games after dinner. Harding at one point lost a $4,000 stickpin to a guest. On another evening he gambled away a White House dinner service that had been there since the administration of Benjamin Harrison.

"Prohibition was better than no liquor at all," people said,[13] and nowhere was this more true than in the higher levels of government. In Washington, the president could get his drinks from Taylor, his butler at the house he kept near the Chevy Chase Club, or from his attorney general, Harry Daugherty, who had large quantities of seized liquor delivered by Justice Department employees to his infamous Little Green House on K Street.[14]

When Wheeler called on him that day in June, President Harding was about to leave for Alaska, part of a tour of the West in which he hoped to bolster his failing popularity. Wayne Wheeler was also an Ohioan, a bulky muscle man who had learned the art of political blitzkrieg. Harding welcomed Wheeler into the sanctum sanctorum, the Oval Office built by President William Howard Taft at the center of the White House West Wing. Harding had since appointed Taft to be chief justice of the United States Supreme Court.

Built and decorated with an eye to posterity that would make Ozymandias blush, the large oval room was dominated by the huge, wooden pedestal desk that had been designed by Charles McKim for Teddy Roosevelt. The desk stood at the room's large windows, which were draped in silk velvet olive-green curtains to match the Taft color scheme. The visitor's chairs were upholstered in caribou leather with brass studs, and a spindly potted palm stood behind the president's wooden chair. It was a warm day, and through the large windows, Wheeler could see the gardens and the White House lawn.

Armed with the power of the Anti-Saloon League which stood for many of the things Harding had opposed—anger at immigrants, racism, fear of cities—Wheeler urged him to sign a pledge, to promise that he, the leader of the country, the president of the United States, would stop drinking. Harding, of all people, should be on the moral high ground when it came to Prohibition. Wheeler menaced and wheedled and coaxed. Harding may have been afraid of losing the "dry" support he certainly would have needed for a second term, but at first he turned Wheeler down.

After all, he tried to explain to this unwelcome emissary, his drinking was merely part of the entertaining he was required to do as a president. It was his job! He had to be welcoming to people from other countries who expected to have liquor served with dinner. The president's diplomatic skills were lubricated by whiskey. Sometimes visiting statesmen brought gifts of liquor, which they expected to see served at the White House. Wheeler didn't buy it. Harding tried another argument; he had been drinking his entire life, he explained to Wheeler, and he was concerned that a sudden stop in the flow of alcohol to his body and its organs might have negative health consequences. As president, he tried to explain to Wheeler, he needed to be careful about his health and making a sudden change might cause problems. There were medical reasons for his drinking. Wheeler persisted.

So in June 1923, because of Wheeler's pressure and over all his own objections, President Warren Harding agreed to take the pledge and add his voice and his lifestyle to the cause of Prohibition. By July, on a rigorous tour of lectures and campaign stops in the West, Harding complained of severe chest pains that radiated down his legs. By August 2, 1923, he was dead. The doctors said he died of congestive heart failure. Others suspected poisoning.

Did Warren Harding die from alcohol withdrawal? Medically this would be unlikely. Still, the end of his drinking and the end of his life coincided. Harding was under tremendous pressure and traveling through the West in a desperate attempt to regain some of his lost popularity. Certainly losing his beloved whiskey may have increased his stress levels and ultimately contributed to his death. After Harding's death, Vice President Calvin Coolidge was sworn in. Coolidge was a quiet, restrained, abstemious Vermonter who didn't drink alcohol; his favorite beverage was a carbonated sugary concoction called Moxie.

Warren Harding was not the only victim of Prohibition. For all the general lack of seriousness with which many Americans took the Eighteenth Amendment, it began to have some severe negative consequences. Desperate to drink and unwilling to stop, Americans in every state dabbled in creating their own liquor or buying "bathtub gin" that had been made by neighbors and illegal distillers. Some of this stuff only tasted like poison. Some was actually lethal.

In the first year of Prohibition, 1920, the death toll from people drinking poisonous liquor was 98. That was just the beginning. By 1926 in New York City almost 800 people died of drinking illegal liquor, and in 1925 the toll nationally rose to 4,145. Part of the problem was Wayne Wheeler's insistence on a law that allowed industrial alcohol to be manufactured—as long as it was made undrinkable by the addition of 4 percent of methanol, or "wood alcohol." Thus much of the alcohol available was deadly. Columbia University president Nicholas Murray Butler called the use of methanol in alcohol "legalized murder."[15] Humorist Will Rogers cracked, "Governments used to murder by the bullet only. Now it's by the quart."[16]

Jamaican Ginger, called "jake," had been a patent medicine that was known to be intoxicating. The government beginning in 1920 prohibited it, unless it had a sufficient solid content to make it undrinkable. A pair of bootleggers found that the addition of a plasticizer, TOCP, could make it palatable, and it was soon a popular substitute for unavailable liquor. Jake drinkers began to have problems walking. They had "jake leg" or "jake foot." Between 1920 and 1933, an estimated thirty to fifty thousand people were paralyzed to some degree by the consumption of jake. The Anti-Saloon League and other dry groups had lobbied hard on the health benefits of Prohibition. Now the health liabilities of Prohibition seemed to take them by surprise.

Prohibition was supposed to make the country healthy, but instead it made them sick. Prohibition was supposed to cut down on crime, eradicate poverty, and reunite the American family. Instead it increased crime immeasurably and created organized crime syndicates. "Prohibition had been the catalyst for transforming the neighborhood gangs of the 1920s into smoothly run regional and national criminal corporations," wrote Selwyn Raab in his book about the Mafia, *The Five Families*.[17] Criminals, once fragmented and disorganized, came together around what Prohibition created: one of history's greatest opportunities for creating illegal fortunes. By the time Herbert Hoover was elected in the fall of 1928, Prohibition was not even debated during the campaigns. It had become a national embarrassment, a synonym for corruption and foolishness, and the only amendment to the Constitution ever to be repealed.

Four factors had made Prohibition possible: the institution of the income tax, the power of women's suffrage, and World War I, along with the anti-German sentiment and general xenophobia brought about by the war. Prohibition was only mildly effective when it came to lowering the amount of alcohol people drank. The numbers dipped before Prohibition, but by 1925 Americans were drinking illegal liquor almost as much as they had consumed legal liquor at the turn of the century. Furthermore, it made many people sick, made smugglers and bootleggers prosperous, and created patterns of criminal families and organizations that are still with us today.

CHAPTER 10

THE WRITER'S VICE

Prohibition had a less heralded and more enduring spiritual effect on two generations of American writers. Nineteenth-century American writers did not drink much. Twenty-first-century American writers do not drink much. Twentieth-century writers after Prohibition made up for the generations before and after them. They drank so much that they are still famous for drinking. The coincidence of American writers' alcoholism growing during Prohibition is too obvious to be ignored.

Most writers are observers rather than participants. They stay outsiders in order to see the world clearly, and they sometimes suffer because of what they see. Their imaginative empathy—the quality that enables them to understand other people's lives—makes them vulnerable.

By making alcohol forbidden, Prohibition increased its appeal for American writers. Writers are outlaws. Outlawing liquor gave it a delicious cachet. Part of a writer's job is to question conventional wisdom and illegal gin had a magnetism that legal gin lacked. It is often pointed out that American writers have written about drinking, but many of them—notably Fitzgerald in his novel about a bootlegger *The Great Gatsby*—have also written about the effects of Prohibition. "Writers, even the most socially gifted and established, must be outsiders of some sort," writes historian Olivia Laing, "if only because their job is that of scrutinizer and witness."[1]

The intersection of writers with Prohibition was at its most intense in New York City—the mecca for all talented young men and women in the 1920s. Seven thousand arrests for alcohol possession in New York City between 1921 and 1923 (when enforcement was more or less openly abandoned) resulted in only seventeen convictions.

For some writers, Manhattan, with its habitual speakeasies and after-hours clubs as well as its famous flouting of the law even in restaurants, became synonymous with drinking too much. Eugene O'Neill and F. Scott Fitzgerald were two writers who were only able to stop drinking, or at least moderate their drinking, after they left what one minister called "Satan's Seat."

It is a truth universally acknowledged that writers drink too much and that, at least in America, writing goes hand in hand with a bottle or a brew, a bad liver, and a very bad temper. "Of course you're a rummy," Ernest Hemingway comforted his friend Scott Fitzgerald, "but no more than most good writers are." In the mid-twentieth century, five of the seven Americans who won the Nobel Prize were alcoholics—Sinclair Lewis, Eugene O'Neill, William Faulkner, Ernest Hemingway, and John Steinbeck. The writer Ring Lardner once listed every writer he knew and concluded that at least a third were alcoholics. "There is no question that alcohol ran through the lives and works of great writers," notes journalist Kelly Boler. "Stories of the grand boozy excesses of twentieth-century literature provide a substantial part of our cultural currency."[2]

So prevalent was the combination of writing and alcoholism that when Dorothy Parker went to a famous writer's funeral and a friend commented on how well the man looked in his coffin, Parker remarked that of course he looked well—"he hasn't had a drink in three days."

"There is nothing else in all the countries of the world like New

York Life," New Yorker writer James Thurber wrote to his friend E. B. White from the South of France, where he was relatively safe from his own alcoholism. New York, he wrote, using a comparison to one of the worst battles of World War I, "is just a peaceable Verdun." Thurber's last drunk was at the Algonquin Hotel across from the *New Yorker* offices. "[He] drank nonstop for a month," writes Ann Douglas in *Terrible Honesty*. "He was legally blind and he kept setting himself on fire with his cigarettes."[3] Thurber, on the lam from his wife and home in Connecticut, had dinner at Sardi's on October 3, keeled over in the bathroom, hit his head, and died in the hospital a month later.

"The presence of the disease in so many of our notable writers surely makes it appear that alcoholism is the American writer's disease," writes Tom Dardis in his book on the subject, *The Thirsty Muse*.[4] Famously in the 1950s Sinclair Lewis angrily asked a reporter, "Can you name five writers since Poe who did *not* die of drinking?" Or as another casualty of alcoholism, the poet John Berryman, put it, "Something has been said for sobriety, but very little."

American writers—those who were not too drunk to write—often wrote about alcoholism. In her recent book about writers and drinking, *The Trip to Echo Spring*, Laing points out that my father John Cheever's famous short story "The Swimmer," published in the *New Yorker* in 1964, was fueled by drink and about drink. The swimming pools in the story make up a secret river, a lot like the secret river of the alcoholic, Laing notes, and the protagonist's memory lapses are similar to alcoholic blackouts. "'The Swimmer,' which I would judge among the finest stories ever written, catches in its strange compressions the full arc of an alcoholic's life and it was that same dark trajectory I wanted to pursue," she writes. "I wanted to know what made a person drink and what it did to them. More specifically I wanted to know why writers drink, and what effect this stew of spirits has had on the body of literature itself."[5]

Laing's book is titled for a Tennessee Williams character—Brick in

Cat on a Hot Tin Roof—who uses the phrase "a trip to Echo Spring" as a euphemism for a swig from the bottle of Echo Spring Bourbon in his closet. Her book joins previous work on this subject—a subject that seems to draw writers as a magnet draws iron filings. In the 1980s both Tom Dardis and Dr. Donald Goodwin, in his book *Writers and Alcohol*, explored the subject thoroughly using the famous drunken writers of the mid-nineteenth century as examples. More recently, Laing has covered much of the same territory with her own charm and energy. Her book opens with a trip my father and Raymond Carver took to the local liquor store in Iowa City in 1975, when they were both teaching there.

Laing also explores the way alcohol erodes memory and language skills. She studies the way in which writers wrote about drinking even as they were unable to stop drinking. She puts herself inside the head of many of the writers she profiles. After quoting a long, powerful paragraph of Hemingway's *For Whom the Bell Tolls*, in which Robert Jordan remembers his father's suicide and his own part in getting rid of the gun his father had used, she writes, "Imagine the mixed relief and terror of getting that sequence down. Imagine pressing the words, letter by letter, into the page. And imagine getting up, closing the door to your study, and walking downstairs. What do you do, with that sudden space in your chest? You go to the liquor cabinet and pour yourself a shot of the one thing no one can take away from you: the nice good lovely gin, the nice good lovely rum."[6]

One 1987 statistical study of the phenomenon of writers drinking was done at the University of Iowa Writers' Workshop—the one of the hot centers of writing talent in the United States—by an English Literature Ph.D. and psychiatrist Nancy Andreasen, more than a decade after my father and Ray drank there together. (It was my father's last drunken stand. Within a year he was in rehab, got sober, and stayed sober for the rest of his life.)

Using a sample of thirty established writers, Andreasen found that the writers were significantly more depressed, more manic, and more alcoholic than the nonwriter control group. At the end of the nine-teenth century, Henry James put this another, more eloquent way in his short story "The Middle Years": "We work in the dark—we do what we can—we give what we have. Our doubt is our passion and our passion is our task. The rest is the madness of art."

Tales of drunken writers range from the cautionary to the sweet. Brendan Gill treasured a story about Robert Frost and Wallace Stevens, both attending a literary seminar in Key West, Florida. One night after drinking way too much, the two elderly poets walked home to their resort hotel on a boardwalk that runs just above the sandy beach. One of the men tripped and the other tried to catch him, and soon they were rolling over and over in the sand—each poet con-vinced that he was trying to keep the other one from getting hurt.[7] In the 1930s Edna St. Vincent Millay's fans were sometimes amazed to see her take a long pull from a flask before going onstage and then return to her dressing room to finish it off after her perfor-mance. In 1946, Raymond Chandler decided he could only complete the screenplay of *The Blue Dahlia* for John Houseman if he wrote it drunk. Deadlines had come and gone. Houseman was desperate. He agreed and provided round-the-clock nursing care for Chandler as well as a doctor to give vitamin shots, since Chandler didn't eat while he was drinking. Working in between binges and hangovers, Chan-dler finished the script.[8]

How do writers go from the starry, aspirational idea of the "mad-ness of art" to the squalid, talent-destroying landscape of empty bot-tles, rotting livers, and broken families? In the James story, it is Den-combe's strange, mysterious marriage to his work that seems to kill him. The drinking is not explicit, but the idea—that writing somehow catapults the writer into a land of life and death, truth and beauty, passion and horror that is unknown to normal people—is enough to make any writer want to drink.

"Writing is a form of exhibitionism; alcohol lowers inhibitions and prompts exhibitionism in many people," writes Dr. Donald

Goodwin in his book on the subject. "Writing requires an interest in people; alcohol increases sociability and makes people more interesting. Writing involves fantasy; alcohol promotes fantasy. Writing requires self-confidence; alcohol bolsters confidence. Writing is lonely work; alcohol assuages loneliness. Writing demands intense concentration; alcohol relaxes."[9] Goodwin points out that many other ethnic and professional groups have high rates of alcoholism. "The group, however, with perhaps a higher rate of alcoholism than any other consists of famous American writers."[10]

Alcoholism laid waste to the most talented American writers of the mid-twentieth century. Although many of them made jokes about it, it wasn't really funny. Electric shock treatment, treatment with primitive psychopharmalogical drugs—lithium, Miltown—liver disease and suicide are all common in the American writers of the mid-twentieth century.

Goodwin and Dardis both published in the late 1980s, and they both used the same set of writers to prove their point. More recently, Laing added Raymond Carver and John Cheever to the list of alcoholic writers. My father's earliest memory of being a writer in New York was of going to a party at Malcolm Cowley's apartment during Prohibition and getting so drunk on bathtub gin that he vomited all over the luminaries. When he told this story, it made the anecdote seem both amusing and glamorous. In the story he was a teenager, a small-town boy from the South Shore of Boston, thrown in with the great and near great, and he disgraced himself, but it was a romantic, literary kind of disgrace.

The idea that creativity requires alcohol or drug abuse is not a new one, but it seems to strike some kind of welcoming chord in the cultural unconscious. Baudelaire, a French poet, wrote that in order to write, "[O]ne must always be intoxicated. That's the main thing: it's the only issue. In order to feel the horrible burden of Time which breaks your shoulders and bows you to the earth, you must become intoxicated without respite."[11] Perhaps the idea that writing requires a serious drinking problem gives people an excuse to explain why they are not great writers or great painters—they wouldn't want their family to pay the price of having an alcoholic or addicted member. "If you are an artist," my father wrote, "self-destruction is quite expected of you. The thrill of staring into the abyss is exciting until it becomes, as it did in my case, contemptible."[12] The critic Leslie Fiedler wrote that each literary age had its flaw: Homer's blindness, Byron's incest, and in twentieth-century America, drunkenness.[13]

Dardis, Goodwin, Laing, and all the other writers on the subject of writers and drinking have failed to notice one thing—all the drinking they chronicle occurred in one or two generations of writers: the generations after Prohibition, the 1920s through the 1970s. Although there is scant evidence that contemporary writers drink too much, the myth persists. Even the writers who produce the kinds of big novels that supposedly require a great deal of drinking—Jonathan Franzen, Michael Chabon, John Irving, Donna Tartt—don't drink much. David Foster Wallace had a checkered drinking history, but before that Raymond Carver seems to have been the last old-fashioned writer-drunk, and he got sober. Wallace, a writer who battled the demons of alcohol like few others, and who like Hemingway and Faulkner reinvented the language in which we all write, wrote his greatest book about…getting sober.

Similarly, few nineteenth-century American writers—with the single prominent exception of Edgar Allan Poe—had drinking problems. When the historian F. O. Matthiessen famously pointed out that all of what we call American literature was written in five years between 1850 and 1855, he was referring to a string of writers who had no problems with alcohol: Melville, Emerson, Thoreau, Hawthorne, Longfellow, the Alcotts, and even the exuberant Whitman.

A look at the books that have been written about American writers and their dependence on drinking shows that in order to make the argument that writers drink more than other people, each writer is forced to use the same examples: Fitzgerald and Hemingway, Faulkner and O'Neill, Williams, Lewis, Steinbeck, and, more recent, Carver and Cheever. By the time my father's generation of writers started publishing in the years after World War II, being a writer almost always meant being a drunk. My father embraced this personality with enthusiasm. At the age of seventeen he was expelled from prep school, wrote a story entitled "Expelled," moved to New York from suburban Boston, and sold the story to the *New Republic*.

Even writers who were not alcoholics drank with abandon in the post-Prohibition world. The writer and *New Yorker* editor William Maxwell once told me that he got so drunk at a party at my parents' that he realized, when he got out to his car, that he had literally forgotten how to drive. My father's friend Jack Kahn wrote a memoir in which he mentioned in passing that he got up some mornings and vomited before brushing his teeth—he was amazed at the reaction he got. Not everyone was so hungover they had to vomit in the morning? This discovery became the talk of the suburban party circuit. Who were these abstinent people? Thank God they were far away. Everyone in our world drank and drank until they couldn't drink anymore.

When he went to visit F. Scott Fitzgerald's daughter Scottie, my father came home and reported that she was a terrific woman. She had mixed him a drink, he said, "strong enough to draw a boat." Drinking was not only the way in which this generation of writers sustained themselves; it was used as a standard of judgment for everyone they met. When Brendan Behan came for lunch, and we all wandered— and I mean wandered—down to the swimming pool for a dip, he blundered into the water and was clearly too drunk to remember that he didn't have gills. He seemed to stay on the bottom of the pool for a long, long time. Finally, to everyone's relief, he floated to the surface. Laughter ensued.

Before Prohibition, drinking was something that men did while women wrung their hands and wept. But many of the women who wrote and published in the 1940s and '50s were also drunks. The post-

Prohibition writers who drank too much were women as well as men. Djuna Barnes, Dawn Powell, and Dorothy Parker all showed that being drunk could be ladylike.

In the 1980s, as the entire nation turned away from drunkenness, and as people began running literal marathons instead of having marathon drinking sprees, writers also turned away from drinking. A year-by-year analysis shows that although many famous American writers drank too much, they did that only in the years after Prohibition and World War II.

Prohibition's principal effects were not the ones its proponents and supporters intended it to have. Most of the assumptions that promoted Prohibition—that it would lead to a healthier nation, that it would diminish crime, and that it would be a boon to the long-suffering women who stayed home while their husbands drank—turned out to be topsy-turvy. Most damaging of all, a generation of American writers—the heirs of the relatively sober Melville, Hawthorne, Whitman, Thoreau, and Emerson, to name a few—became drunkards, endangering their mental and physical health and often dying young: Fitzgerald at forty-four, Hemingway a suicide at sixty-one, and the other Nobel Prize winners living only into their early sixties. Of the writers who drank too much in the fifty-year period of American alcoholic literature, four committed suicide. There was nothing glamorous about their drinking. It was, as my father noted, more contemptible than useful. Perhaps there were some glamorous moments looked at from the outside, but in the end the drinking of a generation of great American writers led where drinking usually leads—to psychic pain, electric shock treatments (Faulkner and Hemingway), institutions (Zelda Fitzgerald), and unimaginable suffering and rage on the part of those who care about the alcoholics and cannot understand why they cannot stop killing themselves.

Although drinking may seem to be an aid to writing for a few ephemeral years, it almost always turns on the writer—eating away talent, which leads to inferior and even embarrassing work, and shutting off the flow of genius. A few of the writers lapsed into silence for years, Tom Dardis points out, but "virtually all the rest continued to write, producing increasingly feeble works, a situation suggesting the relevance here of Fitzgerald's much-quoted remark 'There are no second acts in American lives.'"[14] He might as well have written that there are no second acts in alcoholic lives.

Drinking did terrible damage to these writers and their families, and it may have done a subtler and more serious act of destruction on the American ideal of a writer's life. These writers, in spite of their miseries and because of their outlaw status, eloquently glamorized writing and the drinking that often accompanied it. A writer as great as William Faulkner remarked that "civilization begins with distillation." What would Hemingway be without his bottle of whiskey, his macho fearlessness and his savvy swagger. "I have drunk since I was fifteen and few things have given me more pleasure. When you work hard all day with your head and know you must work again the next day what else can change your ideas and make them run on a different plane like whisky? When you are cold and wet what else can warm you? Before an attack who can say anything that gives you the momentary well-being that rum does?" he wrote to his Russian translator, Ivan Kashkin. "It has been said that alcohol is a good servant and a bad master," wrote Christopher Hitchens in an essay—"The Muse of Booze"—on the famous drinking writer Kingsley Amis.

One of the principal drunken writers about the phenomenon of writers and drinking was Charles Jackson, the alcoholic who in 1944 wrote the novel *The Lost Weekend*, which was made into a hugely popular movie by Billy Wilder starring Ray Milland as the drunken writer. Jackson, an alcoholic who was intermittently sober in Alcoholics Anonymous, knew the territory well and described its details with skill and vividness. His story includes the sneakiness of drinkers—it opens with Milland hiding his bottle by hanging it out the window on a string and hauling it up for an occasional slug. He also captures the stinging remorse that besets alcoholics, the morning-after promises and apologies that accompany the splitting headaches and the spotty memories.

Why do writers drink? "The theories writers tend to offer lean more towards the symbolic than the sociological or scientific," Laing writes. Throughout history writers have leaned toward mind-altering substances. The poet Horace wrote about the way that wine encouraged the appearance of the muse. Yet there have been many American writers who seemed unaware of the balm and inspiration of a drink. Thoreau just wasn't interested. Emerson seemed to have no desire to drink more than an occasional glass of port. The Alcotts were too poor to drink. Hawthorne drank, but not habitually.

Something in the world during the middle of the twentieth century made drinking seem like a prerequisite for writing. That impetus was not apparent in nineteenth-century literature. It is not apparent in European or Russian literature, and it is not apparent in contemporary literature. No doubt there were many factors creating an atmosphere of literary drunkenness in those years—the end of World War I and the beginning of World War II, the continuing predominance of men in the field of writing, and most of all the shimmering caul of desirability lent to drinking by the fact that it was outlawed, prohibited, something available only to those smart enough and sly enough to be unconventional, energetic, and to live outside the deadening strictures of bourgeois life.

We live in a twenty-first-century world in which it is more fashionable to be sober than it is to be drunk. These days we go to the gym after work instead of the bar. The kind of drinking and wild behavior that seemed so glamorous and extreme in the mid-twentieth century is no longer tolerated. People no longer get falling-down drunk at dinner parties, grope the hostess, take swipes at the chandelier, and weave their way down the driveway to drive home squinting in order to keep the road's central yellow line in sight. What was normal in the 1950s and even the 1970s is now not done. What changed?

The swings in the way American writers drink are part of a larger series of pendulum swings—changes in the American attitude toward drinking in general. As the world has moved faster, our changes in attitude have also moved faster. Between 1620 and 1820, Americans slowly drank more and more all the time. Then the pendulum reached an apex and began to swing the other way, until in 1920 it reached the other end of the arc—Americans made liquor against the law. At that point the pendulum began to swing toward drunkenness again— but this time the high point of the swing came sooner. By 1980, only fifty years after Prohibition, America had again become a nation of heavy drinkers. Now, even more rapidly, the pendulum is swinging back toward an attitude that drinking should be controlled by the law—should be against the law. The drinking age has been raised in every state. The level of blood alcohol that constitutes drunkenness has fallen year after year. A new brand of temperance organization, from Mothers Against Drunk Driving to the National Council on Alcohol and Drug Dependence, has sprung up to lobby for legal limits on drinking. Educating Americans about drinking is a good idea, but outlawing drinking is a bad idea. Prohibition did not work in 1920 and it will not work now.

"In the 1970s, a good deal less was known about alcoholism than today, either by doctors and psychologists or the population at large," Laing writes. "It had only recently been classified as a disease, and most ordinary people had very little understanding of what it involved. It was also an era considerably more lubricated and less censorious than our own."[15] In the pendulum swing of our love affair with alcohol, we are swinging again back toward limited drinking and away from a tolerance for drunkenness. No one misses the stumbling, vomiting drunks of the 1950s, but we are headed back toward some of the questionable ideas that helped to pass the Eighteenth Amendment.

Today in a world where more and more people aspire to writing, romancing alcoholism is equally dangerous. In the past few years, people have turned to writing as a means of self-expression and self-understanding. One statistic shows that in 1995, five graduate programs offered advanced degrees in creative writing; in 2013, 356 programs offered such degrees. By linking writing with drinking, we encourage a new generation of writers who may fizzle out their talents, court mental illness and liver disease, and end up dying young. Nevertheless, in spite of plentiful legal liquor, passionate desire to write, and the loneliness, exhibitionism, and cravings that characterize many writers, this literary generation shows no signs of romancing the glass or of being a throwback to the literary drunks of the mid-twentieth century. Perhaps only another round of Prohibition could make that happen.

CHAPTER 11

SENATOR JOSEPH MCCARTHY AND
THE COLD WAR

D rew Pearson would never have gone to the dinner if he had
known that Sen. Joe McCarthy was going to be there. The
party, to honor Republican James Duff on December 12, 1950, was at
the exclusive Sulgrave Club near Dupont Circle. Pearson, famous in
Washington for his syndicated *Washington Post* column, titled the
Washington Merry-Go-Round, and his nationally broadcast radio
program, was forthright as a journalist when he felt it was necessary.
Still he was socially reluctant, a man who would rather stay at home
than go to fancy dinners in the capital. That December night he was
persuaded to go by his wife, Luvie.

The result was a series of incidents that became famous for showing
off the drunken behavior of Wisconsin senator Joe McCarthy, who
was enjoying fame and garnering respect by accusing dozens of members of the government, including the State Department, of being
communists or of befriending communists. The handsome ex-Marine
and self-appointed war hero—he had flown combat missions in the
Pacific as an observer—dominated the news.

McCarthy, who had been nicknamed "Tail Gunner Joe" by the
press, was a proud drinker and lecher at a time before Watergate when
the press, including the Washington, D.C., press corps, colluded to
keep politicians' private lives out of the public eye. McCarthy's

occasional drunken scenes, the flask he kept in the men's room of the Senate Office Building, and the sloppiness of his research were never reported in the press. "It was all part of the game," Haynes Johnson writes in *The Age of Anxiety*, his book on the McCarthy years, "an insider game in which press and politician forged a cozy, mutually beneficial relationship. Rules of the game…held that a reporter protected his sources;…[and] did not reveal politician's personal misbehavior (drunkenness or sexual affairs) which might attract public notice."[1]

Drew Pearson did not play this game very well. Pearson, fifty-three, originally had been a supporter of McCarthy in the Senate but had turned on him, revealing in print his financial problems—McCarthy was at war with the IRS as well as with communists. McCarthy had found his calling and his audience while giving a speech at a women's club in Wheeling, West Virginia, early in 1950. There he dramatically held up a sheaf of paper and proclaimed that he had a "list of names that were made known to the Secretary of State as being members of the Communist Party and who…are still working and shaping policy in the State Department."[2] Soon enough he was on the floor of the Senate brandishing more papers—copies of about a hundred dossiers from State Department files. The dossiers were three years old; most of the men were no longer with the State Department, but that didn't matter and remained unreported. McCarthy had discovered that he could substitute angry certainty for accurate facts, and this became the inspiration for his short career as a communist scourge.

As McCarthy's accusations became increasingly heated and increasingly undocumented, Pearson kept after him in the *Washington Post*, sometimes writing daily bulletins of criticism. In a previous encounter, McCarthy had threatened to break Pearson's arm.

Pearson wasn't alone in attacking Senator McCarthy, but in 1950 our fear of communism was so great that McCarthy's accusations were hugely popular. Criticisms and detractions were often overwhelmed by support. It didn't matter if there was no proof of his accusations— they sounded true. What if there *were* communists in the government? Of all politicians, McCarthy biographer Richard Rovere wrote two years after McCarthy's death at the age of forty-eight, "McCarthy was surely the champion liar. He lied with wild abandon; he lied without evident fear; he lied in his teeth and in the teeth of the truth; he lied vividly and with a bold imagination; he lied, often, with very little pretense to be telling the truth."[3]

On that night at the Sulgrave Club in 1950, McCarthy's lies were working well. From his first campaign for a Wisconsin judgeship when he, at age thirty, repeatedly lied about his sixty-six-year-old opponent's age, inflating it to seventy-three or eighty-nine, McCarthy's methods of lies, bluster, and intimidation had made him one of the most popular politicians in the country. Protected by an affable press, in a career lubricated by drunken charm and by powerful Roman Catholic supporters, McCarthy got away with extraordinarily bad behavior.

With no open mike or Internet to show him in action, McCarthy cleverly kept his real tactics just below the radar of public knowledge. A poll showed that 50 percent of Americans were in favor of his anti-communism campaign. McCarthy became a celebrity in an age before celebrity. Crowds of fans, many of them women, followed him around Capitol Hill hoping to chat with the great man or even touch him.

During the milling around before dinner on that night at the Sulgrave Club, Pearson, a slender man who rarely drank, encountered a blustering, hostile McCarthy who was clearly already impaired. When the two men ran into each other for the first time that night, McCarthy announced to Pearson that he was giving a speech on the Senate floor the next day in which he was going to tear him to pieces and "rake the bejesus" out of him, adding, "I am going to murder you."[4] With the single-mindedness that always characterized his accusations, McCarthy—who was seated at the same dinner table as the Pearsons—repeated again and again that he was going to attack Pearson in the Senate the next day. He hectored Luvie Pearson, too, telling her that her husband was a communist and that she should divorce him. Pearson later characterized McCarthy's attacks as "the way I have heard these Nazi or Gestapo inquisitions are carried on, just pounding home, pounding home, pounding home, trying to get under someone's skin."[5] Pearson escaped to the dance floor, but when the music stopped McCarthy was back at his side. Now he addressed the whole table, telling them that he was going to destroy Pearson on the Senate floor the next day. Dinner was served. McCarthy kept at it. When Pearson finally retaliated by mentioning McCarthy's financial problems, the stocky senator grabbed him by the back of the neck between his thumb and index finger and gouged so hard that Pearson staggered back off his chair.

Later, as Pearson recalled in the deposition for the $5 million lawsuit he brought against McCarthy, McCarthy continued to bait him. At the cloakroom as the two men were leaving the dinner, McCarthy pinned Pearson's hands down against his sides and kneed him in the groin. The newly elected senator Richard Nixon tried to come between the two men. ("Let a Quaker stop this fight," he reportedly said.) Undeterred by Nixon, McCarthy then hit Pearson in the face, knocking him to the floor. Pearson was barely able to scramble to his feet and escape as Nixon ran interference against the growling, seemingly homicidal McCarthy. Nixon and McCarthy spent the next half hour trying to find McCarthy's car—he was so drunk he didn't know where he had parked it.[6]

Although McCarthy was often drunk, people who agreed with him took him seriously. After bragging about punching Pearson, McCarthy took more than a dozen congratulatory calls from other senators. An admirer from Missouri presented him with a watch inscribed "For combat duty on the 12th of December above and beyond the call of duty." Sen. Arthur Watkins of Utah reportedly put an arm around McCarthy in the Senate elevator and said, "Joe, I've heard conflicting reports about where you hit Pearson. I hope both are true."[7]

But McCarthy often turned on his friends as well as his enemies.

Later on, Senator Watkins, who eventually led the Senate committee to censure McCarthy in 1953, was not sufficiently supportive. So every time McCarthy passed Watkins's seat in the Senate chamber he would lean over and hiss, "How is the little coward from Utah?" in Watkins's ear.

McCarthy's promised Senate attack on Pearson the next day was as exaggerated and untrue as many of his accusations, typically delivered as if McCarthy were Moses on Mount Sinai preaching to a reverent public. On the Senate floor, McCarthy called Pearson a "Moscow directed character assassin," a liar, and a fake, and he urged everyone to stop buying Adam Hats, a brand of hat that Pearson had endorsed in a world where all the men wore hats all the time. Anyone who buys an Adam Hat, McCarthy growled, is contributing to the cause of international communism. Adam Hats quickly fired Pearson as a spokesman.

McCarthy's attack on Pearson wasn't the first time a drunken politician had physically attacked someone who disagreed with him. In May 1856, during a time when slavery was actually being debated in the United States House of Representatives, a congressman from South Carolina, Preston Brooks, took a heavy cane and began to bludgeon Charles Sumner, an abolitionist senator from Massachusetts. Trapped behind his desk—Senate desks were bolted to the floor—Sumner struggled to escape and was almost killed.[8]

Seen today, McCarthy's antics almost reach the level of slapstick. At the time his accusations were taken as deadly serious. The fear of communism that swept this country in the 1940s and 1950s caused behavior that seems irrational and even criminal in retrospect. The postwar years in the United States were years of grotesque panic about an imaginary enemy with the power to blow up the world—the Soviet Union. We were a nation living in fear, and men like McCarthy fed those fears.

These were the years when the House Un-American Activities Committee interrogated anyone under suspicion about their communist connections and demanded that they name the names of their friends and colleagues—supposedly communist "fellow travelers." If they refused, they were often jailed for contempt of court. Although many senators criticized the committee, which famously persecuted Hollywood stars and directors and ended up blacklisting and incarcerating some of the country's most talented actors and writers, both liberals and conservatives voted to fund it year after year until the end of the decade. On the say-so of the committee a few hundred people were persecuted and hauled off to prison. Thousands lost their jobs. More than a hundred college teachers were fired for refusing to cooperate. Writer Mary McCarthy observed that the purpose of these purges was not to identify communists, but to convince Americans to accept "the principle of betrayal as a norm of good citizenship."[9] More predictably, left-wing journalist I. F. Stone condemned the tendency to turn a whole generation of Americans into "stool pigeons."[10]

Although McCarthy also targeted homosexuals—he was an equal-opportunity bully—it was his undocumented attack on communism that made him famous. In the 1950s the threat of communism was both horribly real and entirely imaginary. The Russians were armed and ready to attack us. The Russians would come marching down Main Street past our white picket fences. The Russians were in submarines just off the Atlantic Coast waiting to take over our suburbs.

Drew Pearson reported that President Harry Truman's secretary of defense, James Forrestal, stoked on pills and alcohol, was discovered in the street in his pajamas in a state of terror because he believed the Russians had invaded Bethesda. "The Russians were coming!" yelled Forrestal until the police came and took him away. Truman fired Forrestal and Forrestal killed himself, jumping from his sixteenth-floor room at Bethesda Naval Hospital. What had Forrestal known? What if he had information that had been denied to the public? If the Russians weren't about to land, they were armed to begin a catastrophic war that would lead to the end of the world. Nuclear winter was unavoidable.

McCarthy's license to attack, maim, and hurt the innocent began a politics of reaction to threats, which is very much a feature of our modern world. Since September 11, 2001, we have been living with the same kind of fear that characterized the 1950s. They were fighting a war on the terror of communism; we are fighting a war on the terror of jihad. "Political repression and threats to liberty neither began nor ended with Joseph McCarthy," Haynes Johnson writes. "Examining McCarthyism and terrorism in light of one another is imperative as Americans face a new Age of Anxiety and the ever more difficult task of balancing the needs of national security with those of personal freedom."[11]

The American public is still, as it was then, easy to manipulate with uncertainty and fear. "The judgment of the years," Arthur Watkins wrote later, "is that McCarthy exploited McCarthyism as an instrument to power and personal glory. As a skilled bell ringer, he played all the changes and excited his numerous followers with variations of alarm and patriotism with a skill that has seldom been equaled by any demagogue."[12]

Was President George W. Bush our generation's Joe McCarthy? Both men had drinking problems, and both solved those problems in the way condoned by the culture of the time: McCarthy drank himself to an early grave; Bush gave up drinking for the woman he married. There are other similarities between the two: the replacement of false certainty for accuracy as in Bush's famous "Mission Accomplished" speech and performance, and the facile way in which truth got trampled on to serve a decision that had already been made for other reasons.

In October 2002, President Bush convinced everyone who would listen that Iraq's leader Saddam Hussein was stockpiling weapons, nuclear and otherwise, and that it was imperative that the United States go to war with Iraq. In fact Iraq had no such weapons and posed no threat. By timing the vote to attack Iraq right before the midterm elections and threatening to brand everyone who didn't go along as

cowardly and unpatriotic, President Bush and his administration got
what they wanted. On October 11, the Senate voted 77–23 to autho-
rize the use of force, getting yes votes from both Hillary Clinton and
John Kerry. Of course there are plenty of differences between Bush
and McCarthy—one was a two-term president and the other a flash-
in-the-pan firebrand, but both danced with the devil of alcoholism
and both contributed hugely to our culture of fear.

McCarthy came first. Formed in the nervous years after World
War II and ignited by a drunk behaving exactly like a drunk, our country developed a line of defense against communism that included a
narrowing of individual rights. That line of defense is still in place.
From the Patriot Act to the excesses of the National Security Agency,
our reaction to threats still owes its tone to one of the most embarrassing moments in American history. "Whatever McCarthy's personal
qualities, McCarthyism in one form or another outlived the man,"
writes Johnson. "Its impact on our politics, and on the way Americans
view their leaders and their government, has been profound."[13]

McCarthy's drinking and his arrogance were finally his downfall—
he flew too close to the sun. As chairman of the Senate's Permanent
Subcommittee on Investigations, he went after the State Department
and the Voice of America. His tactics were always the same—bluster
replaced reason. Finally, in 1954, he went too far. He began hearings
to investigate communists in the military. When he began attacking
the army generals, he lost support from Republicans as well as
Democrats. Televised, the Army-McCarthy hearings also exposed his
antics and erratic behavior to many people who had previously taken
him seriously.

By this time, McCarthy's alcoholism was alarming to even his
friends. He had become paranoid and carried a gun on Capitol Hill.
He had put on weight. The hearings themselves showed McCarthy
to the whole world as the bully that he was. He had pushed for pub-
licity and he got it. Fame drove him. "He was verbally brutal where
he should have been dexterous and light," wrote Roy Cohn in his

memoir. "He was stubbornly unwilling to yield points where a little yielding might have gained him advantage; he frequently spoke before thinking of the effect of his words; he was repetitious to the point of boredom."[14]

The television coverage of the Army-McCarthy hearings, one of the first televised Senate debates, revealed what the press had held back. Called for by McCarthy who claimed that the Army brass was hiding "known communists," it was his most famous moment and also his most infamous. It didn't take long for McCarthy's drinking and intoxicated behavior to catch up with him. Senator Watkins, that little coward from Utah, was appointed head of the Select Committee to Study Censure Charges against Senator Joseph McCarthy.

In November 1954, after days of interruptions, counteraccusations, and disruptions to the process, McCarthy was condemned by the United States Senate, the ruling body that had once given him his immunity and his public platform, the place where he had felt so at home that he hid his flask in the men's room. The resolution, passed by a Senate vote of 67–22, censured McCarthy for conduct "contrary to Senatorial ethics and [which] tended to bring the Senate into dishonor and disrepute, to obstruct the constitutional processes of the Senate, and to impair its dignity; and such conduct is hereby condemned."[15]

In writing about the censure process, Watkins explained that his committee began by dropping charges that they determined would not lead to censurable behavior. "In this category we chose to eliminate such interesting but legally insufficient allegations as McCarthy's personal claims as to his war record, wounds received, and that fact that he referred to himself as savior of the country from communism, and the fact that he had never turned up (or turned over to the Justice Department evidence against) a single alleged communist of the numbers he claimed to have knowledge."[16] The morning after the vote to condemn, President Eisenhower called

Watkins before breakfast and asked him to come to the White House. There the president personally thanked the senator from Utah for conducting an orderly process in the Senate when it came to the very disorderly McCarthy.

His colleagues disowned his senatorial misbehavior, but many of them continued to believe that the communist threat was real, terrifying, and omnipresent. The vote to condemn Senator McCarthy carefully avoided any criticism of McCarthy's hunt for communists in the government. Both Lyndon Baines Johnson and John F. Kennedy believed that McCarthy had been more or less right about the menace communists posed to American government and American life. After all, it was not McCarthy but the liberal Truman administration that had prosecuted Ethel and Julius Rosenberg and sentenced them to die in the electric chair in 1953. In 1950, President Truman's attorney general, J. Howard McGrath, had expressed it well: "There are today many communists in America. They are everywhere—in factories, offices, butcher shops, on street corners, in private business—and each carries in himself the germs of death for society."[17]

McCarthy, condemned by his colleagues, was suddenly not news. As he was one of the first celebrities, he became one of the first celebrities to experience the brevity of the news cycle. His wild speeches, usually featuring piles of paper with names which turned out to be innocent names and which had reliably generated news, became boring. His famous lists of communists were exposed as fakes. This, as much as the Senate condemnation, seemed to be the final blow. "He had died, then, of a broken heart," writes Rovere. "If he had been a Hitler, he might have burned down the Senate. Being McCarthy he had hired a lawyer and sought an acquittal." Yet in the end it was the failure of his liver rather than the failure of his crusade against communism that killed him. "He died because he could not lay off liquor," Rovere writes.[18]

By 1957, friends who hadn't seen him in a while were shocked by McCarthy's vacant stare, his shaking hands, and his breathing problems. He had at least one bout of delirium tremens at Bethesda Naval Hospital. He clung to his obstreperous personality. When his best friend, Urban Van Susteren, begged him to cut down on his drinking, McCarthy came to life and spat out, "Kiss my ass." Those were some of his last words. He died on May 2, 1957.

CHAPTER 12

A FEW SECONDS

At 12:30 p.m. on November 22, 1963, bullets fired into the open roof of the presidential limousine tore through John F. Kennedy's body. The first shot went through the president's neck but did not kill him. A second, fatal shot ripped through his brain and his skull almost four seconds later. During the critical time between the two shots, seconds in which the president's life might have been saved, the Secret Service agents within a few feet of the man they were duty bound to protect failed to take the evasive actions they had been trained to do.

Roy Kellerman, the leader of the security detail, riding in the passenger seat of the limousine, wasn't sure what was happening. He turned to see the president grasping his neck. William Greer, at the wheel of the presidential limo, did not at first speed up or swerve away from the noise. Neither Paul Landis, on the running boards of the vehicle trailing Kennedy's, nor Jack Ready in front of him jumped forward to protect the president. Lyndon Johnson, riding two cars back, was startled by the sound of the first shot. "Others in the motorcade thought it was a backfire from one of the police motorcycles, or a firecracker someone in the crowd had set off," writes Robert Caro in his biography of Lyndon Johnson, *The Passage of Power*.[1]

Even the official commissions disagree about what happened that day. Were there three shots or four? Did all the bullets come from the window of the Texas School Book Depository—where assassin Lee Harvey Oswald stood with his 6.5-millimeter Carcano Italian infantry carbine? Did the first bullet pass through President Kennedy and continue on to wound Texas governor John Connally, who was sitting in the forward jump seat of the limousine with his wife, Nellie? Whose decision was it to forego using the main limo's plastic bubble, built to shield those in the passenger seats? Why were there no Secret Service agents on the running boards of the president's car?

Those fatal seconds, although they were caught on film by several amateur cameramen, still elude our understanding. But one thing about those moments—one thing on which all the commissions agree—has gone relatively underreported during the five decades since. Nine of the twenty-eight Secret Service men who were in Dallas with the president the day he died had been out in local clubs until the early hours of the morning—in one case until five a.m. Three of the Secret Service agents riding a few feet from the president in the follow-up car had been, by their own accounts, up very late and drinking, an activity prohibited in the Secret Service rulebook.[2]

A week after the events in Dallas, President Lyndon Johnson ordered the first official investigation of the assassination. Its chairman: Earl Warren, the chief justice of the Supreme Court, who had had a distinguished career as the governor of California. The Warren Court, during his fourteen years as chief justice, had heard many pivotal cases, including *Brown v. Board of Education* in 1954, with its landmark civil-rights decision. With an already established reputation and an eye on the political thicket that would surround an investigation into Kennedy's assassination, Warren hesitated to accept Johnson's mandate. Johnson prevailed.

Three days after reluctantly taking the job, Warren learned that Secret Service agents had been out on the town socializing and drinking until early morning the day of the assassination. The revelation came not from depositions but from a radio report followed up by

a December 2 newspaper column in the *Washington Post* by Drew
Pearson, the establishment journalist (and close friend of Chief Justice Warren) well known for speaking truth to power. Pearson wrote
that the Secret Service agents had visited the Fort Worth Press Club
after midnight and that six of them had proceeded to an offbeat place
called the Cellar Coffee House. Some of the agents were out until
nearly three a.m. and "one of them was reported to have been inebriated," Pearson wrote.[3] Pearson explained that his information had
come to him through Thayer Waldo, a *Fort Worth Star-Telegram* reporter who didn't think his editors would dare publish a story casting
aspersions against Secret Servicemen or the Fort Worth club owners,
employees, and patrons. "Obviously men who have been drinking until nearly three a.m. are in no condition to be trigger-alert or in the
best physical shape to protect anyone,"[4] Pearson wrote about the Secret Service agents in the Kennedy motorcade.

The Warren Commission duly questioned the Secret Service
agents in question about their activities the night before the assassination and found they had been drinking. But in the 1960s the pastime
of drinking with peers or colleagues was considered normal, accept-
able behavior in many circles. Because of the lack of social stigma
associated with drinking, it was hard for the panel's members to know
how to react. Philadelphia assistant district attorney Arlen Specter,
who had reluctantly taken the Warren Commission job, and who de-
briefed the agents for the Warren Commission, didn't consider their
behavior a severe problem. Indeed, the agents themselves were already
devastated by their failure to protect the president, who most of them
had revered. Although the agents had broken the rules, many involved
with the commission were eager to protect them from going down in
history as the men who had made the mistakes that may have doomed
the president.

Chief Justice Warren, however, was outraged. His ire finally found
a voice in June 1964, when the commission questioned James Rowley,
the director of the Secret Service. Under oath, Rowley admitted that

Drew Pearson's column had been more or less accurate. Some had been drinking scotch; others, "two or three" beers. After forcing Rowley to read the agency's regulations that "the use of intoxicating liquor of any kind…is prohibited,"[5] General Counsel J. Lee Rankin hammered him. Even though drinking was a firing offense, according to the manual, Rowley had fired no one. "How can you tell," Rankin asked, that the men's actions "the night before…had nothing to do with the assassination?" Rowley bobbed and weaved. He had thought about punishment, he admitted. On the other hand, he had not wanted to blame the agents for the assassination—he did not want to "stigmatize" them or their families.

These answers seemed to infuriate Warren. "Don't you think that if a man went to bed reasonably early, and hadn't been drinking the night before, he would be more alert than if he stayed up until three, four, or five o clock in the morning, going to beatnik joints and doing some drinking along the way?"[6] Warren noted that some citizens along the route of the motorcade, waiting for the president to pass by, had actually seen a gun barrel pointed out of the sixth-floor window of the Texas School Book Depository. None of the Secret Service agents had noticed it. "Some people saw a rifle up in that building," Warren went on. "Wouldn't a Secret Service man in this motorcade, who is supposed to observe such things, be more likely to observe something of that kind if he was free from any of the results of liquor or lack of sleep than he would otherwise? Don't you think that they would have been more alert, sharper?"[7]

Long work shifts and a tolerance for partying and drinking had become entrenched in the Secret Service during JFK's years in office, and this extended to the men in charge of the president's security. Although there have been a handful of Secret Service drinking scandals since then, the early 1960s seem to have been a particularly difficult time for Secret Service agents. "Agents acknowledged that the Secret Service's socializing intensified each year of the Kennedy administration, to a point where, by late 1963, a few members of the presidential detail were regularly remaining in bars until the early morning hours,"[8] investigative journalist Seymour M. Hersh would note in his book *The Dark Side of Camelot*. Hersh reported that things were so loose that at least three of the Kennedy women—sisters and cousins from the president's large family—had propositioned various agents. [9]All of this rule-breaking behavior among members of the extended Kennedy family should have made the Secret Service more alert and more responsible. Instead, it seemed to have the opposite effect.

Whether or not they were hungover on November 22, several agents were certainly sleep deprived, a not-uncommon state among Secret Servicemen at the time. Agent Gerald Blaine, also in the Dallas motorcade, remembered struggling to stay awake on numerous occasions and spoke of being afraid to sit down or lean against a wall lest he nod off: "Working double shifts had become so common since Kennedy became president that it was now almost routine. The three eight-hour shift rotation operated normally when the president was in the White House, but when he was traveling…there simply weren't enough bodies."[10] Not only did many agents lack sleep, they rarely had time to eat. In his flight bag, along with extra ammunition and shoe polish, Blaine typically kept a few bags of Planters peanuts— sometimes the only thing he ate all day.

The Secret Service, one of the oldest federal law enforcement agencies, was founded in the nineteenth century to investigate financial crimes and curb counterfeiting after the Civil War. The department's formation was one of the last things President Abraham Lincoln approved in a conversation with Secretary of the Treasury Hugh McCulloch the day of his assassination. (Lincoln's bodyguard, John Parker, was taking a break at a bar across the street when John Wilkes Booth approached the presidential box and fired a single, mortal shot.)

Then, in 1881, President James Garfield, waiting at the Washington, D.C., railroad station for a train meant to take him on a visit

to New England—and unaccompanied by any kind of bodyguard—
was assassinated by a man who thought God was telling him to kill
the president. It wasn't until the administration of Grover Cleveland,
when a stranger walked into the White House and hit the president
across the face, that the Secret Service became part of a unit intended
to guard the nation's chief executive.

The first twenty-five U.S. presidents had bodyguards but no official
security detail, and the idea of protecting a leader from his own people
was, at first, an unpopular one. Yet the need for close security became
a governmental necessity in 1901, when an anarchist in Buffalo, New
York, approached President James McKinley, who was loosely flanked
by three Secret Service agents, and fatally shot him from only a few
feet away.

By the 1960s the Secret Service had evolved into an elite corps of
physically impressive men, adept in the use of firearms and ready to
meet all emergencies, even at the cost of their own lives. Despite the
agency's stature, two problems have always undermined it. One has
been the desire of presidents to be physically accessible to the American public, but the other is more serious, especially when things go
wrong.

From the beginning, the macho pride of the armed men of the
service has made it a culture that has masked its weaknesses. Pride is
not flexible and it does not ask for help. And since tough guys don't
complain, problems have often been downplayed. Sleep and careful
eating were for sissies. Training was for beginners. In certain cases in
the 1960s, physical fitness requirements were just a matter of filling
out forms. Being a man who could hold his liquor was part of the MO.
Indeed, First Lady Betty Ford liked to joke that when she got sober,
some members of her Secret Service contingent who had to accompany her to Alcoholics Anonymous meetings ended up getting sober
as well.[11]

Even in recent years, this machismo mindset has bedeviled the
agency. Though the agency has gone through repeated reforms, the

past decade has seen nearly nine hundred incidents in which officials were charged with misconduct. In the past three years alone, three reprimands for misbehavior turned into public scandals. In 2012, agents doing advance work for an official visit to Colombia by President Obama cavorted with strippers in their hotel; thirteen were investigated, and four were demoted or fired. In 2013, a Secret Service supervisor in the president's detail picked up a woman at the bar of the Hay-Adams hotel in Washington, D.C., then went upstairs with her to a hotel room, leaving behind a bullet from his Sig Sauer semiautomatic pistol when he left. And in March 2014, in Holland, after a Secret Service squad went out well into the night and one Counter Assault Team member was found drunk and passed out in a hotel hallway, three agents were shipped back stateside and put on leave.

President John F. Kennedy, beginning his campaign for a second term, traveled more than any previous president. Traveling had always been a nightmare for the Secret Service, especially when it involved the First Lady and other eminent guests and their families. "Motorcades were the Secret Service's nemeses," agent Gerald Blaine would write. "There were an endless number of variables…and you could never predict how a crowd would react." In Dallas, against department regulations, the president and the vice president—Lyndon Johnson—would ride in the same motorcade, making the situation even more unstable in the eyes of the men there to keep them from harm.

Kennedy wanted to be physically close to his constituents. And for all his personal courtesy to his guardians, including his motorcycle escorts, he made it clear that he was impatient with those who wanted to hem him in with security, especially the chosen few whose assignment brought them near enough to touch him. At the start of his administration, four agents would typically ride along on the side of the president's vehicle, balanced on running boards affixed to the car. Their positions, however, often blocked well-wishers from approaching the president for a handshake or from having a direct line of sight to him. At one point a few days before his death, Kennedy commanded his Secret Servicemen—whom he affectionately called a bunch of "Ivy League charlatans"[12]—to stay off the exterior footrests because he felt they boxed him in.

It was the prospect of a good meal that led the Secret Service agents out of the Hotel Texas in Fort Worth the night of November 21. The president and the First Lady had retired to their suite, and the men had had no dinner; some of them hadn't eaten since breakfast in Washington, D.C. Word got out that there was a buffet with food a few blocks from the hotel. In fact, local journalists had kept the Fort Worth Press Club open so that visiting White House reporters could go and grab a bite. It was after one in the morning when nine of the twenty-eight agents in the presidential detail walked over in search of food. There was none. Though the kitchen at the club was closing, the agents stayed around for scotch and sodas, and a few cans of beer. Three of the agents then headed back to their rooms; six continued with the festivities.

CBS newsman Bob Schieffer—then a young night police reporter for the *Fort Worth Star-Telegram*—remembers the evening well. "I went to the club when I got off at two a.m.," he recalls. Nearby was a legendary hangout called the Cellar Coffee House. "The Cellar was an all-night San Francisco–style coffee house down the street and some of the visiting reporters had heard about it and wanted to see it. So we all went over there and some of the agents came along. The place didn't have a liquor license, but they did serve liquor to friends— usually grain alcohol."[13] (Fort Worth was a dry city in 1963, so the Cellar officially offered only fruit juice.)

Six Secret Service members stayed at the Cellar until close to three in the morning; one didn't leave until five a.m. "Every one of the agents involved had been assigned protective duties that began no later than 8:00 a.m. on November 22, 1963,"[14] observed Philip Melanson, an expert on incidents of politically motivated violence who would oversee the archive of the Robert F. Kennedy assassination.

On November 22, a morning mist had burned off, and bright sunshine greeted the presidential party, who had flown from Fort Worth to Dallas. Instead of getting in the limousine, President Kennedy and the First Lady walked along the chain-link fence separating the airfield from the public, shaking hands and chatting with the spectators. Secret Service agents Clint Hill and Paul Landis scanned the crowd for trouble. Neither had had more than a few hours of sleep; both had been drinking into the early hours of the morning.

That morning, nine agents were specifically responsible for guarding the president. In the lead car—at the front of the motorcade, directly in front of Kennedy's limousine—sat agent Winston Lawson, along with Dallas police chief Jesse Curry. Behind them in the presidential limousine—the second car of the motorcade—the driver and passenger seat were occupied by Secret Service members William Greer and Roy Kellerman. The limousine, a 1961 midnight-blue four-door Lincoln (code-named the SS-100-X), had been modified by the Ford Motor Company for presidential use. Four retractable side steps and two steps with handles on the rear of the car had been added to allow security personnel to jump on or off, or be escorted along. The side steps had been retracted. Modifications had widened the car's wheelbase and increased its weight from 5,200 pounds to almost 7,800 pounds. Even for an experienced driver like Greer, who had been a chauffeur in Boston, it was a difficult vehicle to maneuver, especially on a route like the one in Dallas, which included some sharp right-angle turns.

Riding along that day were the Kennedys (code-named Lancer and Lace) and the Connallys. The third car, also configured with protruding footrests, was a 1956 black Cadillac convertible (code-named Halfback), driven by Secret Service agent Sam Kinney. It was Kinney's job to stay a few feet behind the presidential limousine at all times: close enough so that the two cars couldn't be separated by someone lunging between them, but not so close as to cause a collision. Paul Landis, Jack Ready, and Clint Hill rode the running boards along the sides of this follow-up car. Inside sat agents George Hickey, Emory Roberts, Glenn Bennett, and senior aide Ken O'Donnell.

Agent Hill—poised just a few feet behind the Kennedys, who sat in the backseat of the car in front of him—was nervous. The motorcade kept speeding up and slowing down, speeding up and slowing down. That morning, he frequently jumped off the running board to jog alongside the vehicle. Kinney, right behind him in Halfback's driver's seat, watched him struggle to keep pace with the cars.

Clint Hill had been assigned to the First Lady's detail; his job was to focus on her, not on the president. According to Hill, in *Mrs. Kennedy and Me*, one of two books he has written about the Kennedys, he and Mrs. Kennedy had developed a solid friendship. They had first become good friends, he noted, after a propitious encounter. One day when he was in the passenger seat next to the driver while she was being chauffeured to Middleburg, Virginia, where she had rented a small estate for riding horses, Hill lit up a cigarette. She leaned forward and asked Hill to ask the driver to pull over. Hill was baffled when she invited him to ride with her in the backseat. Perhaps she didn't like his smoking? Instead, with an impish look on her face, she asked Hill if she could have one of his cigarettes. Hill reached for his pack of L&M's and lit one for the First Lady. "She was like a giddy teenager who was getting away with something, and I was her cohort in crime," Hill writes.[15]

Hill's laser focus on the First Lady may have also stemmed from a deeper affection for her, evident in the tenderness with which he would later write about her. After the first and second shots rang out, it was Hill who acted, climbing onto the rear of the Kennedys' limousine and pushing the First Lady—who had crawled onto the back of the car—back into her seat. It was already too late to save the president.

Across from Hill on the other side of the follow-up car, agent Jack Ready was also on the footboards, feet from the president. Behind him, in similar proximity, was Paul Landis, also from Mrs. Kennedy's detail. Both men seemed paralyzed for a few moments. All three—along with Glenn Bennett, who was inside their chase car—had gone to the press club and then the Cellar the night before. Hill, Ready, and Bennett had stayed until after two a.m.; Landis, until five.

The fourth car in the motorcade, containing Vice President Lyndon B. Johnson and his wife, was guarded by other agents, including Rufus Youngblood. Youngblood had not joined the others the previous evening. And at the sound of the first shot, the agent, in line with his Secret Service training, pushed Johnson to the floor of the car and covered him with his own body, a move that none of the other agents would make in those precious few seconds to protect the president, the governor, or their wives.

The situation in Dallas, surely, had been exacerbated by President Kennedy's fearlessness—even recklessness—a charge later levied by some in his protective detail. It was the president who wanted to ride in an open car without the protective bubble. It was the president who insisted on going to Dallas, a staunchly conservative stronghold, even though a fellow Democrat, Adlai Stevenson, had recently been attacked there. "Dallas is a very dangerous place," Kennedy had been told by his friend Arkansas Democrat senator J. William Fulbright, according to journalist Ronald Kessler in his book *In the President's Secret Service*. "I wouldn't go there. Don't you go." (Ironically, that first shot was fired at Kennedy at the very moment Nellie Connally had turned to the president to comment about the friendly Dallas crowds.)

Agent William Greer, who had served in the Navy during World War II, was clearly undone by the events of the day, although he had not been out with the other agents the night before. "Greer was tormented by his actions in the motorcade, including his failure to hit the accelerator immediately after hearing the first shot," journalist Philip Shenon writes. Witnesses remember seeing the car's brake lights illuminate at around the time the bullets were fired. Later, Greer said he had been waiting for instructions from Roy Kellerman, the

Secret Service agent in the passenger seat of the limousine. (Kennedy's two main escorts, Greer and Kellerman, were fifty-four and forty-eight at the time, respectively. In a department which prized speed and reflex—and in which forty was considered the age limit—the plum spots were often awarded to senior staffers.)

It would later become clear, however, that Greer, from the first, worried about his culpability. At Dallas's Parkland Hospital, where the president's body was rushed, Greer tearfully apologized to Jacqueline Kennedy, according to William Manchester, who interviewed the agent for his book *The Death of a President*. Greer, who died in 1985, admitted he had told the First Lady: "Oh, Mrs. Kennedy, oh my God, oh my God. I didn't mean to do it. I didn't hear, I should have swerved the car, I couldn't help it. Oh. Mrs. Kennedy...if only I'd seen in time. Oh!"[16]

His sense of guilt was echoed by Clint Hill, who in a TV interview with newsman Mike Wallace would break down in tears. "It was my fault," he admitted. "If I had just reacted a little bit quicker...I'll live with that to my grave."

The famous and horrific film sequence of the assassination—twenty-six seconds of eight-millimeter footage taken by a bystander named Abraham Zapruder—shows that the rest of the Secret Service agents, those in the presidential limousine and those riding behind in Halfback, seemed to be taken by surprise. "The men in Halfback were bewildered," according to Manchester. "They glanced around uncertainly. Lawson, Kellerman, Greer, Ready, and Hill all thought that a firecracker had been exploded...Even more tragic was the perplexity of Roy Kellerman, the ranking agent in Dallas, and Bill Greer, who was under Kellerman's supervision. Kellerman and Greer were in a position to take swift evasive action, and for five terrible seconds they were immobilized."[17]

Kellerman, who was riding in the passenger seat of the presidential limousine, also behaved oddly after the first shot rang out. Instead of moving back to protect his passengers, he stayed in the front, relaying radio messages to Greer, who was sitting a foot away, on his left. The commission's Arlen Specter was not impressed. Kellerman, Specter said, "was the wrong man for the job—he was 48 years old, big and his reflexes were not quick."[18]

The response of the Secret Service to Drew Pearson's allegations was fast and thorough. In an appendix to the Warren Commission report, Inspector Gerard McCann in Washington, D.C., and Secret Service agent Forest V. Sorrels, the special agent in charge of the Dallas office, canvassed everyone they could find who was at the Hotel Texas, the Fort Worth Press Club, or the Cellar Coffee House that night, including its manager, Jimmy Hill, and owner Pat Kirkwood, and a reporter who had also been at the party with the Secret Service agents.

Their conclusions? Letter after letter states that no one at Fort Worth that night was intoxicated. Letter after letter repeats that of the nine Secret Service agents at the press club and the Cellar, only three were due to report for the eight a.m. shift. A dozen times in the report, respondents state that the Cellar was a dry club that served no alcohol. However, Philip Melanson writes, "At many clubs and restaurants in the Dallas–Fort Worth area, it was customary, given local liquor laws, for patrons to bring their own liquor, with the management providing setups."[19]

Every agent on duty in Fort Worth and in Dallas was asked to write an account of his whereabouts and activities in the early morning hours of November 22. The agents say they went to the press club because they were hungry; none confesses to more than a drink or two. At the Cellar, the agents say, they drank fruit juice—mostly grapefruit juice. Two of them mention drinking a juice concoction called a "Salty Dick."

It took Pat Kirkwood, the Cellar Coffee House owner, more than twenty years to tell more details of what happened the night of November 21. In the letters he wrote in 1963, he claimed that none of the Secret Service agents in his establishment had been drinking.

But in 1984 he wasn't so sure. Kirkwood was fatally ill at the time, and the truth may have come to seem more important than it had before. In an article recalling the glory days of the club, he explained that although he did not "officially" serve liquor, he actually dispensed large quantities of booze, especially to people like lawyers and politicians and policemen who might later be helpful. Cellar manager Jimmy Hill would later own up as to the truth of what happened as well. After the assassination, he recalled in Jim Marrs's book *Crossfire*: "After the agents were there, we got a call from the White House asking us not to say anything about them drinking because their image had suffered enough as it was. We didn't say anything, but…they were drinking pure Everclear."[20] (Everclear is 190 proof, a popular spike for a drink like the Salty Dick.)

How could the president's protectors have been so careless? What possessed the men guarding John F. Kennedy's life to think it was not unreasonable to drink and stay out most of the night before taking up their positions in a noontime motorcade? Life can only be understood backward, but it must be lived forward, as Kierkegaard wrote. Of course none of the Secret Service agents knew on the warm night of November 21 in Fort Worth, Texas, that their movements were going to be scrutinized for decades. None of them could have imagined that every move they made on that innocent Thursday night would be something they were called to account for minute by minute and second by second for the rest of their lives.

CHAPTER 13

PRESIDENT RICHARD NIXON
1968–1973:
"OUR DRUNKEN FRIEND"

The last weekend of August 1969 was to be a lazy weekend of relaxation for Richard Nixon, who had, after many setbacks and detours, finally been elected president of the United States in the fall of 1968. Nixon had wanted to be president for decades, and everyone close to him knew it. He was a tightly wound Quaker with a longing for power; one night in 1960 he even got drunk and seriously told his Catholic staffers what a great Pope he could be and how well he could run the Vatican. "There was no doubt among his friends…that from 1952 onward Nixon's determination to be president had been no mere fantasy but a controlled and consuming ambition which occupied the greater part of his waking life," writes historian Fawn Brodie in her biography of Nixon.[1]

In the 1950s Nixon had been Dwight D. Eisenhower's vice president, and in the fall of 1960 he had been narrowly defeated by JFK for president. Now, at long last in the position he had dreamed of, Nixon was relaxing in the hot August sun in Key Biscayne, Florida—where a compound on Bay Lane had become the Winter White House. He had spent most of the month in Key Biscayne, where he watched sports and fished with his hard-drinking best friend and next-door neighbor, Charles "Bebe" Rebozo. The Cuban-American businessman had met Richard Nixon in the 1950s. The two were sometimes joined by Robert Abplanalp, another wealthy Nixon crony who had invented the modern aerosol valve and also had a house on Bay Lane.

Nixon's idyll in the sun was soon interrupted. On August 29, worlds away from the loose and slightly drunken atmosphere at the golf-playing, football-game-attending, chilled-martini-drinking compound in Key Biscayne, two members of the Popular Front for the Liberation of Palestine—Leila Khaled and Salim Issawi—hijacked TWA flight 840 from Rome, Italy, to Tel Aviv. The hijackers forced the pilot to divert the plane to the airport at Damascus, Syria, and set off an international incident. Khaled and Issawi had hoped that Israeli ambassador Yitzhak Rabin was on the plane—he was not. In exchange for their hostages (who were eventually released) they demanded the freedom of Popular Front comrades held in Israeli prisons.

Nixon's national security adviser, Henry Kissinger, knew that the decision about the role the United States should play in this violent drama would be up to his president. He reached the president on the telephone after dark as Nixon shuttled between the beach and his house. As usual, Nixon's rage—fueled by a drink or two—was evident. He didn't wait for Kissinger to give him details. He wasn't interested in a suggested course of action. He exploded: "Bomb the airport!" he yelled into the phone. Appalled, and fearful—a United States bombing of the Damascus airport was impractical and foolhardy and might well start a larger war—Kissinger and Defense Secretary Melvin Laird had to scramble. They found a creative way around the president's order. They ordered two American aircraft carriers into position in the Mediterranean so that they could say they were preparing to bomb the Damascus airport. As Nixon repeatedly and drunkenly called and hectored them through the long night—had the airport been bombed yet?—Kissinger hemmed and hawed. Laird got on the telephone and told the president the current weather conditions made bombing impractical at that moment.

Throughout Nixon's presidency this was often Henry Kissinger's role. "National Security Adviser" became a euphemism for being a ubiquitous nanny to a man who was occasionally too drunk to be coherent or sometimes too drunk to function at all. "Kissinger was the only man in Nixon's ever-changing entourage…who knew how to keep his intellect from becoming threatening," writes Brodie. "He flattered; he effaced himself with wit and drollery; he insinuated ideas and gave Nixon credit."[2] Most of all Kissinger hid his contempt for his boss behind an unctuous façade of admiration. No wonder. On the morning after his orders to bomb Syria, Nixon had forgotten all about the hijacked airplane.

Again and again during the next two years, as airliners were hijacked and war threatened to break out in the Middle East, and decisions had to be made about the war in Vietnam, Kissinger, Laird, and White House Chief of Staff H. R. Haldeman danced around the president's homicidal, drunken orders to bomb the shit out of this or nuke the shit out of that—orders usually not even remembered the next morning. "If the president had his way," Kissinger told his aides, "there would be a nuclear war each week!"[3]

There are many kinds of drinking problems, and many types of drinkers. Early temperance crusaders defined *abstaining* as only drinking wine and beer. Later, the definition of *abstinence* narrowed. As the definition of *problem drinking* has changed and changed again, our citizens have run the gamut from the overt drunkenness of being passed out under a hedge in an "uncivil and beastly manner," like one resident of the Plymouth Colony, to a more clandestine kind of drunkenness. President Richard Nixon, with a drunkenness that was both secret and hidden, brought this country to the brink of World War III and changed forever the way we view our government. The president's drinking was not well understood even by those closest to him. His drinking also did damage closer to home. Drinking and domestic violence are often linked, and there is some evidence that Nixon had hit his wife, Pat, on many occasions.

"I'm not talking about a smack," wrote Nixon aide John Sears. "He blackened her eye."[4]

But all this was private. No one knew. The pre-Watergate 1960s were a time when the United States press conspired with public figures to keep their domestic lives hidden. Naturally, Nixon's drinking was not a secret to anyone who worked with him. "People who knew about the slurred voice and the nights beyond reach seem to have a range of contrasting motives for silence," wrote one Nixon aide, Roger Morris. "It was after all…only an occasional problem."[5] But often those occasions, especially as time drove Richard Nixon forward to his own miserable destiny, were the very occasions when he needed to be clearheaded, well informed, and available.

Born in 1913 to a mother who was a saintly Quaker and an often angry Irish-American father who converted to the Quaker church, Nixon grew up in southern California, first in Yorba Linda and then in Whittier, as one of five sons. The Nixon family was a family on a very short leash. As Quakers they did not drink, smoke, swear, lie, or cheat. They did live in fear of their father's temper, but they grew up in a world where unconditional respect for parents and corporal punishment were normal. The Nixons were poor, but Richard—named after King Richard the Lionheart—was the smart one. He earned a scholarship to Harvard from Whittier High School, but stayed home instead to help his parents run their grocery store and to help care for his brother Howard, who eventually died of tuberculosis—a disease that his parents believed was caused by dissolute living.

Nixon stayed home and went to Whittier Community College and later to Duke University School of Law on a scholarship. Although the scholarship was granted only for the first year of law school, he excelled and it was extended. He graduated third in his class and hoped to join the FBI, but instead became a partner in a local California law firm. In 1938, cast as a male lead in a Whittier Community Players production, he fell in love with the female lead, Pat Ryan. She did not fall in love with him. Perhaps she had a premonition of what life with a brilliant, temper-driven, power-mad husband would be like. It took Nixon two years to persuade her to marry him, but soon the couple had two daughters, Tricia and Julie.

In 1943, as a naval officer, Richard Nixon sailed for the South Pacific on the USS *President Monroe*. The Navy was the first time he had been far from the restrictions of home—whether they were the rules of his parents, or his expectations of himself as a husband. The freedom changed him. There were nine officers in his bunkroom. One of them taught him how to play poker, another taught him how to swear. They all got together and taught him how to drink. Nixon left the Navy a lieutenant commander, having acquitted himself with honor and having learned that a few drinks were delightfully relaxing and inspiring.

Was Richard Nixon an alcoholic? His drinking, which took place in binges during which he was entirely incapacitated or filled with irrational rage, was not a daily occurrence. Nixon's drinking was not the drinking of a bloated, wounded character who died of liver disease in middle age. Nixon never lost his iron sense of personal discipline. Most of the time he didn't drink at all. He seemed, however, to be allergic to alcohol—and this is a sign of alcoholism. A few drinks, a cocktail and wine with dinner, would render him drunk, slurring, stumbling, and rambling irrationally before he finally passed out. The next morning he would have little memory of what had happened the night before.

Most of the time Nixon was able to control whether or not he would drink; what he could not control was what happened after the first cocktail. A drink or two could feel great—or result in embarrassing late-night calls to aides, huge mood swings, fits of weeping, protestations of love and admiration, and being unconscious and dead to the world when the world needed a strong, alert U.S. president. Nixon's many extraordinary accomplishments will always be overshadowed by the crassness, drunkenness, racism, and bad judgment that often followed a drink or two.

As president, Richard Nixon had many triumphant moments. He

opened relations with China, he put a man on the moon, he helped end the war in Vietnam, and he brought the Soviets close to détente. However, these are not always the things for which we will remember him. Instead his erratic, irrational behavior, his self-pity, his moods— in short, his drinking—damaged his personal reputation. Sometimes he sounded more like a bullied elementary school kid—when he announced, for instance, that the voters and the press wouldn't have him to "kick around anymore"—than one of the most powerful statesmen in the world.

The changes in the way voters came to see Richard Nixon reach beyond the personal. Because of the problems of his presidency and the resulting Watergate scandal and impeachment proceedings, the United States' reputation in the world began to shift in ways that are becoming clearer fifty years later. Our role as a powerful and benevolent nation is no longer unquestioned. We citizens feel that we can no longer trust our leaders. During Nixon's presidency, the role of government began to change from that of a trusted structure to that of a hated and mocked group of corrupt rich men. Although Nixon is not famous for drinking, his drinking became a problem early on in his career and was a cause of profound destruction to the office he held and the country he led.

As early as 1968, when Nixon wanted to hire a successful Seattle land use lawyer named John Ehrlichman, who had worked on a few of his campaigns, his drinking was an issue. Ehrlichman, a nondrinking Christian Scientist with little tolerance for drunks, had been in Nixon's entourage enough to identify the problem. Clear-eyed himself at forty-three, a decade younger than the man who was trying to hire him, Ehrlichman had seen Nixon get "pie-eyed" after the Republican National Convention that nominated Barry Goldwater. Earlier, in 1962, he had seen Nixon stumble and slur while giving important speeches. Summoned to New York City to talk with Nixon, soon to be the president elect, Ehrlichman bluntly told Nixon that he didn't want to work for a drunk.

"You are highly susceptible to alcohol. I'm not interested in coming away from my practice and my family and going out and beating my brains out if this is going to be a problem," Ehrlichman told Nixon.[6] Ehrlichman was right to hesitate. In the end, Nixon's drinking destroyed Ehrlichman's life, and Ehrlichman seemed to have known that might happen. A straight arrow who had been an Eagle Scout, graduated from Stanford Law School, and was a decorated World War II flight navigator, Ehrlichman could have had a lucrative and satisfying career. Instead, Ehrlichman's service as Nixon's White House counsel and as his chief domestic adviser developed a loyalty to his drunken boss that had terrible consequences. During the Watergate hearings he was charged with conspiracy, obstruction of justice, and perjury, and he went to jail for a year and a half. Afterward, as a convicted felon, he was no longer allowed to practice law.

In 1968, instead of arguing, Nixon made Ehrlichman a solemn promise that he would no longer drink. Nixon had gone beyond the earliest stage of alcoholism—denial—and entered the second stage when the alcoholic thinks his or her drinking is a problem, but a problem that can be controlled. Like many alcoholics, Nixon was able to keep his promise…for a while. He did not drink during the 1968 campaign. But by August of his first year as president, that day in New York with Ehrlichman and his promises of the campaign seemed far away.

Nixon was not a quantity alcoholic. He rarely drank more than two or three drinks—a drink or two before dinner and wine with dinner was typical. Still, the alcohol he did drink had a huge effect on his life and on the well-being of the United States. "Physiologically, this fellow has a disability," Ehrlichman wrote later. "One drink can knock him galley west if he is tired. Even if he is not tired, about two and a half drinks will do it. So he is much more susceptible than a lot of people I have met." Men who were close to President Nixon, like his speechwriter Ray Price, often bridled at the idea that Nixon had a drinking problem. He did not drink like a drunk. His personal discipline was admirable. Yet even Price admitted to Tom Wicker that when Nixon was tired or if he had taken a sleeping pill—a common occurrence—even one drink could make him "appear drunk."[7]

"Nixon's inability to handle more than one drink was well known to his intimates," write Bob Woodward and Carl Bernstein in *The Final Days*. "During campaigns he had wisely chosen not to touch alcohol. But now, on too many afternoons, he started sipping in his office with Rebozo. He was moody and sometimes didn't come into the office until noon. At a small dinner for a few friends on December 21, 1972, he got more and more emotional and unclear, more than once asking Bryce Harlow to explain what he meant to another guest, Barry Goldwater. On some days he vowed he would never be driven from office. On others he told his daughter Julie's husband, David, that he might as well resign."[8]

As Nixon's presidency faltered in 1973, his drinking got worse. Another crisis was more frightening than anything that had gone before. On October 6, 1973, Soviet-backed Arab armies mounted a surprise attack on Israel, crossing the Suez Canal and entering the Sinai Peninsula and the Golan Heights on Yom Kippur—the holiest day in Judaism. The president's drinking had already been a public relations problem a few months earlier. In August, covering a speech he gave in New Orleans, even the *New York Times* reporter noticed that there was something wrong with the president. "He stumbled over his words…His voice fluctuated in volume and speed."[9] Someone commented that Nixon looked like Ed Sullivan on speed.

At this point, the president's medications combined with his drinking may have been wreaking havoc with his body. He was taking Dilantin prescribed by a doctor as well as "relaxing" with a few drinks prescribed by his friend Bebe. Nixon seemed to be coming apart. Kissinger, who had plotted with Nixon to keep the Vietnam War going as a campaign strategy through the 1972 presidential race, began to refer to the president as "our drunken friend." The combination of drinking, pills, and the pressures of office as the Watergate situation unraveled seemed to affect his brain. The press began writing about mental health issues. On television he got so angry with his press secretary, Ron Ziegler, that he shoved him as the whole world watched. "Who can forget the picture of a president so out of control of himself that he expresses it by laying angry hands on a member of his staff in public?" asked Nicholas von Hoffman in the *New York Times*.[10]

At night, after a few drinks, Nixon was often passed out or incoherent. So when a massive American airlift was sent to help the attacked Israelis on October 6, Nixon was not at the helm of government. As usual Kissinger was desperately trying to act as a go-between for his drunken president and whatever crises the world was bringing in. Columnist Max Lerner noted, "Kissinger was in effect carrying the burden of the presidency."[11] Now, as a Soviet-backed Arab army clashed with an American-backed Israeli army, the threat of nuclear war became real.

During this time of cease-fires and violated truces in the Mideast, Washington also exploded with scandals. Vice President Spiro Agnew resigned and was eventually replaced by Gerald Ford. During the Saturday Night Massacre, Nixon fired Watergate Special Prosecutor Archibald Cox. Attorney General Eliot Richardson and Deputy Attorney General William Ruckelshaus resigned in protest.

Then on the night of October 24, when the Mideast war had been going on for more than two weeks, Kissinger became convinced that the Soviets were about to send troops into Israel. As tensions built, Soviet president Leonid Brezhnev had Soviet ambassador Anatoly Dobrynin read Kissinger a letter that sounded like an ultimatum. If the conflict in the Middle East wasn't settled immediately, there would be unilateral action, Brezhnev threatened.

When Kissinger tried to call the president, Alexander Haig said he wasn't available. Kissinger called a meeting in the White House Situation Room. The military was put on the alert. "At U.S. air bases, B-52s loaded with nuclear weapons lined up nose to tail," writes Anthony Summers. "In missile silos, launch commanders buckled themselves into their chairs. Nuclear-armed submarines sped to secret positions off the Soviet coast."[12] The President was still "asleep." "We had to go on nuclear alert without his permission," Chief of Naval Operations Admiral Elmo Zumwalt recalled of the night of the alert. "The reason we had to do that was because he could not be awakened. Nixon obviously had too much to drink…I was told at the time that they were not able to waken him."[13] The Soviets eventually backed down and the moment passed.

On October 25, an effective cease-fire was called between the Israelis and the Arabs. But the implications for the United States' relations with the Soviet Union as well as the dramatic erosion of the respect this country held in the rest of the world were dramatic and far-reaching. "The inescapable conclusion, well bodyguarded by meticulous research and footnotes," wrote Christopher Hitchens in his *New York Times* review of *The Arrogance of Power*, Anthony Summers's book about Nixon, "is that in the Nixon era the United States was, in essence, a 'rogue state.' It had a ruthless, paranoid, and unstable leader who did not hesitate to break the laws of his own country in order to violate the neutrality, menace the territorial integrity, or destabilize the internal affairs of other nations. At the close of this man's reign, in an episode more typical of a banana republic or a 'peoples' democracy,' his own secretary of defense, James Schlesinger, had to instruct the Joint Chiefs of Staff to disregard any military order originating in the White House."[14]

Although many American presidents have been drinkers—Jefferson, Harrison, and Grant, to name a few—no twentieth-century American president had allowed the leadership of the country to be changed by drinking. No other president had been *hors de combat* during a nuclear alert. No other president had been unavailable because of drinking during a national crisis. No other president's judgment had been this much thrown off by his drinking. Bad decisions are one symptom of alcoholism, and as Nixon's drinking increased, his judgment failed—whether it was deciding to fire Archibald Cox, deciding to lie his way through the Watergate crisis, or deciding to tape everything in the Oval Office.

In the spring of 1973 Nixon decided that he had to cut his losses.

He would get rid of his closest friends and aides, John Ehrlichman and H. R. Haldeman, and blame the Watergate mess on them. (Remember the way the charming Charles Adams, after stealing his brother John Quincy Adams's money, complained about how awful it had been for him to have to lie about it?) Nixon summoned both men to Camp David. In breaking the bad news to Haldeman, who kept a journal of that day, he took some blame on himself. Then, as the two men stood outdoors, Nixon turned to Haldeman and told him he had never shared what he was about to say. Every single night, Nixon told Haldeman, he had dropped to his knees and prayed for guidance. More recently, he confided, he had prayed that he would not wake up in the morning. His life had become unbearable. Haldeman was deeply touched by this confidence... until he compared notes with Ehrlichman and found that the president had told him exactly the same thing.[15]

"Just how serious was Nixon's drinking problem?" asked Seymour Hersh in an article in the *Atlantic Monthly*, which was part of his book on the Nixon presidency, *The Price of Power*. "Many of his former associates and aides, such as Charles W. Colson, dismiss its significance by saying that the president had a notoriously low capacity for alcohol, and would slur his words and appear to be somewhat drunk after one or two highballs."

Another close aide to Kissinger recalls, however, that Nixon always seemed to be experiencing the results of his "low capacity" during his many weekends at the Florida White House in Key Biscayne. On those weekends, according to an aide's interview with Hersh, Nixon spent an inordinate amount of time drinking martinis with two old cronies, Rebozo and Robert Abplanalp. "Kissinger's main concern during those Florida weekend trips, which were working weekends for the National Security Adviser and his staff, was avoiding social encounters with the Nixon entourage," Hersh writes.

One night in Miami, Nixon stopped an attractive woman as he left a restaurant—after having had a few drinks too many—and offered her a job in the White House. "She looks like she's built for you, Henry," the president said. The Kissinger aide learned of the encounter from a Secret Service man. "Hearing this kind of a thing made my veins hurt," the aide says. "The president of the United States, drunk in a restaurant, making crude remarks and engaging in familiarity with a strange woman in a public place— all clearly attributable to martinis..." Nonetheless, the aide says, "I didn't think of his drinking as a real problem—although you sort of wondered what would happen if there was ever a nuclear threat." Most of the time, he says, "it was one of the things you knew about in terms of handling papers—'Oh, no, this is not the time to get him to sign these.'"[16]

Many of the people closest to Nixon only realized how much he had been torn apart by his drinking when it was too late—in his final days as president. National Security Adviser Henry Kissinger's deputy, Lawrence Eagleburger, who eventually served under Presidents George H. W. Bush and Ronald Reagan, was shocked when the president turned to Kissinger for help with the emotional price of his resignation. After a long, teary, and drunken conversation— Nixon sobbed and Kissinger insincerely reassured him—Nixon hung up. Later he officially called Kissinger on the phone to tell him that he had decided to resign. When the phone rang, Eagleburger picked up an extension to listen, write Woodward and Bernstein in *The Final Days*. "That was the custom—Kissinger rarely took a call alone. Eagleburger was shocked. The president was slurring his words. He was drunk. He was out of control."[17]

CHAPTER 14

RECOVERY

The United States' history with alcohol is the story of the tension between two poles: temperance and intemperance, drinking and abstinence, liquor and sobriety, addiction and recovery. Our country has been, at times, the drunkest country in the world; our country has been, at times, one of the least drunk countries in the world.

Although the United States has been famous for drunkenness, it is also the birthplace of the world's most effective temperance movements, movements with very different goals: Alcoholics Anonymous and Mothers Against Drunk Driving.

Founded in 1980 by a woman named Candace Lightner whose daughter was killed by a drunk driver, Mothers Against Drunk Driving has had a huge impact on the way our culture understands drinking. Drunk-driving accidents have been cut in half as MADD lobbies for higher drinking ages and more severe punishments for driving drunk. Nevertheless almost thirty people a day and more than ten thousand a year are still killed in drunk-driving accidents and millions of people admit to driving drunk. MADD estimates that the price tag for drunk driving is about $132 billion a year. Drunk drivers, as MADD points out, affect not just the people they injure and kill but everyone in the families and workplaces of those they injure and kill.

One of the most powerful arguments against cigarette smoking, an activity that has gone from being almost universal to exceptional in a few decades, is that it hurts others as well as the smoker. Secondhand smoke is dangerous. Smokers hurt others, innocent people, as well as themselves. But secondhand drinking is also dangerous. Like smoking—even more violently than smoking—drinking inflicts collateral damage with even more violent effects on family members and innocent people who cross paths with a drinker. No one in an alcoholic's family is safe from psychological consequences. Secondhand drinking can be every bit as deadly as secondhand smoke.

Alcoholics Anonymous is one of the best known movements that counteracts drunkenness. Although it has a different goal than MADD, it has many of the same results. With millions of members, this movement, which grew out of the nineteenth-century temperance movements, was started in the most American way imaginable. It grew from the mutual need of two white men—a failed businessman and a drunk physician—who were thrown together by a series of all-American coincidences in the hinterlands of Akron, Ohio.

What began with William James, the aristocratic Harvard professor scion of one of America's many alcoholic dynasties, was passed on to meetings in church basements all over the country. "James sponsored several patients-rights movements in his own lifetime, and the fellowship of Alcoholics Anonymous, founded by a New York stockbroker named Bill Wilson in 1935 and destined to become the most important self-help group therapy in the world, sprang directly from his thought," writes Ann Douglas. "The medical establishment, including Freud, had long judged alcoholism a disease impervious to treatment, but alcoholics could apparently do for one another what doctors could not do for them."[1]

William Griffith Wilson was born in 1894 in East Dorset, a small quarry town in Vermont, just as the American temperance movement gathered steam again after the Civil War. This pre-Prohibition heyday featured dozens of visiting temperance speakers who railed against what drinking had done to the American family. P. T. Barnum's famous circus with its sideshow *Ten Nights in a Bar-Room* was the most popular entertainment in the country. Nightly meetings of temperance clubs in every town urged the men of the town to "take the pledge," and stop the mindless destruction caused by their drinking habits.

At the little school in East Dorset, Wilson had classes in temperance that featured horror stories about drunken men who spent their week's paycheck in the local bar before they even got home. His family owned the Wilson House, a hotel that included one of the local bars, and he had been born on the north side of the house—in a room behind the bar. Wilson watched as the men of his town backslid and had sober epiphanies. His uncle found God while climbing on Mount Aeolus, the granite mountain that loomed over East Dorset, and stopped drinking. Other cousins accepted the idea of temperance but were unable to practice it. Like many of its neighboring states, Vermont was dry from 1853 to 1902, and Wilson had heard every argument against drinking that anyone in New England could muster before he was in high school. He also saw how difficult it could be to give up drinking once someone took the first drink.

Drinking was a man's game in those days, and Wilson's father had been one of its players. Gilly Wilson was from an old East Dorset family that had run the hotel on the town green for generations. A quarryman in the marble quarries of East Dorset and Granby, Wilson moved his family from town to town and finally, when his son was ten, drove his wife, Emily, to a level of distraction and rage that caused her to sue him for divorce—a move unheard of in a small town in New England at the turn of the century. Gilly Wilson went west, and his son didn't see him for years. Emily moved to Boston, leaving her children with her parents, the sober Griffiths, who lived in a small gray house on the other side of the East Dorset green. As a kid whose family life had been shattered by his father's drinking, the young Bill Wilson swore he would never drink.

Without alcohol, Bill Wilson was at the mercy of his fears and feelings. He was anxious and depressed. His grandfather, a prescient man who clearly took his responsibilities to Bill seriously, enrolled him in the local prep school—Burr and Burton—where slowly he succeeded and eventually excelled. The untimely death of the girl he loved catapulted Bill Wilson back into the darkness of his younger years. East Dorset and neighboring Manchester were popular summer resorts, and Bill next fell in love with an older woman who was summering there with her family—Lois Burnham of Brooklyn, New York. Lois, a somewhat motherly girl who was four years older than the gawky teenage boy she met at the local lake, had a stabilizing influence on Bill. Soon the two were engaged to be married.

Another stabilizing influence was the United States Army, which Wilson joined as a second lieutenant in the Sixty-Sixth Coast Artillery Corps. Wilson's psychological difficulties were far from over. Although he was a crack shot from hours of hunting in the Vermont woods, he thought that he had joined the weak man's part of the army. His moods cycled through depressions punctuated by panic attacks. Once on a train, convinced that he could not breathe, he rode while lying down in the aisle with his mouth against the bottom of the door to get more air. His unit was about to be shipped out to France. He was afraid.

By the time he was stationed at Fort Rodman in New Bedford in 1917, his resistance to drinking had worn thin, and his need for something to take the edge off had grown irresistible. The soldiers were invited everywhere and at a fancy cocktail party where he felt acutely uncomfortable, Wilson accepted a Bronx cocktail—a lethal concoction of gin, vermouth, and orange juice. The first drink didn't seem to have a big effect, but the second Bronx cocktail changed his life.

Wilson's awkwardness and fear fell away. "I could talk well. I could actually please the guests. I was part of things at last," he remembered.

"Oh, the magic of those first three or four drinks."[2] He had found the elixir of life, the magic potion that changed him from being awkward to being charming, from being afraid to being at home in the world.

The next fifteen years of Bill Wilson's drinking were typical as well as extreme. He made and lost two fortunes in the stock market in the United States and Canada. He turned down a job from Thomas Edison—probably the best job he was ever offered—because he didn't want to commute to New Jersey. He burned through the Burnham money as well as his own, and he caused the family to lose their houses in Manchester, Vermont, and on Clinton Street in Brooklyn. Prohibition didn't make any difference at all. He made his own wine fermenting huge crocks of grapes in the basement of the Burnham townhouse. He became a regular at local speakeasies. All this drove Lois crazy, and he filled pages of their family Bible with promises to stop drinking, promises that were never kept. He made many attempts to stop drinking: He found religion at Calvary Church, he went to rehab at Towns Hospital in New York City, he joined a movement called the Oxford Group. He kept on drinking.

By December 1934, everything he had tried seemed to come together while he was at Towns Hospital for the third time. He was desperate. He was reading William James's *The Varieties of Religious Experience*, with its suggestions that epiphanies can come in any form. The book had been brought to him by his sober friend, Ebby Thatcher, who had joined the Oxford Group. Dr. Duncan Silkworth, who was treating him, had explained that alcoholism was an obsession of the mind and an allergy of the body.

As he lay in bed at Towns Hospital, he remembered all the temperance education he had absorbed during his childhood. He had heard from his old friend Ebby that it was possible to stop drinking and thrive on sobriety. He had experienced both at Calvary Church and in meetings of the Oxford Group, the power of a group of like-minded souls. He had heard from Dr. Silkworth that alcoholism was a disease, a disease activated by the power of the first drink. That December afternoon in Towns Hospital, Bill felt a powerful wind and his room filled with a strange light. Wilson, who had struggled with alcohol for more than a decade, never had another drink.

The United States treasures individual liberties, but it is also a place founded on the potential of group efforts. On the frontier, each family staked out their own land. Then they got together to raise roofs and plant crops. Although he tried to preach what he was practicing, Bill Wilson's success in helping others was limited during the first months of his abstinence from alcohol. He liked to tell people what to do, but they didn't seem to like being told what to do.

It was a coincidental trip to Akron, Ohio, where he had gone to try to consolidate some business—at that point he was selling tires—that pushed him to the next level. The deal in Akron fell through. Feeling like a failure, Wilson was attracted by the lovely sound of clinking glasses and pouring whiskey echoing from the bar off the lobby of the Mayflower Hotel where he was staying. Desperate, he tried calling a list of local ministers asking if they knew of any drunks he could help. "I'm a rumhound from New York," he told the strangers whom he reached on the old-fashioned rotary phone. "I'm looking for a drunk I can help." Not surprisingly, the first few calls were fruitless. Finally Wilson reached a minister who had recently spoken with a woman who knew someone whose husband needed help.

Dr. Robert Smith, a fellow Vermonter from St. Johnsbury in the northern part of the state, was drinking himself out of his medical practice and his family's affections. The son of a prominent judge, he had gone to Dartmouth. Although he was beginning to have problems because of his drinking, he was able to get into medical school in Chicago, do well, and marry his childhood sweetheart. After medical school the Smiths moved to Ohio, where he began a practice as a proctologist and surgeon. He and Ann had two children, Bob and Sue. Smith's family was in the typical state of an alcoholic family—angry, desperate, and baffled. Ann Smith confided in her friend Henrietta Sieberling, who in turn was known at one of the churches Bill Wilson telephoned from the Mayflower Hotel lobby pay phone.

They met in Henrietta Sieberling's living room. Smith was drunk and claimed he had only fifteen minutes to spare for this out-of-towner. Instead of preaching the benefits of his own behavior or condemning drinking, Bill Wilson told his own drinking story as simply as he could. Smith was convinced that Wilson could help him, and Wilson moved into the Smiths' white, gabled house in Akron. Smith did not stop drinking right away. He drank again and got sober again. His last drink, on June 10, 1935, is the date of the founding of Alcoholics Anonymous.

Within fifteen years, the program, which was eventually called Alcoholics Anonymous after the book the group wrote and published, had spread to thousands of men and women all over the country and eventually all over the world. AA does not oppose drinking; it is only a way for people who think they have a drinking problem to help themselves—it has changed the way we think about addiction. Both Bill Wilson and Bob Smith agreed on two important principles that set them apart from movements like the Washingtonians or the Oxford Group, of which both men were briefly members: no temperance and no politics. They had one purpose. They hoped to help other self-identified alcoholics get better by showing them how to stop drinking.

Alcoholics Anonymous is quintessentially American. AA is a true grassroots democracy based on the principle of "one person, one vote." Both Wilson and Smith had experienced this kind of democracy in the Vermont town meetings of their youth, and both saw how necessary it would be for any organization—or lack of organization—involving recovery from alcoholism. There is no hierarchy in AA. As Bill Wilson wrote, in AA leaders are on tap, not on top. All positions rotate, usually more than once a year. To avoid the kind of power wielded by financial contributions and preserve the purity of the democratic process, AA limits monetary gifts—currently to $3,000 a year.

The drinking habits that followed prohibition have slowly reversed themselves again. National Institutes of Health numbers show that overall we are drinking less, with a few exceptions—college students and the military. We seem to be veering back toward the idea that drinking should be outlawed or at least controlled by laws, as drugs have unsuccessfully been for years. In a world that successfully controls what we smoke through taxes and blue laws, the idea of Prohibition seems to make sense again. So many celebrities have publicly gone to rehab that getting sober now seems more fashionable than staying drunk. At the same time, in spite of the growth of the recovery movement, the stigma of alcoholism seems to have dimmed very little.

CONCLUSION

In the second week of December 1620, almost a month after the *Mayflower*'s landing on Cape Cod, after braving almost unimaginable hardships—the journey, the failed explorations of the inhospitable Cape Cod sands, a winter storm that almost wrecked the sailing shallop they were using to explore the coast—a dozen men including Bradford, Winslow, and the soldier Miles Standish landed in what would come to be named Plymouth Harbor. Although Plymouth was also sandy with scrubby trees, it boasted freshwater brooks and some fields, and it was clearly destined to be the Pilgrims' new home.

For Bradford, the Pilgrim's story was parallel to the biblical story of Exodus. "New World Israelites, they had, with God's help, finally found their Canaan," Philbrick writes.[1] Bradford's view of history, like many of his companions on the *Mayflower*, was entirely shaped by his knowledge of the King James Bible Old Testament, which had been completed just a few years earlier. Every sea was the Red Sea. Every voyage was the voyage of the Israelites. Every hardship was biblical. Bradford's worldview made him an effective leader and a resilient soul. Whatever happened to the Pilgrims happened in a larger spiritual and historic context, overseen by an erratic but ultimately loving God. This was the controlling idea through which he saw, understood, and wrote about everything. Bradford took history personally.

The opening sentences of the Mayflower Compact, a message and an apology to King James for landing in the wrong place—not Northern Virginia but what would become Eastern Massachusetts—show the importance of God in Bradford's thinking:

Having undertaken, for the glory of God and advancement of the Christian faith and honour of our king and country, a voyage to plant the first colony in the northern parts of Virginia, do by these presents solemnly and mutually in the presence of God and one of another, covenant and combine ourselves together into a civil body politic.

This is as far from the way we understand history today as Plymouth was from Leiden in the seventeenth century. Although we live in a religious country, our serious historians rarely bring the perspective of religion to bear on their explorations of the past. They do not believe that God has a plan for humankind and that everything that happens is part of that plan.

As political and religious movements have come and gone over the last four centuries, historians have written from dozens of different perspectives. Some have written with economic bias, to prove capitalism corrupt or Communism ineffective, others have written to demonstrate the brilliance of specific groups of men—the founding fathers, for instance—still others to prove a point about the shifting balance between man and nature.[2]

Modern history, for the most part, claims to be objective. Our great historians from Goodwin to McCullough to Catton to Smith write as if they are reporting events with an unbiased eye. This happened and then that happened. This is our modern equivalent of God's will, an observant neutrality occasionally punctuated with some wise commentary. There are many advantages to this kind of history—the historian ostensibly has no ax to grind, no idea to sell, no political point to make. But there are disadvantages. One is that in taking a broad, dispassionate view, historians miss a lot. Their emphasis is on the sweep of time, not on the moments that make up our lives. They are never personal. Their opinions and the assumptions on which they base their lives are hidden. Their history is as far away from memoir as it can get.

In understanding history we are severely limited by this perspective. We see the panoply of history through the narrow keyhole of our own day and time, our own beliefs and knowledge. We are stuck in the first quarter of the twenty-first century, and looking back over the past four hundred years is like trying to make out the details of a ship on a far horizon in a storm. Historians make many decisions about how to deal with this—should we bring modern knowledge to bear on the characters we write about, what kind of language should we use, and how will we acknowledge the differences in language between then and now, how will we factor our own tolerance for women's rights or racial integration into times when those were unheard of?

One of the things many of our modern historians miss are the effects of alcoholism. I have read hundreds of indexes and tables of contents, and dozens of books on American history, and few historians even mention drinking and its effect on the events they write about.

What is history?: a way to sift through the past in an effort to comprehend the world we live in; a way to understand ourselves; a way to make meaning of our lives by finding meaning in the past. How can we do that without acknowledging something many of us do every day, the thing that we use to punctuate our lives in celebrations and in sadness; how can we do it without acknowledging that glass of wine or whiskey neat or dry martini that has been such a powerful and invisible part of our life as a nation?

What if our drinking history was different?

What if the gathering places in eighteenth-century Boston had been schools and churches with their emphasis on obedience, instead of taverns where opinions run hot and action is very close to words, especially after a few drafts of rum? The colonists were already fighters—otherwise they never would have survived Cape Cod. Without the *Mayflower* landing in Provincetown, would there have been a fury over taxation without representation? Would there have been an American Revolution?

Or what if Lincoln had not decided to fire Gen. George McClellan, a teetotaler, and hire Gen. Ulysses S. Grant, who was already famous for drinking too much? Would the Union have lost the Civil War? It was Grant's refusal to admit defeat at Shiloh, his understanding that war requires all or nothing, his alcoholic stubbornness and his determination that won the war.

Grant missed the first day of fighting at Shiloh; he had injured his foot when his horse fell on him. Many of his men thought he had been drinking. When he reached the battlefield, instead of calling for a retreat, he had a drink and spent the night visiting the men who had been injured in the battle. A rational man might have turned in to get some rest, but Grant was unstoppable, as many drinkers are. He had the hard-bitten, crazy courage men can get from brandy. And the Confederate Army, which had been winning the war, began to lose.[3]

What about Prohibition, the amendment to the Constitution that was supposed to be a great boon for women—women who had to deal with their drunken husbands. Women wanted the vote, but the temperance movement overwhelmed them. What if, a few years later, the forces of temperance had not pushed the cause of women's rights aside and railroaded in Prohibition? What if women had the vote in 1890 instead of thirty years later in 1920? Would we have had a different array of presidents? A different set of laws?

Or what if the men in the Kennedy detail of the Secret Service had been more alert on that awful morning of November 22, 1963? What if one of them had seen Oswald's gun barrel poking from the high window of the book depository, or if Bill Greer had stomped on the accelerator when he heard the first shot, taking the president out of range?

What if, at the very beginning, the Pilgrims had been able to land on the welcoming shores of Virginia where other colonies were already thriving? Would we Americans have been a more relaxed, southern, accepting kind of people? Cape Cod, even to the peaceable Henry David Thoreau, is a fighting kind of landscape. "Cape Cod is the bared and bended arm of Massachusetts," he writes in *Cape Cod*. "The shoulder is at Buzzard's Bay; the elbow, or crazy-bone, at Cape Mallebarre; the wrist at Truro; and the sandy fist at Provincetown,— behind which the State stands on her guard, with her back to the Green Mountains, and her feet planted on the floor of the ocean, like an athlete protecting her Bay,—boxing with northeast storms."

History is made of small moments, and the Pilgrims wading into the sandy shore on an icy November day—blown forward by their fears about running out of beer, about their failure to land farther south, about the low wooded land around them—is our first American moment. Imagine them that afternoon with salty air and the sound of water lapping against their heavy boots, the creaking of the *Mayflower* rigging, and the foaming of breakers on the other side of the bar. There they are, stranded on what Thoreau calls the sandy fist, ready to fight all comers. They will have to work alone and in small groups if they are going to survive.

What creates a national character? "America is another name for opportunity," wrote Ralph Waldo Emerson. It's an opportunity that starts with the Pilgrims' taking the opportunity and landing in the wrong place. The American attitude toward legal strictures, the American attitude toward hardship, the American insistence on doing things to benefit the individual, all come from that cold afternoon. Character is a combination of environment and experience, and the American character is being formed in those minutes when the Pilgrims finally, exhaustedly, reach the beach.

To survive, they will have to develop a fierce individualism and a craving for individual freedom that will spread down from the bent arm of the Cape toward what will become the Louisiana Purchase and westward to where their feisty spirit will settle huge tracts of land and explore seemingly impassable rivers and mountain ranges. The American character has been formed by a hundred forces—defining it, as someone has written, is like trying to nail jelly to a wall. Still, it began with New England, with the Pilgrims landing that afternoon in what is now Provincetown Harbor, driven by many forces both natural and man-made. One of those forces, a force of both pleasure and pain, a force of both brilliance and incompetence, was their passionate connection to drinking.

NOTES

PROLOGUE

1 "Alcohol and Public Health"; Millstein, "Drinking Kills 1 in 10 Working-Age Adults."
2 This is about the same number of fatalities as guns cause in a year and twice as many deaths as breast cancer causes in a year.
3 Milam and Ketcham, *Under the Influence*, 21.
4 Ibid., 22.
5 Rogers, *Proof: The Science of Booze*, 202.
6 Ibid.
7 Graham, *Vessels of Rage*, 148.

CHAPTER 1. THE *MAYFLOWER*: A GOOD CREATURE OF GOD

1 Quoted in Philbrick, *Mayflower*, 46, from *The Mayflower Papers: Selected Writings of Colonial New England*, 12.
2 Ibid., 31. Philbrick is himself an experienced blue-water sailor.
3 After one of many arguments with Thomas Weston, the con man who had acquired the *Mayflower* in the first place, the Pilgrims had to sell off most of sixteen firkins of butter—about two hundred pounds—in order to pay harbor duties in Southampton.
4 Bradford, *History of Plymouth Plantation*, 29.

5 Philbrick, *Mayflower*, 28.

6 Bradford, *History of Plymouth Plantation*, 59.

7 Although Murphy's Law would not be coined for centuries, its adage—"Anything that can go wrong will go wrong"—could easily be applied to these seventeenth-century travelers.

8 Nickerson, *Land Ho! 1620*, 12.

9 Bradford and Winslow, *Mourt's Relation*, 2.

10 Smith, *Beer in America*, 31.

11 Beer historian Bob Skilnik has written that the Pilgrims' relationship to beer was invented as PR by Anheuser Busch and the U.S. Brewer's Association. Certainly ads and stories in the 1930s with headlines like "Beer, Not Turkey, Lured Pilgrims to Plymouth Rock," were meant to give beer an aristocratic, ancestral patina. Nevertheless, the Pilgrims did have a severe beer shortage, and this caused much dissension as well as being a factor in their decision to land on Cape Cod.

12 Quoted in Philbrick, *Mayflower*, 38.

13 Ibid., 39.

14 Bradford, *History of Plymouth Plantation*, 106.

15 Ibid., 91.

16 Ibid., 92. Captain Jones was right to worry about the beating his ship was taking as she lay at anchor in Cape Cod Bay. Her trip back to England in April was her final voyage—she was too battered and broken to sail again and was dismantled in the shipyard at Rotherhithe.

17 Smith, *Beer in America*, 11.

18 Devers, "A Pilgrim's Drunken Progress."

19 The full title of the book usually referred to as *Mourt's Relation* is *A Relation or Journal of the Beginning and Proceedings of the English Plantation Settled at Plimoth in New England*, published by George Morton—or Mourt—in London.

CHAPTER 2: THE AMERICAN REVOLUTION, THE TAVERNS OF THE NEW WORLD

1 Quoted in Salinger, *Taverns and Drinking in Early America*, 3.

2 Ibid.

3 Holland, *The Joy of Drinking*, 56.

4   Leaving little John Bradford behind when his parents sailed on the *Mayflower* was done with the best intentions—the dangerous voyage and the travails of the New World would have been dangerous for him. Yet his absence may have contributed to the despair that drove his mother to drown. Later, after William Bradford remarried and his new wife brought her children to the New World, Bradford sent for John, who joined them in Plymouth.

5   Conroy, *In Public Houses*, 11.

6   Burns, *The Spirits of America*, 9.

7   Sismondo, *America Walks into a Bar*, 4.

8   Rorabaugh, *The Alcoholic Republic*, 5.

9   Behr, *Prohibition*, 9.

10   Ibid.

11   Conroy, 40–41.

12   Sismondo, 21.

13   Quoted in Burns, *The Spirits of America*, 23.

14   Quoted in Behr, 7–8.

15   Sismondo, 17.

16   Salinger, 86.

17   Ibid.

18   Devers, "A Pilgrim's Drunken Progress."

19   Burns, *Infamous Scribblers*, 11–12.

20   Ibid., 12–13.

21   W. J. Rorabaugh, quoted in Burns, *The Spirits of America*, 22.

22   Ibid., 23.

23   Ibid., 23.

24   Okrent, *Last Call*, 8.

25   Adams, *Diary of John Adams*, vol. 2, http://www.masshist.org/publications/apde/portia.php?id=DJA02d100.

CHAPTER 3: PAUL REVERE: "THE BRITISH ARE COMING!"

1   Carl Risen, "Back in the Mix: New England Rum," *New York Times*, October 30, 2012. http://www.nytimes.com/2012/10/31/dining/rum-returns-to-new-england.html?_r=1

2   A century later in 1919, a huge molasses holding tank near the Boston

waterfront burst open, sending a twenty-five-foot-high wave of the sweet, brown liquid cascading through town at about thirty-five miles an hour. Twenty-one people were killed and more than a hundred injured.

3   A hogshead can be a hogshead-shaped cask or mug—it is also used to designate about sixty-three gallons in British trade.
4   Quoted in Philbrick, *Bunker Hill*, notes for chapter 6, 321.
5   Philbrick, *Bunker Hill*, 120.
6   Fischer, *Paul Revere's Ride*, 105.
7   Ibid., 120.
8   Fleming, *Alcohol: The Delightful Poison*, 51.
9   Philbrick, *Bunker Hill*, 120.
10 Ibid., 125.
11 Ibid.
12 Ibid., 126.
13 Ibid., 128.
14 Botkin, 296.
15 Ibid., 295.
16 Randall, *Ethan Allen*, 308.
17 Lt. Jocelyn Feltham to Gen. Thomas Gage, June 11, 1775, quoted in Randall, 310.
18 Randall, 529.
19 Quoted in Burns, *The Spirits of America*, 55–56.
20 Barr, *Drink*, 203.
21 Ibid., 59.

CHAPTER 4: ALEXANDER HAMILTON AND THE WHISKEY
REBELLION, JOHN AND ABIGAIL ADAMS'S SONS AND GRANDSONS

1   Burns, *The Spirits of America*, 16.
2   Liquor is still a military perk today when, according to the Department of Defense, 20 percent of soldiers say they indulge in alcoholic binges—more than five drinks a day.
3   Burns, *The Spirits of America*, 16.
4   Ibid.
5   Ibid.
6   Ibid., 43.

7   Ibid., 42.

8   Ibid., 44.

9   Barr, 321.

10   Quoted in Burns, *The Spirits of America*, 45.

11   Smith, *The Shaping of America*, vol. 1, 231.

12   Ibid.

13   Zinn, *A People's History*, 101.

14   Veach, *Kentucky Bourbon Whiskey*, 14.

15   Conroy, 313–314.

16   Conroy, 230.

17   Smith, *The Shaping of America*, vol. 3, 680.

18   Burns, *The Spirits of America*, 26; also Barr, 310.

19   Jacobs, 273.

20   *Alcoholics Anonymous*, 122. This book has no official author. Wilson wrote a first draft in 1938, which was then edited by the dozen or so men who were the earliest members of AA.

21   Wineapple, 5.

22   Smith, *The Shaping of America*, vol. 3, 680.

23   Letter from JQA at Harvard to his parents from AA. See founders .archives.gov/documents/Adams/03-02-02-0003-0002.

24   Ibid.

25   McCullough, 365.

26   Ibid., 514.

27   Ellis, 199.

28   McCullough, 529.

29   Ibid.

30   Jacobs, 418.

31   Shepherd, 210.

32   "The Olden Time," in Pasko, 438.

33   Smith, *The Shaping of America,* vol. 3, 780.

34   Nagel, 122.

35   Ibid.

36   Ibid., 173.

37   Ibid.

38   Ibid., 173, 174.

39   Ellis, 241.

40   Burns, *The Spirits of America*, 16.

41 Califano, "Wasting the Best and the Brightest."

42 McCullough, 236

CHAPTER 5: JOHNNY APPLESEED, THE AMERICAN DIONYSUS

1   Pollan, *The Botany of Desire*, 9.

2   Ibid.

3   Ibid., 16. Emphasis in the original.

4   Ibid., 37.

5   The measurement of how much people drank was inaccurate at best in the nineteenth century. Most twentieth-century surveys, especially after Prohibition, divide the amount of pure alcohol purchased by the number of residents over fifteen years of age. Seven gallons a year may not seem overwhelming at five fifths to the gallon, but because of the differences in proof and percentage of alcohol, a gallon could be far more than five bottles as we would buy them today. Writing about the early twentieth century before Prohibition, Daniel Okrent explains the "average consumption of pure alcohol ran to 2.6 gallons per adult per year—the rough equivalent of 32 fifths of 80-proof liquor." (Okrent, 373.)

6   Katherine A. Chavigny, "Reforming Drunkards in Nineteenth-Century America," in Tracy and Acker, 110.

7   Ibid.

8   Lincoln, 176, 177. This address was given to the Washingtonians on the 110th anniversary of the birth of George Washington.

9   Wineapple, 77.

10 Ibid.

11 Quoted in Werner, 107.

12 Quoted in ibid., 109.

13 Ibid., 110.

14 Burns, *The Spirits of America*, 74.

15 Quoted in ibid., 76

16 Ibid., 74.

17 Ibid.

18 Quoted in Peter C. Mancall, "I Was Addicted to Drinking Rum," in Tracy and Acker, 91.

19   Quoted in ibid., 92.
20   Ibid., 101.
21   Anne Bradstreet, "Meditations," in Miller, 277.
22   Burns, *The Spirits of America*, 71; Fleming, 106.
23   Fleming, 65.
24   Rorabaugh, 202.
25   Frederick Douglass, 100.
26   Ibid., 101.

CHAPTER 6: THE CIVIL WAR

1   Gugliotta, "New Estimate Raises Civil War Death Toll."
2   "Civil War Facts," Civil War Trust, http://www.civilwar.org/education
     /history/faq/.
3   Carey, "Liquor Lifts Spirits, Helps Wounded."
4   Williams, 210.
5   Wiley, 131.
6   Ibid., 31.
7   Ibid., 252.
8   Grant, 657.
9   Omarzu, "Whiskey and the War."
10   Billings, 140.
11   Carey, "Liquor Lifts Spirits, Helps Wounded."
12   Hubbell, Geary, and Wakelyn, 347.
13   Wiley, 252.
14   Lowry, 82. Lowry's research shows that 22.4 percent of Irish soldiers'
     courts-martial involved alcohol. For German soldiers the percentage was
     18 percent and for Americans 15 percent.
15   Carey, "Liquor Lifts Spirits, Helps Wounded."
16   Grant, 657.
17   Brands, 73.
18   Grant, 254.
19   Brands, 184.
20   Grant, 216.
21   Will-Weber, 145.
22   Talbott, 16.

23   Bonekemper, 411.

24   Brands, 247.

CHAPTER 7: THE GREAT AMERICAN WEST

1   Liquor played two parts in Lincoln's death. The president, a teetotaler whose father had worked in a distillery and who called alcohol "the great devastator," was shot from behind by Booth, who had so much to drink at the Star Saloon, run by Peter Taltavull, next to Ford's Theatre that people standing around as he raced onto the stage and out of the theater said he reeked. Lincoln's bodyguard had also left the theater during intermission and was drinking at the Star Saloon when Booth snuck into the presidential box, jammed the door with a piece of wooden lathing, and assassinated the president. Booth "just walked into the bar and asked for some whiskey," Taltavull testified later. "I gave him the whiskey, put the bottle on the counter…I saw him go out of the bar…from eight to ten minutes before I heard the cry that the president was assassinated." (Will-Weber, 132.)

2   Smith, *The Shaping of America*, vol. 3, 510.

3   Morgan, 26.

4   Smith, *The Shaping of America*, vol. 3, 545.

5   Morgan, 37.

6   Ibid.

7   Billington, 385.

8   Morgan, 137–138.

9   Rorabaugh, 157.

10   *How Booze Built America*, episode no. 2, "Westward, Ho!"

11   Ulysses S. Grant was one of the best generals this country ever had and one of the worst presidents. The drunkenness that seemed to feed his ability to lead as the 1860s progressed was at the same time being haphazardly controlled by the presence of his adored wife, Julia. Perhaps the drink turned on him. Perhaps the qualities that make a great general do not make a great politician. As president he was hapless and invested money in ways that provoked a series of congressional investigations. Combined with the panic of 1873, Grant's financial mismanagement made his name a synonym for corruption and dishonesty. He also lost all his own money,

and at the end of his life he hurried to write a best-selling memoir whose royalties would help support his family after his death.

12 Turner, 21.

13 Isenberg, 40. Unrelated to Isenberg, as a side note, William "Buffalo Bill" Cody was another westerner who took the story of the frontier and ran with it. Born two years before Earp, Cody was a legitimate hunter and Army scout whose family moved from Iowa to Kansas. Cody fought in the Civil War, was a Pony Express rider, and panned for gold in Colorado. But his real talent was theater. In 1892 he traveled to Chicago to be part of Ned Buntline's Wild West shows. Billed as a fearless Indian fighter, Cody also performed displays of shooting. Within a decade he was running his own shows that toured Europe and the United States with horses, Native American actors, and guest stars like sharpshooter Annie Oakley.

CHAPTER 8: THE END OF THE NINETEENTH CENTURY AND THE NEW TEMPERANCE CRUSADERS

1 Philbrick, *The Last Stand*, xviii.
2 Okrent, 15.

CHAPTER 9: PROHIBITION

1 Abbott, *American Rose*, 113.
2 Coffey, 4.
3 "This Day in History: 16 January—Prohibition Goes into Effect." Abbott, *American Rose,* 113.
4 From 1920 to 1927 when it became a separate agency, the Prohibition Unit fell under the aegis of the Internal Revenue Service.
5 Douglas, 24.
6 This story is told in Karen Abbott, "Prohibition's Premier Hooch Hounds."
7 Lender and Martin, 107.
8 Okrent, 3.

9   Smith, *The Rise of Industrial America*, vol. 6, 554.
10   Pipes, 67.
11   Lincoln, *In War's Dark Shadow*, 284.
12   Kobler, 214.
13   Okrent, 128.
14   Ibid., 129.
15   Coffey, 197.
16   Ibid., 198.
17   Quoted in Okrent, 345.

CHAPTER 10: THE WRITER'S VICE

1   Laing, 55. Laing begins her book with a story about my father and Ray Carver drinking in Iowa City in the 1970s—two drunks kiting checks at the local liquor store. But this was the end of an era. My father got sober in Alcoholics Anonymous in 1975. Raymond Carver got sober in Alcoholics Anonymous a few years later. And my father's closest friend at Iowa, the young John Irving, was not a serious drinker and is one of the most brilliant writers of his generation, a generation that includes very few drunks. Irving took friendly care of my father in the semester he was teaching at Iowa, probably saving his life by inviting him to family dinners, and sometimes literally carrying him to his room at Iowa House and putting him to bed.
2   Boler, 13.
3   Douglas, 24.
4   Dardis, 3.
5   Laing, 7.
6   Ibid. 173.
7   Quoted in Hall, 190.
8   Quoted in ibid., 224.
9   Goodwin, 47.
10   Ibid., 173.
11   Ibid., 183.
12   Ibid., 184.
13   Ibid., 185.
14   Dardis, 5.
15   Laing, 247.

CHAPTER 11: SENATOR JOSEPH MCCARTHY AND THE COLD WAR

1 Johnson, 141.
2 Zinn, *The Twentieth Century*, 166.
3 Rovere, 53.
4 Johnson, 199.
5 Ibid., 200.
6 Ibid., 203.
7 Ibid., 204. Johnson's book contains the best account of this evening.
8 Stauffer, 153–154. In the endnotes, Stauffer quotes the reformer Gerrit Smith: "But for liquor [Brooks] would never have committed his enormous crime." (Ibid., 372n105.)
9 Stone and Kuznick, 232.
10 Ibid.
11 Johnson, xii.
12 Watkins, 198.
13 Johnson, 460.
14 Quoted in ibid., 293.
15 Watkins, 150.
16 Ibid., 78.
17 Zinn, *The Twentieth Century*, 172.
18 Rovere, 251, 252, 253.

CHAPTER 12: A FEW SECONDS

1 Caro, 313.
2 Shenon, 259.
3 Ibid., 139.
4 Ibid., 138.
5 Dornan, 375.
6 Shenon, 376.
7 Ibid.
8 Hersh, 244.
9 Ibid.
10 Blaine, 12.

11 Interview with the late Loretta Barrett.
12 Manchester, 37.
13 Bob Schieffer in an interview with David Friend of *Vanity Fair*.
14 Melanson, 67.
15 Hill, *Mrs. Kennedy and Me*, 59–60.
16 Manchester, 290.
17 Ibid., 155–156.
18 Dornan, 257.
19 Melanson, 66.
20 Marrs, 230–231.

CHAPTER 13: PRESIDENT RICHARD NIXON 1968–1973: "OUR DRUNKEN FRIEND"

1 Brodie, 377.
2 Ibid, 476.
3 Summers, 372.
4 Ibid, 235.
5 Ibid., 370.
6 Wicker, 392.
7 Ibid., 393.
8 Woodward and Bernstein, 103, 104, 424.
9 Summers, 455.
10 Quoted in ibid., 456.
11 Quoted in ibid., 457.
12 Ibid., 460.
13 Ibid., 461–462.
14 Christopher Hitchens in the *New York Times Book Review,* October 8, 2000.
15 Summers, 448–449.
16 Hersh, "Kissinger and Nixon in the White House."
17 Woodward and Bernstein, 424.

CHAPTER 14: RECOVERY

1   Douglas, 138–139.
2   Cheever, 75.

CONCLUSION

1   Philbrick, *Mayflower*, 75.
2   Jon Krakauer's *Into Thin Air*, for instance, shows a degraded Mount Everest taking revenge on the climbers who degraded her, and Nathaniel Philbrick's *In The Heart of the Sea* makes it clear that the white whale that stowed in the ship *Essex* was a force of nature pushing for redress against the destruction caused by men.
3   Grant's drinking was so well known that another drinker a century later, the writer James Thurber, wrote a famous short story about Lee's surrender to Grant at the Appomattox Court House. In the story, Grant is convincingly drunk; he mistakes Lee for the poet Robert Browning, and he has trouble finding his socks. Thurber, who knew all too much about drunkenness—its ability to loosen the soul and its ability to muddle the mind—staged his worst spree at the Algonquin Hotel, where he locked himself in and drank for a month in the fall of 1961 when he was sixty-six. He died in the hospital a month later.

BIBLIOGRAPHY

Abbott, Karen. "Prohibition's Premier Hooch Hounds." Smithsonian.com. January 10, 2012. http://www.smithsonianmag.com/history/prohibitions-premier-hooch-hounds-16963599 /?no-ist.

Abbott, Karen. *American Rose: A Nation Laid Bare: The Life and Times of Gypsy Rose Lee.* Random House. New York. 2012.

Adams, John. *Diary of John Adams.* Vol. 2, The Adams Papers. Massachusetts Historical Society. http://www.masshist.org/publications/apde2/volume-toc?series=dja&vol=2 (main page).

"Alcohol and Public Health." Centers for Disease Control and Prevention. http://www.cdc.gov /alcohol/.

Alcoholics Anonymous. 4th ed. Alcoholics Anonymous World Services. New York. 2001.

Ames, Azel. *The Mayflower and Her Log: July 15, 1620–May 6, 1621—Complete.* Filiquarian. Lexington, KY. 2013.

Barr, Andrew. *Drink: A Social History of America.* Carroll and Graf. New York. 1999.

Barrows, Susanna, and Robin Room, eds. *Drinking Behavior and Belief in Modern History.* University of California Press. Berkeley. 1991.

Behr, Edward. *Prohibition: Thirteen Years That Changed America.* Arcade. New York. 1996.

Belzer, Richard, and David Wayne. *Hit List: An In-Depth Investigation into the Mysterious Deaths of Witnesses to the JFK Assassination.* Skyhorse. New York. 2013.

Benton, Sarah Allen. *Understanding the High-Functioning Alcoholic: Breaking the Cycle and Finding Hope.* Rowman and Littlefield. Lanham, MD. 2010.

Billings, John D. *Hardtack and Coffee: The Unwritten Story of Army Life.* Corner House. Williamstown, MA. 1980. First published in 1887 by George H. Smith.

Billington, Ray Allen. *Westward Expansion: A History of the American Frontier.* Macmillan. New York. 1974.

Black, Rachel, ed. *Alcohol in Popular Culture: An Encyclopedia.* Greenwood/ABC-CLIO. Santa Barbara, CA. 2010.

Blaine, Gerald, with Lisa McCubbin. *The Kennedy Detail: JFK's Secret Service Agents Break Their Silence.* Gallery Books/Simon & Schuster. New York. 2010.

Bogosian, Eric. *Drinking in America.* Vintage/Random House. New York. 1987.

Bolden, Abraham. *The Echo from Dealey Plaza: The True Story of the First African American on the White House Secret Service Detail and His Quest for Justice After the Assassination of JFK.* Harmony Books. New York. 2008.

Boler, Kelly. *A Drinking Companion: Alcohol and the Lives of Writers*. Union Square. New York. 2004.

Bonekemper, Edward H., III. *Grant and Lee*. Regnery. Washington, DC. 2012.

Botkin, B. A., ed. *A Treasury of New England Folklore*. Bonanza Books, a division of Crown. New York City. 1965.

Bradford, William. *History of Plymouth Plantation*. Little, Brown. Boston. 1856.

Bradford, William, and Edward Winslow. *Mourt's Relation, or Journal of the Plantation at Plymouth*. John Kimball Wiggin. Boston. 1865.

Brands, H. W. *The Man Who Saved the Union: Ulysses S. Grant in War and Peace*. Anchor Books/ Random House. New York. 2012.

Brinkley, Douglas, and Luke Nichter, eds. *The Nixon Tapes: 1971–1972*. Houghton Mifflin Harcourt. Boston. 2014.

Brodie, Fawn. M. *Richard Nixon: The Shaping of His Character*. W. W. Norton. New York. 1981.

Brogan, Hugh. *The Penguin History of the United States of America*. Penguin. London. 1985.

Bugliosi, Vincent. *Four Days in November: The Assassination of President John F. Kennedy*. W. W. Norton. New York. 2007

Burns, Eric. *Infamous Scribblers: The Founding Fathers and the Rowdy Beginnings of American Journalism*. PublicAffairs. New York. 2006.

———. *The Spirits of America: A Social History of Alcohol*. Temple University Press. Philadelphia. 2004.

Califano, Joseph A., Jr. "Wasting the Best and the Brightest: Alcohol and Drug Abuse on College Campuses." CASA Columbia. May 28, 2007. http://www.casacolumbia.org /newsroom /op-eds/wasting-best-and-brightest-alcohol-and-drug-abuse-college-campuses.

Carey, John E. "Liquor Lifts Spirits, Helps Wounded." *Washington Times*. January 13, 2006. http://www.washingtontimes.com/news/2006/jan/13/20060113-085716-3727r /?page=all.

Caro, Robert A. *The Passage of Power: The Years of Lyndon B. Johnson*. Vintage Books/ Random House. New York. 2012.

Cheever, Susan. *My Name Is Bill: Bill Wilson—His Life and the Creation of Alcoholics Anonymous*. Washington Square Press. New York. 2004.

Coffey, Thomas M. *The Long Thirst: Prohibition in America, 1920–1933*. Norton. New York. 1975.

Conroy, David W. *In Public Houses: Drink and the Revolution of Authority in Colonial Massachusetts*. University of North Carolina Press. Chapel Hill. 1995.

Cornog, Evan. *The Birth of Empire: DeWitt Clinton and the American Experience, 1769–1828*. Oxford University Press. New York. 1998.

Crowley, John W. *The White Logic: Alcoholism and Gender in American Modernist Fiction*. University of Massachusetts Press. Amherst. 1994.

Crutchfield, James A., ed. *The Way West: True Stories of the American Frontier*. Forge/Tom Doherty Associates. New York. 2005.

Custer, Elizabeth B. *The Boy General: Story of the Life of Major-General George A. Custer*. Edited by Mary E. Burt. Charles Scribner and Sons. New York. 1901.

Daniels, Bruce C. *Puritans at Play: Leisure and Recreation in Colonial New England*. St. Martin's Press. New York. 1995.

Dardis, Tom. *The Thirsty Muse: Alcohol and the American Writer*. Ticknor and Fields. New York. 1989.

Davis, William C. *The American Frontier: Pioneers, Settlers, and Cowboys, 1800–1899*. University of Oklahoma Press. Norman. 1992.

Deetz, James. *In Small Things Forgotten: An Archaeology of Early American Life*. Rev. ed. Anchor Books/Random House. New York. 1996.

Denzin, Norman K. *Hollywood Shot by Shot: Alcoholism in American Cinema*. Aldine Transaction. New Brunswick and London. 2004.

Devers, A. N. "A Pilgrim's Drunken Progress." *Lapham's Quarterly*. March 14, 2013. http://laphamsquarterly.org/roundtable/pilgrims-drunken-progress.

Dornan, Michael. *The Secret Service Story*. Delacorte Press. New York. 1967.

Douglas, Ann. *Terrible Honesty: Mongrel Manhattan in the 1920s*. Noonday/Farrar Straus and Giroux. New York. 1995.

Douglass, Frederick. *Narrative of the Life of Frederick Douglass, an American Slave, Written by Himself*. Pocket Books/Simon & Schuster. New York. 2004. First published 1845 by the Anti-Slavery Office.

Douglass, James W. *JFK and the Unspeakable: Why He Died and Why It Matters*. Touchstone/Simon & Schuster. New York. 2010.

Ellis, Joseph J. *First Family: Abigail and John Adams*. Vintage/Random House. New York. 2011.

Emerson, Ralph Waldo. *Representative Men: Seven Lectures*. Modern Library. New York. 2004.

Epstein, Edward Jay. *Inquest: The Warren Commission and the Establishment of Truth*. Bantam Books. New York. 1966.

Faust, Drew Gilpin. *This Republic of Suffering: Death and the American Civil War*. Vintage/Random House. New York. 2008.

Fischer, David Hackett. *Paul Revere's Ride*. Oxford University Press. New York. 1994.

———. *Washington's Crossing*. Oxford University Press. New York. 2004.

Fisher, Paul. *House of Wits: An Intimate Portrait of the James Family*. Henry Holt. New York. 2008.

Fisher, Vardis. *Suicide or Murder? The Strange Death of Governor Meriwether Lewis*. Alan Swallow. Denver, CO. 1962.

Fitzgerald, F. Scott. *On Booze*. New Directions Pearl. New York. 2011. First published in 1931 by Charles Scribner's Sons.

Fleming, Alice. *Alcohol: The Delightful Poison*. Dell. New York. 1975.

Forbes, Esther. *Paul Revere and the World He Lived In*. Houghton Mifflin Harcourt. New York. 1999.

Garrison, Jim. *On the Trail of the Assassins: One Man's Quest to Solve the Murder of President Kennedy*. Skyhorse. New York. 2013. First published in 1988 by Warner Books.

Gateley, Iain. *Drink: A Cultural History of Alcohol*. Gotham Books/Penguin. New York. 2008.

Gilmore, Thomas B. *Equivocal Spirits: Alcoholism and Drinking in Twentieth-Century Literature*. University of North Carolina Press. Chapel Hill. 1987.

Goodwin, Donald W. *Alcohol and the Writer*. Andrews and McMeel. Kansas City, MO. 1988.

Gopnik, Adam, ed. *Americans in Paris*. Library of America. New York. 2004.

Graham, James. *The Secret History of Alcoholism: The Story of Famous Alcoholics and Their Destructive Behavior*. Element Books. Rockport, MA. 1996.

———. *Vessels of Rage, Engines of Power: The Secret History of Alcoholism*. Aculeus Press. Lexington, VA. 1994.

Grant, Ulysses S. *Personal Memoirs of U. S. Grant*. Konecky and Konecky. Old Saybrook, CT. 1991. First published in 1885 by Charles L. Webster.

Gugliotta, Guy. "New Estimate Raises Civil War Death Toll." *New York Times*. April 2, 2012. http://www.nytimes.com/2012/04/03/science/civil-war-toll-up-by-20-percent-in-new-estimate.html?pagewanted=all&_r=0.

Hall, Donald, ed. *The Oxford Book of American Literary Anecdotes*. Oxford University Press. New York. 1981.

Harris, Jonathan. *This Drinking Nation*. Four Winds Press/Macmillan. New York. 1994.

Haslam, Edward T. *Dr. Mary's Monkey: How the Unsolved Murder of a Doctor, a Secret Laboratory in New Orleans, and Cancer-Causing Monkey Viruses Are Linked to Lee Harvey Oswald, the JFK Assassination, and Emerging Global Epidemics*. TrineDay. Walterville, OR. 2007.

Hersh, Seymour M. *The Dark Side of Camelot*. Back Bay Books/Little, Brown. New York. 1997.

———. "Kissinger and Nixon in the White House." *Atlantic Monthly*. May 1982. http://www.theatlantic.com/magazine/archive/1982/05/kissinger-and-nixon-in-the-white-house/308778/.

Hill, Clint, with Lisa McCubbin. *Five Days in November*. Gallery Books/Simon & Schuster. New York. 2013.

———. *Mrs. Kennedy and Me*. Gallery Books/Simon & Schuster. New York. 2012.

Holland, Barbara. *The Joy of Drinking*. Bloomsbury. New York. 2007.

How Booze Built America. Episode no. 2, "Westward, Ho!" First broadcast September 26, 2012, by the Discovery Channel. Narrated by Mike Rowe.

Hubbell, John T., James W. Geary, and Jon L. Wakelyn, eds. *Biographical Dictionary of the Union: Northern Leaders of the Civil War*. Greenwood. Westport, CT. 1995.

Isenberg, Andrew C. *Wyatt Earp: A Vigilante Life*. Hill and Wang/Farrar, Straus and Giroux. New York. 2013.

Jacobs, Diane. *Dear Abigail: The Intimate Lives and Revolutionary Ideas of Abigail Adams and Her Two Remarkable Sisters*. Ballantine Books/Random House. New York. 2014.

Janik, Erika. *Marketplace of the Marvelous: The Strange Origins of Modern Medicine*. Beacon Press. Boston. 2014.

Jersild, Devon. *Happy Hours: Alcohol in a Woman's Life*. Cliff Street Books/HarperCollins. New York. 2001.

Johnson, Haynes. *The Age of Anxiety: McCarthyism to Terrorism*. Harcourt. New York. 2005.

Johnston, Ann Dowsett. *Drink: The Intimate Relationship Between Women and Alcohol*. HarperCollins. New York. 2014.

Katz, Sandor Ellix. *The Art of Fermentation: An In-Depth Exploration of Essential Concepts and Processes from Around the World*. Chelsea Green. White River Junction, VT. 2012.

Ketcham, Katherine, and William F. Asbury, with Mel Schulstad and Arthur P. Ciaramicoli. *Beyond the Influence: Understanding and Defeating Alcoholism*. Bantam Books. New York. 2000.

Kobler, John. *Ardent Spirits: The Rise and Fall of Prohibition*. Putnam. New York. 1973.

Korda, Michael. *Ulysses S. Grant: The Unlikely Hero*. Atlas Books/HarperCollins. New York. 2004.

Laing, Olivia. *The Trip to Echo Spring: On Writers and Drinking*. Picador. New York. 2013.

Leamer, Lawrence. *Sons of Camelot: The Fate of an American Dynasty*. William Morrow/HarperCollins. New York. 2004.

Lee, Jean Butenhoff. *Experiencing Mount Vernon: Eyewitness Accounts 1784–1865*. University of Virginia Press. Charlottesville. 2006.

Lender, Mark Edward, and James Kirby Martin. *Drinking in America: A History*. Free Press. New York. 1982.

Lendler, Ian. *Alcoholica Esoterica: A Collection of Useful and Useless Information as It Relates to the History and Consumption of All Manner of Booze*. Penguin. New York. 2005.

Lerner, Michael A. *Dry Manhattan: Prohibition in New York City*. Harvard University Press. Cambridge. 2007.

Lewis, Oscar, ed. *The Autobiography of the West—Personal Narratives of the Discovery and Settlement of the American West*. Henry Holt. New York. 1958.

Lincoln, Abraham. "Better Than a Gallon of Gall." *Lapham's Quarterly*. Winter 2013.

Lincoln, W. Bruce. *In War's Dark Shadow: The Russians Before the Great War*. Dial Press. New York. 1983.

Lowry, Thomas P. *Irish and German—Whiskey and Beer: Drinking Patterns in the Civil War*. Self-published. 2011.

Manchester, William. *The Death of a President: November 20–November 25, 1963*. Back Bay Books/Little, Brown. 2013. First published in 1967 by Harper and Row.

Marrs, Jim. *Crossfire: The Plot That Killed Kennedy*. Rev. ed. Basic Books. New York. 2013.

McCullough, David. *John Adams*. Simon & Schuster. New York. 2001.

McKnight, Gerald D. *Breach of Trust: How the Warren Commission Failed the Nation and Why*. University Press of Kansas. Lawrence. 2005.

Meade, Marion. *Bobbed Hair and Bathtub Gin: Writers Running Wild in the Twenties*. Harvest Book/Harcourt. New York. 2004.

Melanson, Philip H., with Peter F. Stevens. *The Secret Service: The Hidden History of an Enigmatic Agency*. Rev. ed. Basic Books. New York. 2005.

Milam, James R., and Katherine Ketcham. *Under the Influence: A Guide to the Myths and Realities of Alcoholism*. Bantam. New York. 1983.

Miller, Perry, ed. *The American Puritans: Their Prose and Poetry*. Anchor/Doubleday. Garden City, NY. 1956.

Millstein, Seth. "Drinking Kills 1 in 10 Working-Age Adults: 19 Signs That America Has a Drinking Problem." Bustle.com. http://www.bustle.com/articles/29699-drinking-kills -1-in-10-working-age-adults-19-signs-that-america-has-a-drinking-problem.

Morgan, Ted. *A Shovel of Stars: The Making of the American West—1800 to the Present*. Touchstone/Simon & Schuster. New York. 1995.

Morrow, Lance. *Evil: An Investigation*. Basic Books. New York. 2003.

Murdock, Catherine Gilbert. *Domesticating Drink: Women, Men, and Alcohol in America, 1870–1940*. Johns Hopkins University Press. Baltimore. 1998.

Murray, Marr. *Drink and the War from the Patriotic Point of View*. HardPress. Miami. First published in 1915 by Chapman and Hall.

Nagel, Paul. *Descent from Glory: Four Generations of the John Adams Family*. Oxford University Press. New York. 1983.

Nickerson, W. Sears. *Land Ho! 1620: A Seaman's Story of the* Mayflower, *Her Construction, Her Navigation, and Her First Landfall*. Michigan State University Press. East Lansing. 1997.

Nicklés, Sara, ed. *Drinking, Smoking, and Screwing: Great Writers on Good Times*. Chronicle Books. San Francisco. 1994.

Okrent, Daniel. *Last Call: The Rise and Fall of Prohibition*. Scribner. New York. 2010.

Omarzu, Tim. "Whiskey and the War." *Chattanooga Times Free Press*. October 21, 2012. http://www.timesfreepress.com/news/life/entertainment/story/2012/oct/21/whiskey-and -the-war-civil-war/90673/.

Palamara, Vincent Michael. *Survivor's Guilt: The Secret Service and the Failure to Protect President Kennedy*. TrineDay. Walterville, OR. 2013.

Pasko, W. W., ed. *Old New York*. Vol. 1. W. W. Pasko. New York. 1890. http://babel.hathitrust .org/cgi/pt?id=nyp.33433081783213;view=1up;seq=1 (site identifies this as volume 2).

Pegram, Thomas R. *Battling Demon Rum: The Struggle for a Dry America, 1800–1933*. Ivan R. Dee. Chicago. 1998.

Pennock, Pamela E. *Advertising Sin and Sickness: The Politics of Alcohol and Tobacco Marketing, 1950–1990*. Northern Illinois University Press. DeKalb. 2007.

Philbrick, Nathaniel. *Bunker Hill: A City, a Siege, a Revolution*. Penguin. New York. 2013.

————. *The Last Stand: Custer, Sitting Bull, and the Battle of the Little Bighorn*. Penguin. New York. 2010.

————. Mayflower: *A Story of Courage, Community, and War*. Viking Penguin. New York. 2006.

Pipes, Richard. *A Concise History of the Russian Revolution*. Knopf. New York. 1995.

Pollan, Michael. *The Botany of Desire: A Plant's-Eye View of the World*. Random House. New York. 2002.

————. *The Omnivore's Dilemma: A Natural History of Four Meals*. Penguin. New York. 2006.

Powers, William. *Hamlet's BlackBerry*. Harper Perennial. New York. 2011.

Quiett, Glenn Chesney. *They Built the West: An Epic of Rails and Cities*. D. Appleton. New York. 1934.

Randall, Willard Sterne. *Ethan Allen: His Life and Times*. W. W. Norton. New York. 2011.

Ratey, John J. *A User's Guide to the Brain: Perception, Attention, and the Four Theaters of the Brain*. Pantheon Books. New York. 2001.

Risen, Carl. "Back in the Mix: New England Rum," *New York Times*, October 30, 2012. http://www.nytimes.com/2012/10/31/dining/rum-returns-to-new-england.html?_r=1.

Roberts, J. M. *The Penguin History of the World*. Penguin Books. New York. 1976.

Rogers, Adam. *Proof: The Science of Booze*. Houghton Mifflin Harcourt. Boston. 2014.

Root, Waverly, and Richard de Rochemont. *Eating in America: A History*. Ecco. New York. 1981.

Rorabaugh, W. J. *The Alcoholic Republic*. Oxford University Press. New York. 1979.

Rotskoff, Laurie. *Love on the Rocks: Men, Women, and Alcohol in Post–World War II America*. University of North Carolina Press. Chapel Hill. 2002.

Rovere, Richard H. *Senator Joe McCarthy*. Harcourt, Brace. New York. 1959.

Rowlandson, Mary, and Others. *The Account of Mary Rowlandson and Other Indian Captivity Narratives*. Edited by Horace Kephart. Dover. Mineola, NY. 2005.

Rucker, R. D. *Drugs, Drug Addiction, and Drug Dealing: The Origin and Nature of, and the Solution to, the American Drug Problem*. Vantage Press. New York. 1991.

Salinger, Sharon V. *Taverns and Drinking in Early America*. Johns Hopkins University Press. Baltimore. 2002.

Schlesinger, Arthur M., Jr. *The Almanac of American History*. G. P. Putnam. New York. 1983.

Shannonhouse, Rebecca, ed. *Under the Influence: The Literature of Addiction*. Random House. New York. 2003.

Shenon, Philip. *A Cruel and Shocking Act: The Secret History of the Kennedy Assassination*. Henry Holt. New York. 2013.

Shepherd, Jack. *The Adams Chronicles: Four Generations of Greatness*. Little, Brown. Boston. 1975.

Simon, Philip. *Log of the* Mayflower. Priam Press. Chicago. 1956.

Sismondo, Christine. *America Walks into a Bar: A Spirited History of Taverns and Saloons, Speakeasies and Grog Shops*. Oxford University Press. New York. 2011.

Slotkin, Richard. *The Long Road to Antietam: How the Civil War Became a Revolution*. Liveright/W. W. Norton. New York. 2012.

Smith, Gregg. *Beer in America: The Early Years, 1587–1840: Beer's Role in the Settling of America and the Birth of a Nation*. Brewers. Boulder, CO. 1998.

Smith, Jean Edward. *Grant*. Simon & Schuster. New York. 2001.

Smith, Page. *The Rise of Industrial America: A People's History of the Post-Reconstructionist Era*. Vol. 6. McGraw-Hill. New York. 1984.

————. *The Shaping of America: A People's History of the Young Republic*. Vol. 1. McGraw-Hill. New York. 1980.

————. *The Shaping of America: A People's History of the Young Republic*. Vol. 3. Penguin. New York. 1989.

Spiller, Robert E., Willard Thorp, Thomas H. Johnson, and Henry Seidel Canby, eds. *Literary History of the United States*. 2 vols. Macmillan. New York. 1948.

Standage, Tom. *A History of the World in Six Glasses*. Walker. New York. 2006.

Stauffer, John. *Giants: The Parallel Lives of Frederick Douglass and Abraham Lincoln*. Twelve/Hachette. New York. 2008.

Stavely, Keith, and Kathleen Fitzgerald. *America's Founding Food: The Story of New England Cooking*. University of North Carolina Press. Chapel Hill. 2004.

Stewart, David O. *American Emperor: Aaron Burr's Challenge to Jefferson's America*. Simon & Schuster Paperbacks. New York. 2012.

Stone, Oliver, and Peter Kuznick. *The Untold History of the United States*. Gallery Books/Simon & Schuster. New York. 2012.

Straus, Robert, and Selden D. Bacon. *Drinking in College*. Yale University Press. New Haven, CT. 1953.

Summers, Anthony. *The Arrogance of Power: The Secret World of Richard Nixon*. Viking Penguin. New York. 2000.

Tague, James T. *LBJ and the Kennedy Killing*. TrineDay. Walterville, OR. 2013.

Talbott, Strobe. *The Great Experiment: The Story of Ancient Empires, Modern States, and the Quest for a Global Nation*. Simon & Schuster. New York. 2008.

"This Day in History: 16 January—Prohibition Goes into Effect." History Channel (UK). http://www.history.co.uk/this-day-in-history/January-16.

Thompson, Jerry D., ed. *New Mexico Territory During the Civil War: Wallen and Evans Inspection Reports, 1862–1863*. University of New Mexico Press. Albuquerque. 2008.

Tracy, Sarah W. *Alcoholism in America: From Reconstruction to Prohibition*. Johns Hopkins University Press. Baltimore. 2005.

Tracy, Sarah W., and Caroline Jean Acker, eds. *Altering American Consciousness: The History of Alcohol and Drug Use in the United States, 1800–2000*. University of Massachusetts Press. Amherst. 2004.

Tropman, John E. *Conflict in Culture: Permissions Versus Controls and Alcohol Use in American Society*. University Press of America. Lanham, MD. 1986.

Tunis, Edward. *Frontier Living: An Illustrated Guide to Pioneer Life in America, Including Log Cabins, Furniture, Tools, Clothing, and More*. Lyons/Globe Pequot. 2000. First published in 1961 by Thomas Y. Crowell.

Turner, Frederick Jackson. *The Frontier in American History*. Harvard. 1920.

Vander Ven, Thomas. *Getting Wasted: Why College Students Drink Too Much and Party So Hard*. New York University Press. New York. 2011.

Veach, Michael. *Kentucky Bourbon Whiskey: An American Heritage*. University Press of Kentucky. Lexington. 2013.

Vickers, Daniel. *Farmers and Fishermen: Two Centuries of Work in Essex County, Massachusetts, 1630–1850*. University of North Carolina Press. Chapel Hill. 1994.

Walton, Stuart. *Out of It: A Cultural History of Intoxication*. Three Rivers. New York. 2001.

Watkins, Arthur. *Enough Rope: The Inside Story of the Censure of Senator Joe McCarthy by His Colleagues—The Controversial Hearings That Signaled the End of a Turbulent Career and a Fearsome Era in Public Life*. Prentice-Hall. Englewood Cliffs, NJ. 1969.

Werner, M. R. *Barnum*. Harcourt, Brace. New York. 1923.

West, Elliott. *The Saloon on the Rocky Mountain Mining Frontier*. Bison Books/University of Nebraska Press. Lincoln. 1979.

Wicker, Tom. *One of Us: Richard Nixon and the American Dream*. Random House. New York. 1991.

Wiley, Bell Irvin. *The Life of Billy Yank: The Common Soldier of the Union*. Bobbs-Merrill. Indianapolis. 1952.

Williams, David. *A People's History of the Civil War: Struggles for the Meaning of Freedom*. New Press. New York. 2005.

Will-Weber, Mark. *Mint Juleps with Teddy Roosevelt: The Complete History of Presidential Drinking*. Regnery. Washington. 2014.

Wineapple, Barbara. *Ecstatic Nation: Confidence, Crisis, and Compromise, 1848–1877*. Harper. New York. 2013.

Woodward, Bob, and Carl Bernstein. *The Final Days*. Simon & Schuster. New York. 1976.

Zimmerman, Jonathan. *Distilling Democracy: Alcohol Education in America's Public Schools, 1880–1925*. University Press of Kansas. Lawrence. 1999.

Zinn, Howard. *A People's History of the United States: 1492–Present*. Harper and Row. New York. 1980.

———. *The Twentieth Century: A People's History*. Rev. ed. Harper Perennial. New York. 1998.

ACKNOWLEDGMENTS

Without many dozens of other writers, historians, biographers, and archivists—as well as the availability of books and writers through the Internet—this book would have been impossible. The idea began in 2010 when I read Daniel Okrent's marvelous book *Last Call: The Rise and Fall of Prohibition*. "In the early days of the Republic drinking was as intimately woven into the social fabric as family or church," wrote Okrent, quoting W. J. Rorabaugh, who noted that, "Americans drank from the crack of dawn to the crack of dawn." I contacted Daniel Okrent through email, and he generously encouraged me, and referred me to Eric Burns's wonderful book *The Spirits of America* about drinking in early America. This led me to more books, and soon I had borrowed and bought piles of books on almost every aspect of drinking in American life. The books ranged from Nathaniel Philbrick's brilliant and engaging histories of the *Mayflower* and Bunker Hill to his excellent biography of George Armstrong Custer, from David McCullough's majestic biography of John Adams to Olivia Laing's charming *A Trip to Echo Springs* and even to a less-than-persuasive book showing that the Kennedy assassination was linked to New Orleans monkey viruses via Clay Shaw.

I reveled in biographies of General U.S. Grant and General Robert E. Lee, especially those by Michael Korda, who wrote about both great and fascinating warriors. I scoured histories of the frontier—from Frederick Jackson Turner's *The Frontier in American*

History to Ted Morgan's wonderful *Shovel of Stars*—and of Prohibition and American writers, and I searched for links to drinking and stories at the intersection of drinking and history. I studied colonial eating habits and read the Warren Commission Report sections that describe drinking by the Secret Service Agents in the Kennedy detail the night before the assassination—facts to which I was alerted by Philip Shenon's extraordinary book *A Cruel and Shocking Act*. Combing through my own shelves, I rediscovered Page Smith, a historian who had been a favorite of my father's and who seemed to have cogent ideas about almost everything. I dusted off Tom Dardis's *The Thirsty Muse* and William Manchester's *The Death of a President* and Frederick Douglass's short, powerful autobiography. In presuming to write history, I anchored my story to as many excellent books as I could find.

Without my friends and family—my smart, talented children—I would accomplish nothing at all. My son, Warren, is a brilliant and fearless editor and researcher. My daughter, Sarah, is an inspired listener and her comments are always invaluable. Time that I am privileged to spend at Yaddo is always magical and results in a quality of writing and thinking better than anything I expect. Being a member of the Author's Guild and sitting in on our meetings inspires me and makes me feel less alone. I live in a city where you can run into a writer at the drug store or in a coffee shop, where a nearby library—the New York Society Library—offers open stacks for browsing and helpful staff. I like to talk about what I am writing, and my neighbors and friends have been very kind about listening to my ideas and my prose many, many times.

My brilliant editor Deb Futter, who recognized the value of this idea, and my astonishing, loving, and intelligent agent, Gail Hochman, are the pillars of my writing career. Michael DiPaola brilliantly checked every page. I like to say that my real audience is someone who picks up a book of mine in a rented summer house in ten or twenty years—dusts it off, opens the warped cover, reads it, and comes to see the world in a new way. I can almost see her reading in a creaky Adirondack chair on a porch somewhere, perhaps to the sound of the sea. I write for this person, although I may never know her. She and my other readers, both real and imaginary, are the true inspiration and mainstay of everything I write. Thank you, whoever you are.

INDEX

ABOUT THE AUTHOR

Susan Cheever is the author of the biographies *E. E. Cummings,* *American Bloomsbury,* and *My Name Is Bill,* as well as five novels and four memoirs. Her work has appeared in the *New Yorker, New York Times,* and *Newsday,* among other magazines and anthologies. She has been a Guggenheim Fellow, has been nominated for a National Book Circle Award, and won the *Boston Globe* Winship medal. She attended Brown University and has taught at many places, including Yale, Brown, Columbia, the New School, and Bennington College.